John Lloyd CBE is the creator of *QI*, founding producer of *The News Quiz*, *Not the Nine O'Clock News*, *Spitting Image* and *Blackadder*, and the presenter of BBC Radio 4's *The Museum of Curiosity*. An admirer of Socrates, the only man in Athens who knew that he knew nothing, he is alarmed to find chainsaws were invented to assist childbirth (page 54).

John Mitchinson, QI's first researcher, once ran the marketing for Waterstones and now moonlights as a publisher with the book crowdfunding platform Unbound. He was amazed and disappointed to find the Famous Five never drank 'lashings of ginger beer' (page 243).

James Harkin, QI's Head Elf, has, in the course of his Quite Interesting duties, sung karaoke with Bhutanese monks, danced with the world's most advanced humanoid robot and learned how to tear a telephone directory in half. He co-presents the QI Elves' podcast *No Such Thing As A Fish* and co-produces *The Museum of Curiosity*. He was surprised to find out that Bolivia is the place 'where the nuts come from' (page 233).

Andrew Hunter Murray writes for *QI* and *Private Eye* magazine, and performs with improvised comedy group 'Austentatious'. He also co-presents *No Such Thing As A Fish* and (along with James) is part of the team behind the BBC TV spin-off *No Such Thing As The News*. He was astonished to learn where camels come from (page 165).

For more from the team behind *QI*, visit qi.com. You can also follow QI's fact-filled Twitter account @qikipedia and listen to the QI Elves' weekly

A Quite Interesting Book

THE THIRD BOOK OF
General Ignorance

John Lloyd
John Mitchinson
James Harkin
Andrew Hunter Murray

FABER & FABER

First published in 2015
by Faber & Faber Ltd
Bloomsbury House
74–77 Great Russell Street
London WCIB 3DA
This paperback edition published in 2016

Typeset by Palindrome
Printed and bound in England by CPI Group (UK) Ltd, Croydon CR0 4YY

A CIP record for this book
is available from the British Library

ISBN 978–0–571–30901–6

2 4 6 8 10 9 7 5 3 1

CONTENTS

Introduction   xv

Where is the world's largest waterfall?   1
Where is the world's largest river?   2
Where is the world's longest mountain range?   4
Where is the nearest natural rainforest to Britain?   5
Where will the lion sleep tonight?   7
How did Tarzan get around the jungle?   9
Which country has the second-biggest film industry?   11
Name the only country in the world to have been
    officially accused of biological warfare   12
Name a gas used on the battlefield in the Second
    World War   14
Which kind of power station produces the most
    radiation?   16
Why is gasoline called gasoline?   17
Which company is the world's largest manufacturer
    of tyres?   19
What are plastic bags made from?   21
What is marmalade made from?   22
Who invented the grapefruit?   24
What's the world's most popular fruit?   25
Why did Popeye eat spinach?   27
What do beavers eat?   28
What does an elephant drink through?   30

What always happens to couples who get drunk
in Las Vegas? 32
How old do you have to be for a Club 18–30 holiday? 34
When should you report a missing person? 35
How long does it take to play the 'Minute Waltz'? 37
What's the best kind of violin? 39
Which day is added to make a leap year? 41
Who brought the first Christmas tree to Britain? 42
What did Prince Albert invent? 43
Who invented the Nazi salute? 45
In which war did both sides fight under the Union
Jack? 46
What colour are the flags on the Moon? 48
What colour is the dark side of the Moon? 50
What happens nine months after a blackout? 51
When should you be eating for two? 53
What was the first chainsaw used for? 54
What was the best thing before sliced bread? 56
Who invented the sandwich? 58
Which country invented ice hockey? 60
Which country invented the motorway? 61
Why did motorists have to carry red flags in front
of them? 63
What kind of glass does the US president's car have? 64
Would you take a bullet for me? 66
What might you find in the average British
courtroom? 67
What's the oldest profession? 69
Who first wore high heels? 70
Name a traditional Italian bread 72
Who first ate frogs' legs? 73
What happens to most of the world's liquorice? 74

Name the most important vow taken by Trappist
monks   76
Which town hanged a monkey thinking it was a
French spy?   78
What's the northernmost place on mainland Britain?   79
Which country do missionaries go to more than any
other?   81
Where did the *Mayflower* land in America?   82
What was the date of the American Declaration of
Independence?   85
When should you take down your Christmas
decorations?   86
Which holiday is celebrated on 26 December every
year?   87
Which seasonal event was 'Jingle Bells' written for?   89
Who should you visit on Mothering Sunday?   90
How old would Jesus have been in the year AD 2000?   92
What would Jesus' mum have called him?   94
What was the name of the saint from Assisi?   95
When was the name 'Wendy' first used?   96
What kind of reasoning did Sherlock Holmes use?   98
What was the name of the cabin boy in *Captain
Pugwash*?   100
Name a piece of music written by Henry VIII   102
What was the main event in a medieval tournament?   103
Why was the Colosseum called the Colosseum?   105
What is the name of the Queen's official residence?   106
How many English kings named Henry have there
been?   108
What dynasty did Henry VII and Henry VIII
belong to?   110
Which king of Scotland succeeded Macbeth?   111

Which dog stood by his master's grave for 14 years?   113
How did Pavlov get dogs to salivate?   115
Why should you rely on the 'wisdom of crowds'?   116
Why should you avoid feral pigeons?   117
How hot does water have to be to wash the bacteria off
   your hands?   119
What would happen if the world suddenly stopped
   spinning?   121
What is the deepest canyon in the USA?   123
Where is the world's tallest statue of Jesus Christ?   124
What species of tree is the tallest ever?   125
Which way do sunflowers face?   127
What colour is a robin's breast?   129
Could you beat the king of dinosaurs at an arm
   wrestle?   131
Which animal has the most teeth?   133
How many claws does a lobster have?   134
How do crickets make their chirps?   136
How do cuckoos raise their young?   137
How clever are dolphins?   139
Which animal has the most genes?   140
What is junk DNA good for?   142
Who discovered DNA?   143
Who invented the hovercraft?   144
Why was the dishwasher invented?   146
When was the selfie invented?   147
When was 'OMG' first used?   148
Who wrote the first English dictionary?   150
What is literally the most misused word in the
   English language?   152
What does a cowboy call his rope?   154
What kind of hat did they wear in the Wild West?   155

Where is Harris Tweed made? 157

Which bone of a whale is used for whalebone corsets? 158

What's the loudest animal for its size? 160

Where do fish live? 162

Where do penguins live? 163

Where did the camel get its hump? 165

What is Antarctica's largest native land animal? 166

How high could a flea jump if it was the size of a
human? 167

What would happen if the population of China all
jumped at once? 168

Which island could the whole population of the
world stand on? 170

Where is Krakatoa? 171

What's the world's largest body of dead water? 172

How many American Great Lakes are there? 174

What are deserts made from? 175

What is the ozone layer made of? 176

Does the air get warmer or cooler the higher you get? 178

Which humans have been closest to the Sun? 179

How long does light from the centre of the Sun take
to reach Earth? 180

How much does a shadow weigh? 182

What is the strongest creature for its weight in the
world? 183

What's the worst thing a swan can do to you? 185

Name a monogamous bird 186

Name a non-venomous snake 188

Name a vertebrate with no backbone 190

What kind of creature is a Portuguese man-o'-war? 191

How many legs does the average animal have? 192

How many legs does a kangaroo have? 193

How many knees does an elephant have? 195
How many sphincters do you have? 196
Which finger would you sacrifice first if you had to? 198
What happened to Walt Disney's body? 199
What happened to the *Mary Celeste*? 201
Who was the naturalist on board the *Beagle*? 202
What bird did the Ancient Mariner shoot? 204
The sirens were half-woman, half-what? 206
What did the Birdman keep in Alcatraz? 207
Where is most of America's gold kept? 209
How did Roman soldiers receive their salary? 211
What killed most of the population of Pompeii? 213
How many Spartans died at the Battle of
    Thermopylae? 214
How many people were at the feeding of the 5,000? 216
What did Mary Magdalene do for a living? 218
What did Lady Godiva do? 219
When did the first woman vote in Britain? 221
What's the most dangerous sport for girls in
    America? 223
How good was Kim Jong-il at golf? 224
What is the brake man's job in a bobsled race? 226
What's the main rule of walking races? 228
How long are Olympic swimming pools? 229
Name *either* the starting point *or* the finishing point
    of the Paris–Dakar rally 231
Which country is the world's largest producer of
    Brazil nuts? 233
What are the prickly bits of a rose called? 234
What was the main use for pepper in the Middle
    Ages? 237
Would you rather drink pure water or treated sewage? 239

[x]

What's the quickest way to look healthy?   240

How many portions of fruit and vegetables should
  you eat a day?   241

What did the Famous Five have lashings of?   243

Where was Juliet standing when she was wooed by
  Romeo?   244

What did Napoleon say to Josephine?   245

Who coined the phrase 'Elementary, my dear
  Watson'?   248

Who invented Pythagoras' theorem?   250

Fill in the blank: 'The Man in the __ Mask'   252

Which of the following is true of corrugated iron?   254

What happens if you hit a diamond with a hammer?   256

What shape is a snowflake?   258

What happens if you shout in the mountains?   259

When did the First World War get its name?   261

What happened to crime during the Second World
  War?   263

What was the average age of US combat troops in
  Vietnam?   264

Which country's national anthem is 'The Land of
  the Free'?   266

What were the inhabitants of Mexico called before
  the Europeans arrived?   268

Name the first great civilisation to mummify its dead   269

Where would you find the world's largest pyramid?   271

How did Vikings bury their dead?   272

What can you legally do if you come across a
  Welshman in Chester after sunset?   275

What landmark formed the northern boundary of
  Roman Britain?   276

What's the nearest Third World country to the UK?   278

What's the world's most overweight country?   280

Which country has the most time zones?   281

When was 'time immemorial'?   283

How long is an epoch?   285

How fast was the Earth's fastest mass extinction?   286

A note on sources   289

Index   291

INTRODUCTION

*Water is H₂O, hydrogen two parts, oxygen one, but there is a third
thing that makes it water and nobody knows what that is.*

D. H. LAWRENCE

This is the third of the *General Ignorance* trilogy. We've been
thinking about it for three years. We never planned to write a
trilogy: when we started out a decade ago, the idea of filling
even *one* book with things we learn at school that just aren't true
seemed impossible. But today the magic jar of ignorance seems
bottomless. So here it is: *The Third Book of General Ignorance.* The
third leg of the stool. The balancing tome.

We wanted to compile a third volume for three reasons: first,
because we've found so much great new material; second, because
it somehow 'feels' right. There is a third reason, but nobody
knows what that is.

We humans seem mysteriously hardwired to think in threes:
beginning, middle, end; body, mind, spirit; earth, sea, sky; small,
medium, large; red, blue, green; A, B, C; Father, Son, Holy
Ghost; here, there, everywhere; liberté, egalité, fraternité; Tom,
Dick, Harry; snap, crackle, pop!

It's a long and venerable inner waltz. Even our bodies, famed
for their bilateral symmetry, are full of hidden threes: the skin
has three layers (epidermis, dermis, hypodermis); our ears have
three parts (outer, middle, inner); we have three types of teeth
(incisors, canines, molars); there are three parts to our digestive
system (stomach, small intestine, large intestine).

And the QI universe comes in triplicate: squids have three hearts; the lizard-like tuatara of New Zealand has three eyes; kangaroos have three vaginas and, as you will see if you read on, three legs.

The great minds of history have long been drawn to what the Greeks called a *hendiatris* (literally a 'one through three'), or triple motto.

There are three classes of people: those who see; those who see when they are shown; those who do not see. **LEONARDO DA VINCI**

There are three things that are extremely hard: steel, a diamond, and to know one's self. **BENJAMIN FRANKLIN**

You can tell a lot about a person by the way they handle these three things: a rainy day, lost luggage, and tangled Christmas tree lights.
MAYA ANGELOU

No one has yet come up with a convincing psychological explanation for our attraction to threes and we're not expecting one anytime soon.

Pythagoras, the first person to call himself a philosopher (in 520 BC), believed three was the 'perfect number', the symbol of God, but even he struggled to explain why. Instead he advised, 'Do not go to bed until you have gone over the day three times in your mind.'

'Live, reflect, then ask more questions' is the *hendiatris* we follow at QI. We've learned much about many things but we start each new day in cheery ignorance. If this book, or the others in the *General Ignorance* threesome, inspires you to do likewise, our work here is done.

JOHN LLOYD, JOHN MITCHINSON,
JAMES HARKIN AND ANDREW HUNTER MURRAY

Where is the world's largest waterfall?

It's under the sea off Denmark.

In the traditional sense, the tallest waterfall in the world is Angel Falls in Venezuela. It plummets more than 3,000 feet: three times the height of the Shard building in London. The largest in terms of volume is the Guaira Falls, on the border of Brazil and Paraguay: every 90 seconds it dumps enough water to fill Lake Windermere, England's largest lake.

But both of these pale into insignificance when compared with the height and the flow of an underwater waterfall in the Denmark Strait – a section of sea between Iceland and Greenland that connects the Arctic and Atlantic Oceans.

The water in the Arctic is colder, denser and less salty than that of the Atlantic, and when the two bodies of water meet, they don't mix. As a result, when the Arctic water flows over the vast underwater cliffs separating it from the Atlantic, it sinks to the ocean floor. This creates an underwater waterfall almost three times the height of Ben Nevis, carrying 2,000 times as much water as Niagara Falls.

This gigantic water feature isn't there just to irritate pub quiz setters. As cold water flows out of the Arctic Ocean, warmer water is pushed up from the Atlantic along the west coast of the British Isles, with a hugely beneficial effect on the UK's weather. Even though London is further north than the Canadian ski town of Calgary, it's generally a lot warmer.

The Angel Falls are so inaccessible that nobody outside

Venezuela knew about them until the twentieth century. In 1933 an American aviator called Jimmie Angel flew over them; the falls are named after him, not the heavenly beings.

Angel returned to the falls four years later to confirm what he had seen, but when his plane landed it got stuck in mud. This meant Angel became not only the first Westerner to see Angel Falls but also the first person to descend the cliffs down which they fall. The location was so remote that it took Angel and his companions 11 days to get back to civilisation. His plane stayed at the top of the falls until 1970, when Venezuelan helicopters picked it up. Now fully refurbished, it stands in front of the airport terminal at Venezuela's southern capital, Bolivar City.

Where is the world's largest river?

Thousands of feet up in the sky.

Everyone learns at school that the water cycle carries water vapour from the seas up into the atmosphere, from where it returns to Earth again as rain. But it wasn't until 1998 that scientists discovered that it flows in long narrow rivers in the sky. These 'atmospheric rivers' are thousands of miles long and hundreds of miles wide. A large one can carry more water than the Amazon. There are four or five of them in the sky, somewhere in the world, at any one time.

Atmospheric rivers can cause disastrous floods if they suddenly release their water onto a specific area. The ten worst winter floods to hit Britain in the last 30 years were all caused this way. On the other side of the world, the west coast of America is also regularly hit by flooding from an atmospheric river known as the Pineapple Express, which stretches from Hawaii to California. In 1861 an atmospheric river brought 43 days of storms to California and turned its Central Valley into a 600-square-mile lake. Thousands died and the state was bankrupted – and there's no guarantee it won't happen again.

The largest river that's not in the sky is deep underground. The River Hamza flows at just a millimetre an hour, 3 kilometres (2 miles) beneath the Amazon. The Hamza is thought to be the same length as the Amazon, but it's much wider. It's less like a river than a system of porous underground rocks with water flowing steadily through them. Many geographers prefer to call it an aquifer.

Ignoring subterranean and stratospheric exceptions, everyone agrees the Nile is the planet's longest river. It tops all the official lists at 4,152 miles long, followed by the Amazon at 4,000 miles. But the Amazon has recently got longer – a huge blockage at its mouth has forced the water to find a new way to the sea, adding an extra 200 miles and allowing it to overtake the Nile.

STEPHEN *Atmospheric rivers are vast ribbons of water vapour moving water around the world. They appear in different places at different times.*

MARCUS BRIGSTOCKE *Are they the ones that are perfectly timed to coincide with bank holidays?*

Where is the world's longest mountain range?

Most of it's under the sea.

The longest mountain range on Earth is the 40,000-mile mid-ocean ridge, almost all of which is underwater. It's ten times longer than the Andes and circles the globe, stretching from the Arctic down through the Atlantic to the Antarctic, then up again through the Indian Ocean and into the Pacific.

This ridge is where the planet's ten major tectonic plates meet, like the seams on a baseball. Because they are always pulling away from each other, there are near-constant volcanic eruptions and earthquakes along its length. As a result, the mid-ocean ridge is also the planet's largest single volcanic feature. Its thousands of active volcanoes produce three-quarters of the Earth's output of molten rock, or magma.

One part of the mid-ocean ridge that isn't underwater is Iceland. In 1783 the segment of the ridge that rises above sea level there spewed out 8 cubic miles of lava, enough to bury the entire US interstate freeway system more than 30 feet deep. The lava, and the 50 million tons of sulphur dioxide that were released into the atmosphere, ruined crops and killed more than 10,000 Icelanders – a quarter of the population at the time.

We know less about the mid-ocean ridge than the surface of Venus or Mars. Less than 0.1 per cent of it has been studied, but new information is added all the time. In 2014 analysis of radar satellite data indicated the ridge may have as many as 25,000 mountains over 5,000 feet high. This estimate results from the fact that, ignoring temporary features like waves, the ocean's surface is not flat – it mimics the shape of the seabed beneath it. The gravitational effect of huge underwater volcanoes (or 'sea mounts') causes seawater to bunch up over them, and the reverse is true of deep submarine trenches.

The mid-ocean ridge is host to one of the most hostile environments on Earth, yet, in 1977, life was found there. Tectonic movements under the ridge create scalding deep-sea fountains, called 'hydrothermal vents' or 'black smokers'. Here, beset by volcanic eruptions, earthquakes, toxic chemicals, extremes of temperature and pressure – and in total darkness – over 300 new species have been discovered. These include white crabs, foot-long clams and giant tubeworms almost 8 feet long. In 2006 one such new species, found here 7,500 feet below sea level, was dubbed the 'yeti crab' because of the long, silky-looking hair that covers its limbs.

The manned vehicle that first encountered life at the vents of the ocean ridge was called Alvin, after its developer, oceanographer Allyn Vine. Alvin has made over 4,000 dives since it was built in 1964, including, most famously, an exploration of the *Titanic* in 1986. Each passenger gets given one bottle per dive in which to urinate, with an extra attachment for women.

STEPHEN *I think I'm right in saying that Churchill's nanny was called Everest.*

BILL BAILEY *Nanny Everest – the tallest nanny in the world.*

Where is the nearest natural rainforest to Britain?

As unlikely as it sounds, there are rainforests in Britain.

Tropical rainforests like the Amazon are not the only type of rainforest. There are also 'temperate' rainforests, and there are several in the UK. While there isn't a universally accepted definition of a temperate rainforest, most biologists would say it

should combine high rainfall, low average temperature and a tree canopy that blocks out most of the light from the sky.

Britain's rainforests occur in the Furness Fells of Cumbria, the Scottish Highlands, wet coastal areas of Wales and the river valleys of Devon. As the most common tree is the oak, they are also known as Atlantic Oakwoods. They provide habitats for birds like woodpeckers and kites, for flowers like bluebells and primroses, and especially for fungi, ferns and mosses that can grow without much sunlight. The UK's rainforests suffered greatly in the seventeenth to nineteenth centuries, when they were felled for fuel in the Industrial Revolution. Today the Forestry Commission is leading a concerted restoration effort. We hear much about the damage inflicted on the South American rainforests, but we also need to look after our own.

That said, mankind has had a devastating effect on the Amazon rainforest: a fifth of it has been lost in the last 40 years. Though man is now destroying the rainforest, there's some evidence that it was originally man-made. The early Amazonians were selective about the plants they grew. They culled useless species and encouraged useful ones, mixing the soil with charcoal from their fires to make it rich and fertile. The resulting soil is known as *terra preta* and has remarkable regenerative properties: it may be exported to transform the infertile soils of sub-Saharan Africa. Brazilian farmers search it out and sell it as valuable compost but always leave some in the ground, where it retains its power. There is enough of it in the Amazonian rainforest to cover the whole of France or an area twice the size of Great Britain.

Archaeological evidence and the depth and volume of this unique compost suggests that before European contact the Amazon supported an advanced civilisation of 5 or 6 million people, who may have been responsible for planting the seeds of the rainforest and creating the world's largest orchard.

Where will the lion sleep tonight?

It won't be in the mighty jungle.

Lions don't live in jungles and they sleep during the day. Almost all wild lions live on the African savannah (apart from the 400 in Gir Forest National Park in India, which isn't a jungle either). Some lions may have to move as their habitat shrinks – one lioness was spotted in the Ethiopian jungle in 2006, but there's no evidence she was hunting and breeding there.

'The Lion Sleeps Tonight' is the most famous song ever to have come out of Africa. Originally called '*Mbube*' (Zulu for 'lion') it was recorded in 1939 by Solomon Linda and the Evening Birds. During the studio session the Birds sang '*Mbube, uyiMbube*' ('Lion, you're a lion') while Solomon improvised over the top. It sold 100,000 copies in South Africa alone. It has since been translated into Danish, Japanese, Congolese and Navaho, and broadcast on US radio for the equivalent of 300 years of continuous play. It has changed over the years: in 1949 banjo player Pete Seeger misheard the *Mbube* chant as 'a-wimoweh' when he taught it to his band, the Weavers. In 1961 George Weiss, who wrote 'What a Wonderful World', added the lyrics 'In the jungle, the mighty jungle, the lion sleeps tonight' to Solomon's version.

Despite the song's huge success, Solomon was only paid £1 for the recording session. When he died in 1962 his family were so poor his wife couldn't afford a gravestone. The song's popularity increased exponentially when it appeared in Disney's *The Lion King* in 1994. It has been calculated that if Solomon had received a fair share of royalties he would have made $5 million in five years from the Broadway show alone. In 2004 his family sued Disney, who settled out of court, agreeing to backdate the rights to the song to 1987.

The Lion King was called *King of the Jungle* until it was pointed out that lions live on the savannah. The plot is loosely based on Hamlet: screenwriter Irene Mecchi said the story was pitched to her as 'Bamblet' or 'Hamlet in Africa with Bambi thrown in'. The story sees the dark-maned lion Scar trying to overthrow his golden-haired brother Mufasa; in the real world Scar would have been the natural leader. A dark mane is a status symbol for male lions – it shows they are eating well and have high levels of testosterone.

During the mating season lionesses have sex up to 50 times a day for four days and nights in a row with as many as five males – but each bout lasts only ten seconds. Up to 8 per cent of lion mountings are thought to be homosexual.

RICHARD COLES *The Vicar of Stiffkey. Was bitten by a lion. In Skegness. And that was the end of the end of the Vicar of Stiffkey.*
VICTORIA COREN MITCHELL *Are you sure you're not accidentally recounting the plot of a limerick?*

How did Tarzan get around the jungle?

At no point in any of the Tarzan books does Tarzan swing on a vine.

In the original stories, Tarzan swings from branch to branch or makes 20-foot jumps across the canopy. When the first film, *Tarzan of the Apes*, was made in 1918, it became obvious that no human being had the strength required to move like the character in Edgar Rice Burroughs's books. So vine travel was introduced. But, in real life, this wouldn't work either. Vines grow from the ground up and only hang down when they are draped over tree branches – one wrong choice and Tarzan would plummet to Earth.

Swinging from branch to branch is called 'brachiation' (from *bracchium*, Latin for 'arm'). Tarzan supposedly did it because he copied the apes that adopted him, but almost no great apes do this. It's better suited to smaller primates like gibbons, which can move at up to 35 miles per hour and bridge a 50-foot gap in a single swing.

Edgar Rice Burroughs became an author because he couldn't make a living as a pencil-sharpener salesman. He decided to give writing a go after reading pulp fiction and thinking, 'If people were paid for writing rot such as I read in some of those magazines, that I could write stories just as rotten.' In early drafts his hero's name was 'Zantar' or 'Tublat Zan', and his first completed story was written on the back of used letterheads and scraps of paper.

Tarzan of the Apes was published in 1912. It was an immediate success, spawning over 150 films and countless books as well as 'Tarzan bread' (launched in 1934), which sold more than 20 million loaves in four months. Tarzan also inspired Jerry Siegel to create Superman.

The most famous Tarzan was Johnny Weissmuller. Before taking up acting, he was one of the greatest athletes of the twentieth century. After contracting polio as a child, doctors advised him to take up swimming. He went on to win five Olympic gold medals and break 67 world records (fans say it was more, but he got tired of submitting the paperwork). In ten years, he never lost a single race.

From 1934 to 1948 Weissmuller played Tarzan in 12 films. In none of them did he say the immortal line 'Me Tarzan, you Jane' – though he did say it once in an interview. He recorded the original 'Tarzan yell' for MGM, with expert help from master sound engineer Douglas Shearer.

Later versions in RKO movies are clearly just him yodelling, but Weissmuller insisted the MGM yell was all his. It had, he said, saved his life in 1959 when he was stopped at a checkpoint in Cuba during the revolution. Rebel troops only let him go when he convinced them who he was by reproducing it. In the Second World War, American GIs requested it be broadcast on Armed Forces Network radio to remind them of home. The copyright is now owned by Burroughs's estate.

In the books Tarzan is an aristocrat who speaks nine languages and over 20 dialects. Burroughs disliked the grunting 'fairground chump' of the movies. His daughter recalled, 'One time, we saw a Tarzan movie together. After it was all over, although the audience seemed enthusiastic, my father remained in his seat and kept shaking his head sadly.'

Even Johnny Weissmuller himself was moved to remark, 'My lines read like a backward two-year-old talking to his nurse.'

STEPHEN *What's the most famous line from a Tarzan film?*
RONNI ANCONA *Oh, 'Me Tarzan, you Jane.'*
STEPHEN *Yes, except, of course, it never happened.*
DAVID MITCHELL *Why do these films always forget to put their most famous lines in?*

Which country has the second-biggest film industry?

It's not India, or America, but Nigeria.

Many people know that India's Bollywood has overtaken America's Hollywood to become the world's biggest film industry, but it's now run a close second by Nigeria's 'Nollywood'.

According to UNESCO, in 2006 Bollywood released 1,091 feature films, Nollywood made 872, and Hollywood trailed a distant third with just 485. These days, Nigeria makes even more: as many as 2,500 full-length feature films a year, or about 50 a week. Most are made for under £20,000 and shot in just ten days. In Hollywood the average film budget is £6.7 million and production takes at least a year.

Film is now Nigeria's second-biggest employer after agriculture. As of 2014, Nollywood was worth $5.1 billion and made up 5 per cent of Nigeria's GDP. Most people don't see the movies in the cinema – almost all are sold on tape or DVD from thousands of market stalls. They cost the equivalent of £1.80 each.

Nollywood began in 1992, when a trader called Kenneth Nnebue ordered a consignment of blank videotapes. They didn't sell well, so he had a cheap film made with a VHS camera and copied it onto the tapes. *Living in Bondage* was about a man haunted by the ghost of his wife. It sold over 750,000 copies.

Suddenly everyone else started making films too, all on incredibly tight budgets (to film a tracking shot, a director will push his cameraman around in a wheelchair). They have to keep churning them out because piracy is rife – it takes two weeks to make an illegal copy of a new film and distribute it across the country. There are at least five pirate movies in circulation for every official one. Nnebue has since retired from Nollywood to become a preacher, but the industry he founded goes from strength to strength.

Popular Nollywood titles include *Baby Police, Tears of the Dumb, Blackberry Babes 2, Tear My Bra (If You Can), Mama Insurance* and *Margaret Thatcher*. In 2015, for the first time, Nollywood movies will be eligible to compete at the Oscars for the Best Foreign Language Film Award.

Name the only country in the world to have been officially accused of biological warfare

The USA.

The only time the UN has ever invoked the 1972 Biological Weapons Convention – designed to prohibit the use of weapons containing microbes and biological toxins – was in 1996, when the USA was accused of attacking Cuba with a plague of insects.

On Boxing Day 1996 the Cuban Ministry of Foreign Affairs presented the USA with a written accusation of 'entomological warfare'. Both sides agreed on the basics: a US plane had flown over Cuba and released a smoky substance. The Americans said it was a smoke signal designed to alert other aircraft of its presence and so avoid mid-air collisions; the Cubans said it was a swarm of

Thrips palmi, tiny hyphen-shaped insects that destroy citrus, cotton and potato crops. They reproduce frighteningly fast: if Adam and Eve had bred as quickly as *T. palmi*, the Earth would have reached today's population levels just 110 days after they were created.

Cuba's crops were ruined but, after hearing the evidence, the UN's Formal Consultative Meeting concluded that 'due . . . to the technical complexity of the subject and the passage of time, it has not been possible to reach a definitive conclusion with regard to the concerns raised by the Government of Cuba.' This very diplomatic response left neither side particularly satisfied.

Biological weapons date back to antiquity: the Romans threw dead animals into wells to poison their enemies' drinking water. In the second century the city of Hatra repelled the Romans by throwing terracotta pots full of live scorpions at them, but the golden age of biological warfare was the Middle Ages. In the fourteenth century Tatars catapulted the bodies of bubonic-plague victims over the city walls of Kaffa, in modern-day Ethiopia. In 1495 the Spanish tried to poison the French in Naples by mixing their wine with the blood of leprosy patients. (Other than leaving victims with a nasty hangover, this wouldn't have worked: 95 per cent of people are immune to leprosy.) And, in the mid-seventeenth century, the Polish general and artillery specialist Kazimierz Siemienowicz bombarded his enemies with metal spheres filled with the saliva of rabid dogs.

Some commentators have suggested that WMD should stand for Weapons of Minimum, rather than Mass, Destruction. Whether used by armies, terrorists or by accident, biological and chemical weapons are far less destructive than conventional ones. The most widespread use of toxic gas occurred in the First World War, but it still only accounted for 5 per cent of casualties, and victims were ten times likelier to recover than those injured by bombs or bullets.

LINDA SMITH *If any of you do find any weapons of mass destruction under your seats, if you could forward them to the government, because they've looked everywhere. Oh, it'll be the last place they look.*

Name a gas used on the battlefield in the Second World War

No gas was used at any point.

In 1939, on the assumption that gas would be one of Germany's principal weapons, the British government distributed 38 million gas masks across the country. They were never needed. Although the Japanese used gas against the Chinese, chemical weapons played no part in the war in Europe.

One of the main reasons for this was widespread public abhorrence of them. In the First World War they had caused a million casualties, including 90,000 deaths. They were particularly hated for their stealth: they couldn't be seen or smelled until it was too late, and their effects were delayed as well as instant.

The first gas attacks took place in 1915, before gas masks were available. To neutralise the deadly chlorine soldiers were told to soak their socks in urine and wrap them around their faces. Gas masks were quickly developed by both sides and are said to be the reason for Hitler's famous moustache. Before the First World War he'd sported a much bushier, broader 'Kaiser-style' one, but was advised to trim it so it would fit neatly inside his mask.

Mustard gas, the most notorious weapon of the First World War, is not a gas. At room temperature it's a liquid. To be deployed, it has to be finely dispersed by mortars as an aerosol. It was especially lethal because it was strong enough to dissolve the rubber and leather of the gas masks. It smells like horseradish or mustard, hence the name, although the Germans sometimes disguised it with lilac-scented tear gas. Tear gas is also a liquid rather than a gas.

With such experiences still fresh in the memory, it's hardly surprising that the Allies feared gas attacks in the Second World War – and rumours were rife. In Britain it was widely believed that the Germans had filled toy balloons with deadly gas, with which they planned to lure children. In 1941 panic gripped Southampton when fumes that smelled 'like burning onion' filled the town. Everyone put on their gas masks until the smell was traced to a fire at the local pickle factory.

In June 1940 the British media reported that mysterious specks of soot had fallen on towns in south-east England. These were whispered to be the fallout from Nazi 'fog weapons'. Germany's English-language radio station picked up on these rumours and ran with them. It claimed German parachutists had been issued with 'fog pills' that allowed them to create their own cloud which they could float in, invisibly, for up to ten hours. It was pure invention.

Of all the combatants in the Second World War, Britain probably came closest to using chemical weapons. Churchill stockpiled mustard gas in case of a German invasion. The plan was to spray enemy troops with it from the air as they landed on the beaches – which they never did.

Which kind of power station produces the most radiation?

Coal-fired ones: they emit 100 times more radiation than nuclear plants.

Coal contains traces of radioactive uranium and thorium. In small amounts, these present no danger, but burning large quantities of coal for electricity produces 'fly ash' (ash that flies up into the air), in which the radioactive elements are concentrated at up to ten times their original levels. This also contaminates the soil around a conventional power plant. Nuclear waste, by contrast, is contained and safely disposed of.

As a result, people who live near a coal-fired power station may consume crops and livestock with twice as much radiation as those who live near a nuclear plant. But neither represent a serious threat to health. The chance of getting ill from a coal-fired plant is about one in 100 million; with a nuclear plant this drops to one in a billion. You are four times more likely to be struck by lightning than to be affected by radioactivity from any power station.

Areas with large deposits of granite or shale, like Cornwall or Aberdeenshire, contain radon, an invisible, odourless, radioactive gas produced as a natural by-product of the breakdown of uranium. It seeps up through the rock and into houses, where it can pose a serious health hazard if it isn't detected and neutralised. Nuclear power stations cannot be built in Cornwall;

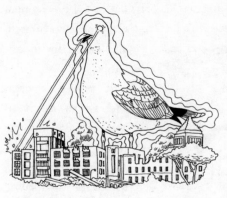

background radiation in the ground is so high that they would automatically breach legal limits before any plant was even switched on.

Another source of natural radiation is the cosmic rays that bombard the planet from space. Most of these are filtered out by the Earth's atmosphere and magnetic field, but the higher you travel, the stronger they become: levels double for every 6,000 feet of altitude gained. As a result, flight crews are exposed to approximately twice as much radiation a year as the rest of us.

The nuclear plant at Sellafield stores radioactive seagulls. It was feared that birds landing on the site might pick up radiation and then fly away, spreading it across the surrounding countryside. The management solved the problem by employing snipers to kill any gulls that did this. The hundreds of dead birds are designated low-level nuclear waste and stored in a freezer.

Why is gasoline called gasoline?

It's got nothing to do with gas.

Gasoline (American English for petrol) gets its name from John Cassell (1817–65), a Mancunian publisher, coffee merchant and temperance campaigner who began importing and distributing crude oil into Britain and Ireland from Pennsylvania in the 1860s.

He called his product Cazeline, after himself, and sold it for indoor lamps.

It proved a great success, so much so that by 1865 he was taking Samuel Boyd, a Dublin shopkeeper, to court for selling counterfeit Cazeline. Boyd had changed the 'c' to a 'g' on all his stock records and then claimed he'd coined the word 'gazeline' himself from *gasogène*, an early French device for making carbonated water. The judge was not impressed and Cassell won the case. But Boyd had the last laugh. Probably because of its similarity to the word 'gas', 'gasoline' caught on and became the preferred name for the product. The last recorded use of the word Cazeline was in 1920.

People have lent their names to many surprising things. Nachos were named after Ignacio ('Nacho' for short) Anaya, who was working in a hotel in Mexico when he threw together some fried tortilla chips topped with melted cheese and jalapeño peppers. This was so popular that customers gave it his nickname. 'Sideburns' were named after the nineteenth-century American soldier (and first president of the National Rifle Association) Ambrose Burnside, who was noted for his unusually bushy facial hair. Gradually this migrated from 'Burnsides' to 'sideburns', probably because they grow from the sides of a man's face.

The word 'dunce' derives from John Duns Scotus, one of the fourteenth century's foremost theologians. He studied and lectured at the universities of Oxford and Paris and died thinking himself one of the wisest men alive. He had many followers but, as his religious theories fell out of fashion, they were ridiculed. First known as the 'Dunsmen', then 'dunses', they were so closed-minded that by 1577 the word 'dunce' had come to mean 'stupid'.

Ferris wheels were named after their inventor, George Washington Gale Ferris (1859–96). Shrapnel was named after the British general Henry Shrapnel (1761–1842), who invented a new kind of exploding shell in the 1790s. The original 'Maverick' was a Texan lawyer and land baron called Samuel Maverick (1803–70), who refused to brand his cattle. In time any cattle in Texas that were unbranded came to be known as 'mavericks'. In 1944 Maverick's grandson Maury coined the word 'gobbledygook'.

JEREMY CLARKSON *Nobody knows what colour petrol is, because it goes into your car and you don't see it. It could be any colour.*
JIMMY CARR *And no one has ever checked.*

Which company is the world's largest manufacturer of tyres?

Not Pirelli. Or Michelin. Or Dunlop.

The world's largest tyre manufacturer is LEGO. They make up to 320 million tyres a year for their toys, far outstripping Michelin's 170 million. LEGO tyres are smaller and not full of air, but they're definitely rubber and they go on the wheels of vehicles.

In Latin *lego* means 'I gather or collect', but that's not the source of the name. The name comes from the Danish *leg godt* meaning 'play well'. The first LEGO bricks were made in 1949, and were copied from an existing toy created by British inventor Hilary Fisher Page. He called his invention the 'Kiddicraft Self-Locking Building Brick' and he filed two patents (for a four- and an eight-stud brick) in 1940 and 1947. Page was one of the first designers to incorporate child psychology into toy design. He didn't live to see the success of his work. He committed suicide in 1957, the year before LEGO launched in the UK.

There are more than 60 LEGO bricks for every person in the world. More than 400 billion have been produced since 1949. Remarkably, all LEGO bricks are fully compatible, whether they were made at the beginning or yesterday.

LEGO human figures were first introduced in 1975, and the early ones were always smiling. Now they display a range of emotions: 'disdain, confidence, concern, fear, happiness and anger', which LEGO says is driven by the increasingly complex 'interaction scenarios' of modern children. In a study of 3,655 figures made between 1975 and 2010, Christoph Bartneck of the University of Canterbury in New Zealand found that the percentage of angry faces has increased.

John Boyd Dunlop patented the pneumatic tyre in 1888, inspired by watching his son bumping across cobbles on his tricycle. Dunlop, a Scottish vet living in Belfast, adapted a leather garden hose to make an inner tube, filled it with water and inserted it between two thin pieces of rubber glued together. Later he replaced the water with air. His patent was rescinded in 1890, because of the earlier claim of another Scot, Robert William Thomson.

Thomson had come up with the idea of an air-filled inner tube (or 'aerial wheel' as he called it) in 1847, but the strong, thin rubber he needed was too expensive to put into mass production. Dunlop's timing was perfect, however. His tyres revolutionised cycling and gave a huge impetus to the developing car industry. The company he founded is now part of the Bridgestone Group, the world's second-largest rubber company after Goodyear.

Wheels on toys are much older than LEGO or Dunlop. The Mayans of Central America made them for their children's playthings, but they never made the connection that they might be useful for adults, such as on barrows, carts or chariots.

What are plastic bags made from?

Gas.

Many people think plastic bags are made from oil. In fact, they're made from natural gas, or ethylene, one of the simplest compounds of hydrogen and carbon. The gas is heated to very high temperatures with a small amount of oxygen: this forms a solid substance – polyethylene, or polythene – from which plastic bags are made.

Polyethylene was discovered by accident in 1899 by German scientist Hans von Pechmann. He didn't see the potential of the new material, and it only became a viable product after work done in the 1930s at ICI. The first item ever made from polythene was a cream-coloured walking stick, but it soon became obvious that the new material was incredibly versatile. It was so useful that its existence was made a national secret during the Second World War. It was used as an insulating material for radar cables, giving Britain a vital advantage in long-distance air warfare.

Today plastic bags are a symbol of people's damaging effect on the planet. In the USA, where the traditional alternative is paper bags, it's not clear they are necessarily better. Plastic bags generate less solid waste and carbon dioxide, and cost 75 per cent less to make than paper bags. The main problem is that people throw them away. If they were all reused or recycled they would be a perfectly green way of carrying one's shopping. So-called 'bags for life' aren't perfect either – in one recent study *E. coli* was detected in half the bags sampled. The researchers said that 'Consumers are alarmingly unaware of these risks and the critical need to sanitise their bags on a weekly basis.'

Despite this, plastic bags appear to be on their way out. San Francisco was the first US city to ban them in 2007. Italy followed in January 2011, and the levy of 15 cents per bag introduced in 2002 has reduced bag manufacture in Ireland by over 90 per cent. It's also produced a huge reduction in 'witches' knickers', the brilliantly descriptive Irish term for discarded plastic bags caught in trees.

What is marmalade made from?

Strictly speaking, marmalade should be made with quinces, not oranges.

Marmalade was originally a quince preserve solid enough to cut with a knife and eat with your fingers. Usually presented in decorative boxes, it was a dessert rather than a breakfast food, and was popular at banquets in the fifteenth century. Its name comes from *marmelo*, the Portuguese word for 'quince' – the earliest version was a Roman quince preserve sweetened with honey. *Marmelada* is still what the Portuguese call quince jelly.

The first printed recipe for modern marmalade appeared in Mary Kettilby's cookbook, *A Collection of Above Three Hundred Receipts in Cookery, Physick and Surgery*, published in London in 1714. It uses whole oranges, lemon juice and sugar. The first commercial marmalade was also flavoured with orange, and was made in Dundee in 1797. The legend goes that a retired merchant called James Keiller bought a few cases of Seville oranges from a Spanish  ship sheltering from a storm in Dundee harbour. He took them home to his wife and she 'invented' marmalade. In fact Janet Keiller ran a sweet and jam-making business and she almost certainly adapted a quince recipe to something more like the soft berry jams she specialised in, made from the raspberries and tayberries in the fields around Dundee and Perth. Her innovation was to add slices of orange rind to the preserve to help it set. TV gardener Monty Don is Janet Keiller's great-great-great-great-grandson.

The Scots probably also invented the tradition of marmalade for breakfast. James Boswell records that he and Dr Johnson were offered morning marmalade on their travels in 1773. Marmalade's heyday was the twentieth century: Captain Scott took it to the Antarctic and Edmund Hillary took it up Everest. Other fans included Winston Churchill (who washed it down with a flute of champagne) and James Bond (who ate it on wholemeal toast).

Marmalade sales have suffered in recent times. Only 7 per cent of people now eat it for breakfast, and over 80 per cent of marmalade consumption is by the over-45s. One such loyalist is Paddington Bear, who keeps marmalade sandwiches under his hat in case of emergency.

STEPHEN *We had the word orange for a fruit, but didn't use it for the colour 'til the sixteenth century.*

SARA PASCOE *Yeah. We always think it was the colour that named the fruit, and it's not, it's the fruit that named the colour.*

DAVID MITCHELL *In those days people would say, what's the name of that red fruit? Oh, the orange.*

Who invented the grapefruit?

According to tradition, it was a legendary figure called Captain Shaddock.

It might sound strange to talk about somebody 'inventing' the grapefruit, but that's exactly what happened. At some point in the comparatively recent past, somebody in the Caribbean took a Jamaican sweet orange (*Citrus sinensis*) and an Indonesian pomelo (*Citrus maxima*) and crossbred them to create the grapefruit. Locals say this 'somebody' was 'Captain Shaddock', who brought pomelo seeds to the islands and bred the first one. Until the nineteenth century all grapefruits were known as shaddocks.

Shaddock is an Anglo-Saxon name, with the same root as the more common 'Chadwick', so it's certainly possible that there was a captain of that name. Whoever was responsible, 400 years ago grapefruits simply didn't exist.

The first documented grapefruit was described in 1750. A Welsh clergyman, Reverend Griffith Hughes, described specimens from Barbados but the fruit wasn't known to be a hybrid until 1940 when it was given the official name *Citrus x paradisi* – the 'x' signifies it's an artificial mixture of two other plants. Barbados has long claimed the invention: grapefruits there are known as one of the 'Seven Wonders of Barbados'.

The grapefruit is not the only citrus hybrid. In fact, none of the familiar citrus fruits – including oranges, lemons and limes – occur naturally in the wild. Some were created by people, others by happy accident – but all are 'genetically modified' foods.

The fruit world is ripe with hybrids. The *Prunus* species, which includes plums, peaches, nectarines and apricots, can be mixed in all sorts of different ways to produce new fruits such as pluots, plumcots and apriums. If you look hard enough in supermarkets, you might come across a 'papple'. It's described as a cross between an apple and a pear, but is actually a cross between two different pear varieties.

The ultimate hybrid plant is the fruit salad tree. These trees are found mostly in Australia, and are created by grafting branches from several plants onto a single rootstock. It's not unusual to grow orange trees with lemons, limes and grapefruit on them, and some trees can support up to six different fruits.

SANDI TOKSVIG *My headmistress at boarding school spent hours teaching us how to eat a banana correctly. She was very worried, and I remember saying, 'Well, how do you eat an orange?', and she looked over the top of her glasses and said, 'No young woman should ever embark upon an orange.'*

What's the world's most popular fruit?

The mango.

More mangoes are eaten worldwide than any other fruit. Ten mangoes are eaten for every apple, and three for every banana.

Mangoes belong to the cashew family, which includes pistachio nuts.

India produces more mangoes than anywhere else. At 15 million tons each year that's a third of the world's supply and four times more than its closest rival, China. Over 98 per cent of India's mangoes are eaten in India rather than exported. Because eating a mango is a notoriously sticky process, it's said that the best way to eat one is naked, standing in the shower.

In a good year a mango tree can give 500 fruits, though one in India's Maharashtra region once bore 29,000 in a single season. In Hinduism mangoes represent fertility. Temples and the front doors of houses are decorated with their leaves and flowers for Hindu New Year. On holy days some Hindus brush their teeth with mango twigs, although this is inadvisable as they're toxic; mangoes are related to poison ivy. People in India used to feed cows mango leaves because it turned their urine a rich yellow and could be used to dye clothes. This is now illegal because the leaves are poisonous to the cows. Burning mango wood severely irritates the eyes.

The USA once banned Indian mango imports for failing pesticide standards – and India banned American Harley Davidsons for failing emissions standards. In 2007 the two countries reached an agreement to relax their respective rules. It was a straight swap: mangoes for motorbikes.

The first mangoes to reach America in the sixteenth century were pickled to preserve them. Soon other pickled fruits became known as 'mangoes': one 1599 recipe explains how to make a 'mango' of walnuts and cucumber. By the eighteenth century the verb 'to mango' meant 'to pickle'. In the Midwest today bell peppers are still sometimes called mangoes.

In 1968, during China's bloody Cultural Revolution, Chairman Mao was left a basket of seven mangoes by a delegation from

Pakistan. He was not a fan of the fruit, so he decided to give them away to the new 'Worker-Peasant Mao Zedong Thought Propaganda Teams' he had recently established to curb the power of the Red Guards. The teams were ecstatic. Rather than eating them, they treated the mangoes like holy relics – enshrining them in glass cases, placing them in formaldehyde (to be preserved for eternity) and parading them through the streets of Beijing. In one factory, a mango was put in a water tank and workers urged to drink from it to imbibe 'the spirit of Mao'. Dissent was not tolerated. One unlucky man who compared the revered fruit to a sweet potato was arrested, tried and executed for his insolence.

DARA O'BRIAIN *No one's ever slid on a banana peel, no one.*
ALAN PUTS HIS HAND UP
DARA *You're kidding me! Of course, the one person . . .*
JIMMY CARR *That is a commitment to comedy Alan, well done.*

Why did Popeye eat spinach?

It wasn't for the iron.

Popeye ate spinach for the first time in 1932, saying, 'Spinach is full of vitamin A an' tha's what makes hoomans strong an' helty.' It does contain plenty of vitamin A: 100 grams (3.5 ounces) provide 187 per cent of your recommended daily allowance. It also contains iron – but no more than other green vegetables such as broccoli. Spinach is also good for your eyesight and boosts muscle tone. In 2002 Japanese scientists implanted spinach genes into a pig to create a healthier and less fatty meat.

The first historical mention of spinach is from sixth-century

Persia, where it was called the 'prince of vegetables'. (It's still known as 'the Persian vegetable' in China.) The Moors brought it to Europe when they conquered Spain. An early French name for the vegetable was *herbe d'Espagne* – the Spanish herb. Spinach didn't catch on in England until the sixteenth century, when it became popular sprinkled with sugar and served in a tart.

Popeye was originally a minor character in a comic strip called *Thimble Theatre*. He soon proved so popular that he got his own comic strip. It became an international phenomenon. At its peak it was published in more than 600 newspapers. Popeye's popularity came as a blessing for farmers. His spinach habit caused spinach sales to rise by a third between 1931 and 1936, insulating many farms from the ravages of the Great Depression.

In 1980 a live-action *Popeye* movie opened in cinemas, starring Robin Williams in the title role. Filmed on Malta, the set has been preserved and is now one of the island's most popular tourist attractions. It can also be hired as a wedding venue, though a little late for Jack Mercer and Margie Hines. The voices of Popeye and Olive Oyl for the cartoon series that ran from 1933 to 1957, they fell in love, married in 1939 and served spinach at their wedding.

What do beavers eat?

All beavers are vegan: they never eat fish.

Beavers primarily eat tree bark and cambium – the soft tissue that grows under the bark – and they supplement their diet with aquatic plants.

They have two front teeth that are orange and never stop growing: they have to grind them together to keep them to a

manageable length — although gnawing tree bark helps. Their lips close *inside* their front teeth, rather than outside, so they can carry wood under water without getting water in their mouths.

A beaver's flat tail is a marvellous instrument. It functions as a rudder when swimming, as a stool to sit on when cutting wood and as an alarm call: when danger is near, beavers slap it loudly on the water to warn their companions. Their tails also make it hard for humans — their main predators — to track them because it drags behind them as they walk, smoothing over their footprints. The tail also acts like a camel's hump, storing fat for times of need.

Beavers build dams to protect against predators and to store food. They are stimulated to build them by the sound of running water. Leave a tape recorder playing the noise of a stream in a dry part of the woods where beavers live, and it'll soon be buried under a heap of mud and sticks.

The largest beaver dam is in Canada's Wood Buffalo National Park. It is 2,800 feet long — more than twice the length of the Hoover Dam. Several generations of beavers have been working on it since the 1970s. Beaver dams are so impressive that humans have been threatened with legal action for building dams that were actually the work of beavers. And it's not just dams; they also construct canals to float logs from one place to another.

In the seventeenth and eighteenth centuries an Englishman's beaver-fur hat was known as his 'beaver'. The best way to tell male and female beavers apart is by the colour of their anal secretions: males' are brown and females' are white. The anal glands of both sexes produce castoreum, which is used in many classic perfumes to suggest the smell of leather, and as a food additive instead of vanilla.

STEPHEN *Don't write to us pointing out that beavers could be mistaken for euphemisms. We never use euphemisms, and we think that people who do are complete front bottoms.*

What does an elephant drink through?

Its mouth — what did you expect?

The Afrikaans word for an elephant's trunk is *slurp*. It can suck up to 12 litres (25 pints) of water. But elephants don't swallow water through their trunks — they use them to squirt it into their mouths. Their trunks are their noses: if they tried to drink through them, they could drown.

The trunk of an adult elephant is over 2 metres (7 feet) long, weighs 178 kilograms (28 stones) and has 40,000 muscles (60 times as many as we have in our whole body). It can lift a third of a ton, knock down trees and floor a lion with a single blow. Yet the two finger-like protrusions on its end are delicate enough to pluck a single blade of grass, and it has a more acute sense of smell than a dog. Elephants can tell which tribe a person belongs to just by sniffing them.

The trunk of a newborn elephant is relatively short and manageable: but baby elephants have to be taught to use it. Scientists have long been puzzled by the evolution of this extraordinary organ. It was once thought that its length and dexterity allowed elephants to reach higher for food. But the current theory is that their ancestors were aquatic. Elephants are the only land mammals with internal testicles (like whales and seals), and elephant embryos have a kind of primitive kidney called a nephrostome, otherwise only found in freshwater fish and frogs. The closest living relatives of elephants are sea cows (dugongs and manatees), and it's now thought that their trunks evolved as a way of breathing under water. Modern elephants still use them as snorkels when they swim.

No other animal has anything like them – and there's nothing so sad as an elephant suffering from the wasting disease called 'floppy trunk syndrome'.

STEPHEN *The king of Swaziland is an absolute monarch, who rules jointly with his mother, known as the Great She-elephant.*

JO BRAND *I know an interesting fact about his mum.*

STEPHEN *The Great She-elephant, yeah?*

JO *Yes, she's got a really good memory.*

What always happens to couples who get drunk in Las Vegas?

They don't wake up married.

The drunken Las Vegas wedding is a familiar plot device from TV and films. At the end of series five of *Friends*, Ross and Rachel get hitched in Vegas after a night of heavy drinking, and in the hit movie *The Hangover* (2009) Stu, played by Ed Helms, wakes up to discover he's married a stripper.

Las Vegas got its reputation for quickie marriages in the 1960s, when Nevada was the only US state that would grant a marriage licence without waiting-time or a blood test. Nonetheless, there are still some safeguards.

For a start, any wedding in the city must be licensed at the Marriage License Bureau, which is quite a distance from the Strip. It won't issue a licence if you appear to be drunk or under the influence of drugs. You will be asked to come back once you've sobered up. The office used to be open 24 hours a day but in 2006 they decided to close between midnight and 8 o'clock in the morning, saving $200,000 a year. So if you do find yourself feeling romantic (but sober), you must collect your licence before midnight. Even so, in 2014 there were 80,700 weddings in Vegas – 220 a day, or nearly 5 per cent of all the weddings in the USA.

One of Vegas's most famous wedding venues is the Little Chapel. For people who want to get married really fast, it has a drive-through facility. It has hosted the nuptials of Sarah Michelle Gellar; Sinead O'Connor; James Caan; Ricki Lake; Judy Garland; Slash from Guns N' Roses; Frank Sinatra and Mia Farrow; and Bruce Willis and Demi Moore. Britney Spears also tied the knot there, though her marriage to her childhood friend Jason Allen Alexander was annulled less than 55 hours later. By contrast Michael Caine wed his wife Shakira there in 1973 – and they are still happily married 42 years later.

Vegas's reputation as the world's top quickie-marriage destination is now being challenged by St Petersburg. In 2011 it began luring Europeans keen on a fuss-free wedding to come to Russia instead. Licences aren't quite as speedy as in Vegas – there's a 72-hour waiting period – but if you prefer picturesque Orthodox churches to drive-through chapels you know where to go.

Vegas is no longer the gambling capital of the world either. Every year since 2006 it has been beaten to the title by Macau, the former Portuguese colony on the south-east coast of China. In 2013 Macau generated gaming revenues more than seven times greater than Las Vegas.

MARCUS BRIGSTOCKE *I was quite impressed. I went to Las Vegas last year and they have those billboard trucks that say they can deliver a hooker to your room in 25 minutes. But the pizza still takes half an hour. So what I worked out is that you could, if you had the resources, get the hooker to pick up the pizza for you.*
STEPHEN *That's absolutely brilliant.*
MARCUS *You still have to pay for extra toppings.*

How old do you have to be for a Club 18–30 holiday?

16–36.

According to the Club 18–30 website, 'The minimum age for travel is 17, the maximum age is 35. To be permitted to travel you must be within this age range on the day of departure.' So, theoretically, you could book your 18–30 holiday while still 16 – two years before you can legally drink or smoke in Greece or Spain – or you could celebrate your thirty-sixth birthday on it.

Club 18–30 adverts have caused a lot of trouble over the years. In the 1990s tag lines included 'Beaver España' and 'It's not all sex, sex, sex. There's a bit of sun and sea as well' – prompting almost 500 complaints. Another featured a picture of a bulging pair of Y-fronts and asked, 'Girls, can we interest you in a package holiday?'

The company has been owned by Thomas Cook since 1999, but it has a very different philosophy from that of the original Thomas Cook (1808–92). The world's first travel agent was an anti-alcohol campaigner and ex-missionary. The first tour he organised took 500 Baptists 11 miles by rail from Leicester to Loughborough to hear a sermon on temperance. The main aim of his trips was to teach 'moral and social lessons' and warn against the evils of drink.

Cook's later excursions included the first round-the-world trip and a tour of American Civil War battlefields. He once led 350 tourists up Snowdon, all the time exhorting them to give up drink with the words, 'Gentlemen, do not invest your money in diarrhoea!' He also established the *Children's Temperance Magazine*, which was 'a cabinet of instruction and amusement of little teetotallers'. It was the first, but not the last, magazine of its kind in England. For grown-ups, Cook wrote temperance hymns, one of which included the immortal lines:

Six hundred thousand drunkards march
To wretchedness and hell;
While loud laments and tears and groans
In dismal chorus swell.

It's a far cry from 'Beaver España': Thomas Cook must be touring in his grave.

When should you report a missing person?

As soon as possible.

It's not true that you need to wait 24 hours before reporting a missing person. You should let the police know as soon as you're worried about them. The first hours are crucial, particularly in the case of missing children.

In 2011 327,000 people went missing in the UK. Two-thirds of them were under 18. Next most at risk are older people with memory problems and the mentally ill. Most people are found within 48 hours, but a third of missing people go missing more than once.

The victims of two child abductions in America have recently solved their own cases. In August 1987 Carlina White became the first infant to be abducted from a New York hospital. She was only 19 days old and being treated for a fever in the Harlem Hospital Center when a woman – later identified as Ann Pettway – stole her by posing as a nurse. She took the baby to Connecticut, only 45 miles away from her birth parents, and changed her name to Nejdra Nance. Growing up, 'Nejdra' became suspicious that she didn't look like her 'mother' and had no birth certificate. She searched the Internet and, aged 23, found a photo on the National Center for Missing and Exploited Children's website that matched her own baby pictures. Subsequent DNA tests proved she was Carlina White and she was reunited with her family in 2011.

Her case inspired fellow American Steve Carter to investigate his own past. He'd been concerned that he knew very little about it, and was puzzled by the fact that his birth certificate had been issued a year after he was born. He visited the same website, found an age-progressed image of a missing boy called Marx Panama Barnes and realised he was looking at himself. It turned out his biological mother had kidnapped him and placed him in an orphanage three weeks later. She had changed his name and birth date, as well as the ethnicity of his father so that he wouldn't be able to trace him.

In 2012 a woman on a coach tour of a remote area of Iceland accidentally joined in a search for herself. She'd got off the bus to freshen up and, shortly after she got back on, the police were called when a passenger was reported missing – a woman described as Asian, around 1.6 metres (5 foot 3 inches) tall, in dark clothing and speaking good English. Not recognising herself from this description, the woman joined in the search, which involved more than 50 people and lasted till three in the morning. It was called off when she finally twigged what had happened and sheepishly told the police. The other passengers hadn't noticed her get back on the bus because she'd changed her clothes . . .

STEPHEN *How long should you wait before reporting a missing person to the police?*
SUE PERKINS *Well, certainly until they're missing.*

How long does it take to play the 'Minute Waltz'?

About a minute and a half.

Chopin never called his whimsical work the 'Minute Waltz'. He called it 'The Little Dog Waltz', claiming the inspiration for the tune came from watching a small dog chasing its tail. The tune's modern nickname was invented by Chopin's publishers – but they didn't intend it to refer to how long it takes to play. 'Minute' also means 'very small' (think 'my-newt', not 'minnit') and simply refers to the fact that the piece is very short.

Like Mozart before him, Frédéric Chopin (1810–49) was a musical prodigy who was prone to eccentricity. He taught himself to play the piano aged seven and in the same year had his first composition published – a polonaise in G minor. The following year Frédéric gave his first public concert, but decided the concert hall was not for him – he only performed publicly 30 times, much preferring the private salon or tutorial. The emotional intensity of his music and his virtuoso technique combined with a tempestuous love life and constant ill health have helped to fix him in the public mind as the archetypal romantic composer. But there was nothing flamboyant about Chopin: he was a private, nervous person who lived for music, and was obsessed with producing the most 'beautiful quality of sound'. Even his signature was in the shape of a musical note. He was beset by neuroses – he believed ejaculation weakened the creative impulse, and he was so scared of premature burial that in his will he requested his body should be dissected before burial. But he died having revolutionised the repertoire for solo piano and left behind one of the best-loved bodies of work of any classical composer.

To play Chopin's 'Minute Waltz' at the speed the composer intended takes around a minute and a half. The great pianist

Liberace disagreed; he 'cut out the dull parts' and managed to play it in 37 seconds. In 2010 the Royal College of Music ran a competition to find the person who could play the 'Minute Waltz' the fastest while still playing the notes distinctively. The winner completed the tune in 53 seconds.

This would have amused Chopin: he never gave his works a name, was famed for his improvisations and prided himself on never playing a piece exactly the same way twice. The names were attached for marketing purposes by his publishers. Occasionally this led to confusion – his 'Second Piano Concerto' was actually written before his 'First Piano Concerto' but the names stuck because they were published in reverse order.

Another famously misattributed work is Purcell's 'Trumpet Voluntary', which is not by Purcell and was written for the organ. The 'trumpet' in the title refers to 'the trumpet stop', a particular valve of a pipe organ. Voluntaries were organ solos played before or after the church service, and were supposed to sound improvised (hence 'voluntary' or 'free'). The piece (more correctly known as 'The Prince of Denmark's March') was written in 1700 by Jeremiah Clarke, the organist at St Paul's Cathedral. It was wrongly credited to his more famous contemporary, Henry Purcell, from the late nineteenth century until the 1940s and has become a standard at English weddings.

Somewhat ironically, Clarke later committed suicide as a result of a 'violent and hopeless passion for a very beautiful lady of a rank superior to his own'. To decide the method he tossed a coin: heads he would hang himself, tails he would drown. The coin landed on its side in a mud patch, so he shot himself.

What's the best kind of violin?

Since 1817 repeated tests have shown that neither amateur nor professional musicians can tell the difference between a Stradivarius and any other make of violin.

In 2010 21 violinists were asked to rate six different violins: three modern ones, two made by Stradivarius and one by his main rival, Guarneri. The three classic violins were worth over 100 times as much as the three new ones. Most of the violinists chose one of the newer instruments as their favourite, and in one instance the Stradivarius came last.

Antonio Stradivarius and his family made over 1,100 musical instruments, 650 of which survive, and 512 of these are violins. In 2011 a Stradivarius once owned by Byron's granddaughter sold for £9.8 million, making it the most expensive violin ever sold. The most highly priced musical instrument of any kind is also a Strad – a viola called the Macdonald. In 2014 Sotheby's put it up for auction at an asking price of £27 million. There were no takers.

Several explanations for the supposed quality of the Stradivarius sound have been proposed. One suggestion is that lower temperatures during the 'Little Ice Age' of the late seventeenth century led to slower tree growth, producing denser wood with superior acoustic properties. Others believe Stradivarius added a secret ingredient to his varnish or used magically endowed wood from ancient churches.

The human tendency to experience expensive things as 'better' is driven by the psychological phenomenon known as 'cognitive dissonance'. We become uncomfortable if reality doesn't live up to our expectations, so we adjust reality accordingly. And it works. If people pay a higher price for an energy drink, like Red Bull, they are able to solve more brain-teasers afterwards than those who paid a lower price for the same drink. They expect the more expensive drink to be more effective, and their brains make reality conform to this expectation.

In one experiment, 54 oenologists (students of wine) were asked to evaluate what they were told was a fine red wine. They all described it with typical red wine words, such as 'jammy' and 'crushed red fruit'. Afterwards, they found out they'd been drinking white wine dyed red.

Which day is added to make a leap year?

24 February.

Until shortly before the birth of Jesus, Rome observed a 355-day calendar – which was obviously imperfect, as it was ten days shorter than the rotation of the Earth around the Sun. To make up for this the priests in charge of the calendar were supposed to add 'leap months' whenever necessary. But they couldn't be trusted. If they disliked a particular senator, they deliberately neglected to add extra months to his rule, and if there was a pressing matter, such as a civil war, they might simply forget.

Over time these errors added up, until eventually summer festivals were starting in the middle of spring and harvest rituals were being scheduled months before the crops were ready. In 46 BC Julius Caesar decided enough was enough and set up a commission to work on reforming the year.

The new Julian calendar, as it later became known, immediately solved most of the problems because it was 365 days long. However, as a year is almost a quarter of a day longer than that, a leap day was still needed every four years, and Caesar decided to add it to February. The extra day was counted as *ante diem bis sextum Kalendas Martias*, meaning 'a second sixth day before the first day of March'.

The sixth day before 1 March was 24 February. Technically speaking, this is the day that gets added even today and the remaining days in February are bumped along by one. In France the leap day is still known as *bis sextum*.

More evidence for the 24th being the extra day comes from Denmark, where by tradition the one day women are allowed to propose to men is 24 February in a leap year. Additionally, until 1970, the Catholic feast of St Matthias was celebrated on 24 February in a normal year and 25 February in a leap year.

If you think adding an extra day in the middle of a month is complicated, pity the poor Romans who lived through the original changes. To bring the year back into step with the new calendar, 46 BC had to be 445 days long. Caesar called that year *ultimus annus confusionis* ('the last year of confusion'), but most people missed out the *ultimus* and just called it 'The Year of Confusion'.

Who brought the first Christmas tree to Britain?

It wasn't Prince Albert.

The first Christmas tree in England went up in December 1800, when Queen Charlotte, wife of George III, gave a children's party. One of the grown-up guests remarked, 'After the company had walked round and admired the tree, each child obtained a portion of the sweets it bore, together with a toy, and then all returned home quite delighted.'

Christmas trees soon became wildly fashionable in high society, but it took 40 years (helped by the popular press) for them to catch on across the country. By then Queen Victoria's husband, Prince Albert, was busy importing them, which is why they are so often associated with him.

Prince Albert and Queen Charlotte were both born in Germany, where families had been bringing evergreen trees indoors and putting candles on them since the sixteenth century. According to legend, the first person to do this was Martin Luther (1483–1546), better known for his role in the Protestant Reformation. One evening, it's said, he looked up at the night sky, saw the stars twinkling between a tree's branches, and decided to recreate the effect in his home. Luther was a controversial figure. He was also said to eat a spoonful of his own faeces every day. The Christmas tree story may be romantic fiction, but the German tradition of decorating trees indoors did begin in Luther's lifetime.

Artificial Christmas trees became popular in Britain after the death of Queen Victoria, when large ostentatious trees suddenly seemed inappropriate. The first ones were made from goose feathers that were dyed green. These were also imported from Germany, where they had become fashionable as a way of conserving the country's fir tree population. But artificial Christmas trees only took off in the 1930s with mass production by the Addis Brush Company. Founded by William Addis, inventor of the toothbrush, they used the same machinery to make bristly branches that they used to make toilet brushes.

Today artificial Christmas trees are seen as an environmentally conscious alternative to the real thing. Unfortunately, an independent study released in 2009 showed that, to be greener than buying a fresh-cut tree each year, you would have to reuse your plastic tree for more than 20 years.

JOHN SESSIONS *Do you think Hitler's Christmas tree only had one ball hanging on it?*

What did Prince Albert invent?

Stop sniggering at the back!

Queen Victoria's husband, Prince Albert, was a very capable man. He set up the Great Exhibition, campaigned against poverty and helped avert an Anglo-American war in 1861. There is no evidence whatsoever that he invented the genital piercing named after him.

[43]

What he *did* invent was a mechanism for the bedroom door, so it could be locked without getting out of bed. He and the queen were very much in love: Victoria later wrote in her diary that their wedding night had been 'gratifying and bewildering'. (Both were just 20 when they married.)

Albert was initially unpopular with the English – Parliament wouldn't give him an allowance and refused him the title of 'Prince Consort'. But he got fully stuck into the business of government, especially during the queen's frequent absences due to pregnancy – at one point they had nine children under the age of 15. Albert drafted her official letters, did all the paperwork, and acted more or less as her PA. He was the one who removed the monarchy from party politics. This caused huge rows between the royal couple; but when Albert died aged just 42 (of typhoid, or possibly Crohn's disease), all was forgiven and Victoria started 40 years of mourning.

Albert was greatly missed. After his death virtually everyone in the country wore a black armband and many people closed their blinds and shuttered their shops. In the countryside even beehives were draped in black. The Queen mourned him for the rest of her life. Until the day she died, her personal notepaper had a black border half an inch thick. She had Albert's rooms preserved, and every morning had his clothes laid out and ordered hot water for him to shave. Whenever the royal family had their photo taken, they were joined by Prince Albert's marble bust.

The mythical name of the eponymous genital piercing dates back no further than the 1970s, concocted by a piercing enthusiast called Doug Malloy. He invented the story that Albert used it to secure his penis to one side to avoid looking indecent in the fashionably tight trousers of the period. Mr Malloy provided no evidence of this beyond his own assertion.

Who invented the Nazi salute?

It was eighteenth-century French artists, not the ancient Romans.

Despite the persistent belief that stiffly holding out the right arm as an act of greeting or loyalty originated with the ancient Romans, there is not a single contemporary statue, painting, coin or literary reference describing such a gesture. Like many other cultures, Romans did use their right hands to swear oaths and loyalty, but not in that way. The first depiction of the so-called 'Roman salute' appeared in *The Oath of the Horatii*, painted in 1784 by the French neoclassical artist Jacques-Louis David. It shows three brothers from a noble Roman family (the Horatii) saluting their father before doing battle with three brothers from a rival city. The government of Revolutionary France so admired this work, with its emphasis on patriotism and self-sacrifice, they appointed David as their official artist.

A hundred years later America needed a salute to accompany the American Pledge of Allegiance, written by the Christian Socialist Francis Bellamy (1855–1931). With the gesture now firmly associated with revolution, Bellamy chose the 'Roman salute', and American schools adopted it from the turn of the twentieth century. For 30 years American schoolchildren reciting the pledge routinely gave what was to become the Nazi salute.

In the 1920s Italian Fascists adopted the 'Roman salute' to symbolise the idea that they had rebuilt Italy on the model of ancient Rome. It was then copied by the National Socialist German Workers' Party, and became the familiar *Heil Hitler* salute. The Nazis invented an alternative history: that it was a revival of the *deutscher Gruß* ('German greeting'), which they claimed was used during ancient gatherings of Germanic peoples. There is no evidence to support this.

The similarity between the Nazi salute and America's Bellamy salute led to confusion, especially during the Second World War. Americans with Nazi sympathies would claim photographs of them giving the Nazi salute actually showed them using the Bellamy salute.

To prevent this, President Franklin D. Roosevelt replaced the Bellamy salute with the hand-over-the-heart gesture, which is now enshrined in US law. During the Pledge of Allegiance and the national anthem, American citizens must stand up, take off their hats and put their hands over their hearts as a mark of respect to the American flag.

However, since 1989 it's no longer an offence not to comply. This is due to the case of Gregory Lee Johnson, who was prosecuted by the state of Texas for burning a US flag outside the Republican National Convention in Dallas in 1984. He appealed on the grounds that his actions were 'symbolic speech' and protected by the First Amendment of the Constitution, which guarantees freedom of expression. The Supreme Court upheld his appeal, ruling, 'Freedom of speech protects actions that society may find very offensive, but society's outrage alone is not justification for suppressing free speech.'

As well as people no longer having to remove their hats during the national anthem, Texas vs Johnson also means that the US Flag Code, adopted in 1923 and forbidding misuse of the American flag, is now treated as advisory. US firms may now use it to promote their products.

In which war did both sides fight under the Union Jack?

It's not the English Civil War: the flag hadn't been invented then.

During the American War of Independence (1775–83), many American rebels fought under the Union Flag (as the Union Jack was traditionally known when not at sea). It was their way of declaring loyalty to King George III while at the same time asserting their independence from the British government.

The first flag of independence raised by the Americans was at General Washington's camp. It had 13 red and white stripes, but the top left corner, or 'canton' – the most important quarter of the flag – bore the Union Flag.

The British flag flew on several other occasions throughout the war. At the Battle of Newton in 1779, both sides fought beneath Union Flag ensigns. The flag of the Federal Colonies had St George's cross in the canton, as did the flag flown by the Americans at Bunker Hill in 1775. Today the Union Flag is still in the canton of Hawaii's state flag – it's the only US state to have kept it.

The Union Flag was designed after James I became king of both England and Scotland. He gave the job to the Earl of Nottingham, who wanted to put the red and white cross of St George and the blue and white saltire of St Andrew next to each other – the heraldic way of denoting marriage. The 'male' arms would go on the left and the 'female' ones on the right.

However, many Scots were unhappy with this, because Scotland was being placed in the wifely position, and 'impaled' (as heraldic jargon puts it) by England. So the current design was adopted, with the two crosses interlaced. Unfortunately, the Scots were unhappy with this too, as the flag of St George was on top of that of St Andrew; they wanted their own Scottish version which was the other way around. The argument was settled when the two kingdoms merged in the Act of Union of 1707 and the Union Flag was formally adopted by both nations.

Flags flying at half mast are not, traditionally, halfway down. They are a single flag's width below the top of the pole. One flag that will never be flown at half mast is the Queen's flag, the Royal Standard. This is because, technically, the sovereign never dies: the new monarch seamlessly takes over at the very moment the previous one dies.

What colour are the flags on the Moon?

There's one red flag with yellow stars, but the rest are almost certainly white.

In December 2013 China's *Chang'e 3* became the first unmanned spacecraft to soft-land on the Moon since the Soviet Union's *Luna 24* in 1976. In Chinese mythology Chang'e is the goddess of the Moon, and the lunar rover was named after her pet Yutu ('jade rabbit'). Yutu emerged from *Chang'e* and took a photograph of her, complete with the Chinese flag attached to her side. It was the first national flag to have appeared on the Moon for over 30 years.

American astronauts planted six flags on the Moon. Five of them are still standing, but none of them will have any markings left. Over the decades, they have been exposed to searing sunlight and

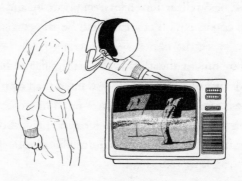

ultraviolet radiation in the Moon's thin atmosphere, which will have caused them to gradually fade to white. Assuming they have prior knowledge of what human flag colours mean, any belligerent aliens who stop off at the Moon en route to invading Earth will assume we've already surrendered.

The most famous flag on the Moon – the one carried by *Apollo 11* and erected during the first Moon landing – is the only one not standing. Buzz Aldrin saw it being blown over by the rocket blast as he and Neil Armstrong left for home. Given the extremes of heat, cold and radiation it will have been subjected to, it's very likely to have disintegrated. Dennis Lacarrubba, whose New Jersey-based company made the flag, has been quoted as saying, 'I can't believe there would be anything left.'

Conspiracy theorists who believe the Moon landings were a hoax often cite the flag in the *Apollo 11* photographs and ask how it could be waving when there is no wind on the Moon. The answer is simple: the flagpole was made of light, flexible aluminium. Because there's so little air resistance on the Moon, when the astronauts let the flagpole go it continued to vibrate, giving the impression of the flag blowing in the wind.

Not everything taken to the Moon has proved so impermanent. Twelve astronauts walked on the surface of the Moon between 1969 and 1972. Their footprints are still there, and will last for centuries. As well as footprints, they left behind six lunar vehicles and 200 tons of litter, including several golf balls and a stowaway cockroach.

There's no news of the cockroach, but a piece of litter from *Apollo 12* still had living bacteria on it three years later, despite temperatures close to absolute zero, and no water or nutrients. Eugene Cernan, the last man to walk on the Moon, wrote his daughter's initials, TDC, in the lunar dust. They are expected to be legible for another 50,000 years.

What colour is the dark side of the Moon?

Turquoise.

The 'dark' side of the Moon is not the same as the 'far' side of the Moon. The far side of the Moon is the part that always faces away from Earth, because the two orbits are locked in sync. The dark side is the one that is currently getting no light from the Sun, and changes all the time. It's strange to think that the far side of the Moon, rather than being permanently dark, is often brilliantly lit by the Sun. It's just that there's rarely anyone out there to see it.

When the dark side of the Moon is facing towards us, it is faintly lit by light reflected from Earth. Researchers at the Mauna Loa Observatory in Hawaii spent two years studying this and showed that, because the light reflected by the Earth is mostly blue, it turns the Moon a bluey-green colour. In other words, the dark side of the Moon – the bit of it that we can see, at least – is turquoise. Rather pleasingly, this light on the Moon is called 'Earthshine'.

Only 24 humans have seen the far side of the Moon with their own eyes – and nobody has seen it since the *Apollo 17* crew in 1972, over 40 years ago. Man has never landed on the far side – six probes have been deliberately crashed there, but no landing craft have touched down.

On the near side of the Moon the tracks of astronauts are still visible even after four decades – the Moon has no atmosphere to wear them away. NASA has mapped Neil Armstrong's and Buzz Aldrin's footprints and found they didn't get very far: they roamed an area hardly bigger than a football pitch. Aldrin mostly stayed in one half.

There are spots on the Moon that are permanently dark. Some craters at the north and south poles are so deep that sunlight never gets to the bottom of them, even when that side is lit. The craters at the south pole are the coldest known part of the solar system, colder even than Pluto – they are permanently at −240 °C. There may even be ice there.

Moon craters were once named after famous astronomers. Now they can be named after anyone. One online service offers to name one after you for a $40 fee. Crater names now include Albert, Boris, Dale, Edith, Igor, Lawrence, Manuel, Norman, Osama, Priscilla, Romeo, Ross, Stella, Susan, Theon Junior, Theon Senior, Vera, Walter and Zach. There's also a Dove, a Fox, a Lamb, a Parrot and a Wolf, as well as a Cannon, a Husband and a Wiener.

What happens nine months after a blackout?

There won't be a baby boom.

No one has ever been able to find documentary proof of a spike in births nine months after a blackout, or indeed after any kind of natural disaster. They are often reported in the newspapers but, under closer inspection, they all fall well inside the expected natural fluctuations in birth rates.

Statistically speaking, these things have a tendency to balance out. While the lack of electricity might encourage one couple to stay in bed and have sex, it might also stop their neighbours from getting home from work on time, and so reduce their chances of conceiving.

The myth seems to have started after a blackout in New York in November 1965. The *New York Times* reported on a 'sharp increase' in births, which actually amounted only to 39 more births than normal, across six hospitals. Five years later, when

Richard Udry of the University of North Carolina studied the figures for the entire city, it became clear there was no significant increase in births, and the *New York Times* issued a retraction. That hasn't stopped the papers running similar stories since then: as recently as 2013, the *Daily Mail* reported that New York's Hurricane Sandy had caused a huge baby boom.

Even if more people did conceive during a blackout, there is unlikely to be a spike nine months later, because most births don't occur exactly nine months after conception. A 2013 study from the US National Institute of Environmental Health found length of pregnancy varied between women by as much as five weeks. Fewer than one in 20 women given a date by their doctor deliver the baby on time, and a quarter are more than ten days out. Some doctors have queried the value of 'due dates' as they make mothers feel unnecessarily anxious if they miss theirs.

Conception and birth rates are pretty constant across the year in Europe and America, with a small spike in births from March to May. This was even more marked in medieval Europe. Despite the suggestive connotations of traditional May Day celebrations, in rural areas conception was more likely to happen in late summer when people were working long hours in the fields at harvest time. What you didn't want during harvest was a woman in the final stages of pregnancy or any breastfeeding newborns. For that reason Advent was regarded as a 'second Lent', and a period of abstinence imposed by the Church – which ran from early November until after Christmas.

STEPHEN *What happens nine months after a blackout?*
ROSS NOBLE *The power company finally give you the cheque for a refund?*

When should you be eating for two?

Not when you're pregnant.

Pregnant women don't need to 'eat for two'. It's more like eating for one and a tenth. According to guidelines from the National Institute for Health and Clinical Excellence (NICE), pregnant women need no extra calories at all for the first six months. During the last three they do need a small increase — about 200 calories a day, or two slices of buttered toast.

The earliest mention of the phrase 'eating for two' appeared in Philadelphia in 1860, in a women's magazine called *Godey's Lady's Book*. It's also the first debunking of the idea, as the author calls it an 'absurd notion'. Women who take 'eating for two' seriously may live to regret it. According to research by Bristol University, women who gain more than the recommended weight while pregnant are three times as likely to become overweight later on, sometimes as much as 16 years after giving birth.

Historical dietary advice for pregnant women was no better than today. In the fifteenth century it was believed that diet affected the baby's looks. Eating hare's heads would give your child a hare lip, eating fish heads would make them look fishy and eating soft cheese would give a baby boy a small penis. Even in the early twentieth century women were told to avoid salty foods, lest their children develop a 'sour disposition'.

Table for one please...

In his book *On Monsters and Marvels*, sixteenth-century surgeon Ambroise Paré advised that, since foetuses are so soft and malleable, if mothers-to-be saw a piece of food they wanted but couldn't eat, the baby might come out looking like it. He also claimed a baby could become 'monstrous' if a pregnant woman had a mouse or frog thrown onto her breasts.

A baby in the womb swallows up to a litre of amniotic fluid every day, and can sense taste from just 13 to 15 weeks of pregnancy. Babies experience any flavour that gets into the mother's bloodstream. Pregnant or breastfeeding women who drink carrot juice can pass a liking for carrots on to their children and a mother's milk can taste of banana just an hour after she eats one.

By the twentieth week of pregnancy, a mother's body has 50 per cent more blood than usual. This is why pregnant women seem to 'glow'. Less glamorously, it can also lead to haemorrhoids, varicose veins and nose bleeds.

JO BRAND *When I got pregnant, my grandma said to me, 'Oh, eating for two are we?' And I said, 'Bog off, I'm not cutting down.'*

What was the first chainsaw used for?

Delivering babies.

In 1783 a Scottish doctor called John Aitken created the first chainsaw – for midwives. It was hand-powered and had a fine serrated chain with a handle at either end. By 1830 this had evolved into the osteotome (from the Greek for 'bone-cutter'), which was also hand-held and had a continuous loop of chain powered by a handle rather like an old-fashioned egg whisk. It is clearly

recognisable as the forebear of the modern chainsaw.

Aitken developed his chainsaw to perform a very tricky operation known as a symphysiotomy. The pubic symphysis is the cartilage that joins the left and right pubic bones (symphysis means 'growing together'). Cutting this joint was an extreme measure used to widen the pelvis in the event of a difficult birth. It often ended up damaging the bladder and urethra and could make walking difficult and painful. It was replaced by the Caesarean section but is still used in remote areas, or where the risk of a Caesarean is too high.

There have been very few innovations in the science of childbirth since the introduction of forceps in the nineteenth century. But recently, in 2008, an Argentinian motor mechanic called Jorge Odon presented a new device to the World Health Organization (WHO). Inspired by a trick his workmates showed him where a cork is removed from an empty wine bottle using only a plastic bag, Odon's device inserts a double layer of plastic into the birth canal to surround the baby's head. Air is then pumped into the bag, inflating a plastic chamber that gently grips the head around the chin (the baby doesn't use its nose to breathe until after birth). The baby is then pulled out without causing damage or bleeding. It could revolutionise birth procedures, especially in developing countries, as the device is simple enough to be used by a midwife without a doctor present. WHO has approved it for a proper trial and it is expected to be in clinical use within the next two years.

Chainsaws were eventually adapted for use on trees. They were a welcome invention for lumberjacks as they replaced a tool called the 'misery whip' – a saw 10 feet long with a handle at either end that had to be operated by two men. Before 1945 most forestry chainsaws were also two-man devices, as they were too cumbersome and heavy for one man to hold.

The record for the most chainsaws caught in a minute is 94, and was set in 2011 by juggler Ian Stewart, using three chainsaws. After his record-breaking success Stewart – who is also a hypnotist – commented, 'I love juggling chainsaws . . . I know that's a little weird, but I really enjoy the noise, I like the action of it and I like that they're so big when I'm throwing them.'

What was the best thing before sliced bread?

Wrapped bread.

The advertisements for Kleen Maid sliced loaves, first sold in 1928, ran, 'The greatest forward step in baking since bread was wrapped: sliced bread.' Not only that, sliced bread was actually invented *because* of wrapped bread.

In the early twentieth century Americans preferred bread from government-owned factories: it was thought more hygienic than traditional bakers' bread. Factory bread was recognisable because it came wrapped in plastic bags. As these were opaque, you couldn't see or smell the bread; all you could do to judge its freshness was feel how soft it was, which became the benchmark of quality. As loaves got softer and softer, it became harder and harder to slice them.

In 1912 a jeweller from Iowa called Otto Rohwedder came up with the idea of pre-sliced bread. To find the ideal width of a slice, he sent out a questionnaire to 30,000 American housewives. Developing the concept took him 16 years. Fearing sliced bread would go stale, he tried fixing the slices together with hat pins. Then one of his workshops burned down. It took him another decade to afford a new slicing machine but, when he'd built it, nobody was interested – it was 5 feet long and 3 feet wide, far too big for most bakeries. Finally, in 1928, someone agreed to buy one, and pre-sliced bread was born.

As one reporter wrote at the launch, 'The housewife can well experience a thrill of pleasure when she first sees a loaf of this bread with each slice the exact counterpart of its fellows . . . here is a refinement that will receive a hearty and permanent welcome.' It was a huge success – the bakery's sales went up twentyfold in a fortnight.

During the Second World War, the US government banned sliced bread to save on the heavy wrappers the loaves needed. There was uproar and within three months the ban was lifted. The first use of the phrase 'the best thing since sliced bread' was in 1969.

In the mid-nineteenth century, a third of all the money spent on food in Britain went on bread. These days, a third of bread bought in the UK is thrown away when it could be eaten. When tested, most people can't tell the difference between two-day-old and six-day-old bread.

ALAN *You shouldn't really feed bread and milk to any mammal, including humans.*
DAVID MITCHELL *We've been drinking milk and eating bread for ages. Why is it suddenly a massive problem? Oh no, actually, we're supposed to live until we're 250 but no, we're eating all this poisoning bread and milk all of a sudden, we can barely live past 98.*

Who invented the sandwich?

It wasn't the Earl of Sandwich.

People have almost certainly been putting food between pieces of bread for as long as bread has existed, but even the oldest documented sandwich pre-dates the famous earl by more than 2,000 years. The sandwich in question was made in the first century BC by a rabbi called Hillel the Elder, and the filling consisted of lamb, horseradish and chutney made of chopped nuts, apples and spices marinated in wine. Variants of the 'Hillel sandwich' are still used by Jews today to celebrate Passover.

Hillel was born in Babylon, but lived in Jerusalem at the time of King Herod, Jesus and Emperor Augustus. He was a radical religious leader and a wise and good man: several of his sayings are repeated almost word for word by Jesus in the Bible. And he invented something even better than the sandwich – 'The Golden Rule', which is at the heart of all great religions, expressed as 'Do as you would be done by' or, in the words of Jesus, 'And as ye would that men should do to you, do ye also to them likewise.'

The man who didn't invent the sandwich was John Montagu, Fourth Earl of Sandwich (1718–92). According to the myth, he was a compulsive gambler who ordered meat wrapped in bread to keep one hand free to play cards. But his biographer, N. A. M. Rodger, says this story is not only untrue but unfair.

The story dates from 1765, a year when Montagu was very busy as First Lord of the Admiralty. It seems much likelier that his fondness for convenience food was due to the fact that he often had to eat a rushed lunch at his desk. He did supply the name, though. Before he came along, sandwiches didn't have one. They were just called 'bread and meat' or 'bread and cheese'.

Montagu came from a long line of gastronomic innovators. His great-great-grandfather, Sir Edward Montagu, First Earl

of Sandwich (1625–72) was a keen collector of recipes. One recommended chocolate, snow and salt to be shaken together. The result was basically a Mocha Frappuccino, 335 years before Starbucks registered their trademark. The current Earl of Sandwich – the eleventh – recently opened a sandwich restaurant called Earl of Sandwich, though its website says they're taking a 'short break' to look for new premises.

The first earl was given a choice of towns to name himself after when he was offered a peerage. He picked the coastal town of Sandwich because his fleet was anchored nearby. It wasn't his first choice – he wanted to be the Earl of Portsmouth. If there hadn't been an existing Lord Portsmouth at the time, we might now all be eating cheese and tomato portsmouths.

STEPHEN *What would be the best flavour for an exploding sandwich?*

TIM VINE *Cheese and hand grenade?*

Which country invented ice hockey?

Sorry, Canadians. It was Britain . . .

Along with lacrosse, ice hockey is Canada's official national sport, and it's a matter of great pride to Canadians that they invented it. The cities of Halifax and Windsor in Nova Scotia both stake a claim, as do Montreal and Kingston, Ontario, but the game was actually invented and first played in England. One of the earliest known players was Charles Darwin.

It's possible that ball games have been played on ice for centuries, but the earliest record of ice hockey is an engraving of a young man skating on a frozen Thames, wearing a top hat and carrying a curved stick. It appeared in a book called *Juvenile Sports and Pastimes* in 1797, almost 80 years before the first official ice hockey match took place in Canada in 1875.

More than two decades earlier, in 1853, Charles Darwin wrote to his son, William Erasmus Darwin, 'My dear old Willy. Have you got a pretty good pond to skate on? I used to be very fond of playing Hocky [*sic*] on the ice in skates.' Darwin wasn't the only famous player: Prince Albert and the Prince of Wales (the future King Edward VII) were also keen participants before English army officers took it across the Atlantic and introduced it to Canada.

While ice hockey was invented in England, the modern game is definitely Canadian. The 'father of ice hockey' was a Montreal lawyer and engineer called James George Aylwin Creighton (1850–1930). It was he who organised the first match in 1875, captained the first official team formed in 1877 and codified the rules the same year. Creighton was an enthusiastic rugby player and, as a result of this, for the first 50 years forward passing wasn't allowed.

Hockey has changed a lot since then. In the earliest matches teams swapped sides each time anyone scored, goals were announced by a man ringing a bell and, oddest of all, the goal mouths faced the sides of the rink rather than each other. Gradually the game evolved into the fast-paced, end-to-end sport we know today.

Genuine Canadian inventions include table hockey, the walkie-talkie and the egg carton.

Which country invented the motorway?

It wasn't Germany: the Americans beat them to it.

The Long Island Motor Parkway (or LIMP) opened in 1908. It was the first road built solely for the use of motor cars, the first to be made from concrete and the first to use overpasses and bridges to avoid intersections. The world's first motorway was 45 miles long and ran from Queens in New York City to Lake Ronkonkoma on Long Island.

It was privately financed by the racing enthusiast William Kissam Vanderbilt II, the great-grandson of Cornelius Vanderbilt (1794–1877), founding patriarch of one of America's wealthiest families. *Automobile* magazine welcomed it with the headline 'First of the motorways is opened – an epoch in motor-driven land transportation'. It wasn't cheap to use – the standard toll was $2 (about $45 today) – and by the mid-1930s it had closed. The explosion in private car ownership had necessitated the building of a public road system (much of it based on ideas that the Parkway had pioneered). Ironically, most of the parts of the Long Island Motor Parkway that survive are now used as a cycle path.

Germany wasn't even the first country in Europe to build a motorway – that was Italy. Mussolini built an 80-mile stretch from Milan to Varese in 1924. The first motorway in Germany was built in 1932, the year before the Nazis came to power. Once in office, they downgraded its status to 'country road' so they could take the credit for building the first German autobahn.

The assumption that Germany built the first motorway is an enduring legacy of the effectiveness of the Nazi propaganda machine. In 1934 Hitler announced Germany would build 1,000 kilometres of autobahn a year, creating 600,000 jobs. Seven years later, only 3,800 kilometres had been completed using just 120,000 people – many of them Russian prisoners of war and Jewish forced-labour squads. By 1942 all construction work had stopped and the following year the almost empty autobahns were opened to cyclists. Despite this, the propaganda films continued throughout the war, showing Hitler opening new motorways built by cheerful German workers.

The UK didn't get its first motorway until 1958, when the 8-mile long Preston bypass opened (it's now part of the M6). The first full-length motorway was the M1, which opened the following year. People had to be taught how to use it and police regularly cautioned people for 'stopping without due cause', 'walking along the motorway' and 'driving backwards'.

When the M25 opened in 1986, it attracted huge interest. Coach tours were particularly popular with people from Norfolk, many of whom had never seen a motorway before, let alone travelled on one. Today Norfolk is one of only five English counties that still don't have a motorway running through them. The others are Suffolk, East Sussex, Dorset and Cornwall.

The idea of an orbital ring road for London had been around since 1905. But at that point it was less a motorway than a horse-and-wagon-way. The Royal Commission's proposals included lining it with water troughs and providing patrols by 'emergency wheelwrights and horseshoe-fitters'.

Why did motorists have to carry red flags in front of them?

They didn't.

In 1865 Parliament passed the Locomotives on Highways Act, which required a man with a red flag to walk 60 yards ahead of all motor vehicles.

However, the only vehicles this applied to were traction engines and steam buses. In 1878 the flag was made optional – and the man only had to be 20 yards ahead – but red flags were never compulsory for cars, because the first car wasn't patented until 1886.

For the first ten years, though, cars did have to have a man walking out in front. He was known as a 'stalker' and was one of three men required for each vehicle – one to steer, one to stoke the engine and one to stalk. The law was often ignored: the engineer Sir David Lionel Salomons of Tunbridge Wells built himself an electric tricycle and drove around solo, in flagrant disregard of the requirement to use a stalker. The speed limit was 2 miles an hour in cities and 4 miles an hour in the countryside.

As cars became smaller and faster the rules became increasingly ridiculous.

In 1896 the speed limit was raised across the board to a blistering 14 miles an hour and the legal requirement for a stalker abandoned for every vehicle below three tons. At this point there were probably only 70 or 80 cars in the UK.

The 1896 act was nicknamed the 'Emancipation Act' and Britain's tiny band of drivers celebrated by holding the first ever London to Brighton Rally. As part of the celebrations a red flag was ritually destroyed, even though one hadn't been compulsory for any vehicle for nearly 20 years. Thirty-three cars competed, of which only 17 made it to Brighton.

The speed limit stayed at 14 miles an hour into the twentieth century and only increased with the Motor Car Act of 1903, which raised it to 20 miles an hour. The act also introduced the new offence of dangerous driving and set the lower age limit for drivers at 17. Driving tests weren't introduced until 1935. The first man to pass one was called Mr Beene.

But early British motoring regulations weren't the silliest in the world. At the turn of the twentieth century, a law in Tennessee required drivers to post a public notice of any impending car trip at least a week before they set off.

JEREMY CLARKSON *So nobody ever had to follow a car [with a red flag]?*
STEPHEN *No.*
JEREMY *I've seen a drawing of somebody doing it. I know drawings aren't necessarily real, but . . .*
JASON MANFORD *I saw a drawing of a unicorn once.*

What kind of glass does the US president's car have?

It's not bulletproof.

Glass manufacturers get very twitchy about the word 'bulletproof'. It implies that something will stop anything fired at it. They prefer to call it 'bullet-resistant glass'.

All the same, bullet-resistant glass is exceptionally tough. It's made of sheets of normal glass interspersed with layers of extremely resilient plastic. These are heated to bind them together. The more layers, the tougher the glass. If a bullet shatters the outer glass, the plastic absorbs and dissipates its energy. Protection from a modern rifle bullet needs 2 inches of bullet-resistant glass. The highest grade is 4 inches thick, but this is extremely heavy and requires specially reinforced window frames.

One neat innovation is 'one-way' bullet-resistant glass: someone firing from the outside can't shoot in, but anyone on the inside can return fire. It's made from a rigid outer layer of glass and a flexible inner one of shock-absorbent plastic. When a bullet enters from outside, the glass shatters, dissipating the bullet's energy, which is then cushioned by the plastic. But a bullet fired from the inside easily punctures the soft plastic and still has plenty of power left to exit the glass.

Armament manufacturers are currently developing liquid bulletproof materials, which harden as soon as they are disturbed. The industry nickname for this stuff is 'bulletproof custard', because while you can slowly sink your hand into a bowl of custard, if you punch it, it feels solid.

The Popemobile has been bullet-resistant since the assassination attempt on Pope John Paul II in 1981. He later asked the media not to use the word 'Popemobile' as he thought it was undignified, but they ignored him. Earlier popes got about in a *sedia gestatoria* (literally 'chair for carrying'). It was a silken throne on a platform shouldered by 12 footmen and last used in 1978.

Pope Francis doesn't bother with a bullet-resistant vehicle. In 2014 he told reporters, 'It's true that anything could happen, but let's face it, at my age I don't have much to lose.'

STEPHEN *How many popes does the Vatican have per square kilometre?*

ALAN *One.*

STEPHEN *No. There's actually 2.27 recurring, because Vatican City is only .44 of a kilometre.*

JIMMY CARR *Well, I think we have it, ladies and gentlemen, the most annoying question ever asked.*

Would you take a bullet for me?

You'd have to be very lucky and inhumanly fast.

We've all seen it happen in cartoons and films: the bad guy pulls a gun on the hero, but as he fires the hero's sidekick throws himself in the way of the bullet, shouting 'Nooooooooooo!' It's a great plot device, but completely impractical.

Bullets move too fast for people to dive in front of them. Handgun bullets travel at well over a thousand miles an hour (and high-powered rifle bullets at up to 1,700 miles an hour). If a gunman fired 30 feet away from the person you wished to save, you'd have only three hundredths of a second to get in the way. That's three times faster than an Olympic athlete is allowed to set off at the beginning of a race without it being given as a false start.

US Secret Service agent Tim McCarthy 'took a bullet' to save Ronald Reagan's life from the assassination attempt by John Hinckley in 1981. But he managed this by getting into position to shield the president after shots had already been fired. In the event that you could get in the way before the gun went off, you would probably succeed in saving your friend: a handgun bullet is unlikely to pass clean through a human body. And, even if it did, it would expend almost all its energy on the way.

When people are shot, they fall over – but not from the force of the bullet. The impact from a bullet is not powerful enough to knock over an average-sized adult. If it were, the same energy would recoil against the shooter, knocking them over backwards as they fired. In energy terms, being hit by a bullet is like being hit by a cricket ball delivered by a fast bowler – it could knock you over, but you'd have to be off balance already.

So why do people fall over when shot? Evidence suggests they only fall over once they realise they've been hit. It's a psychological, rather than a physical, reaction – partly caused by shock and partly by watching too many movies.

STEPHEN *Regardless of bullet, calibre or where they're hit, people who've been shot, but don't know it yet, don't fall over.*
BILL BAILEY *Unless your leg was shot off.*

What might you find in the average British courtroom?

Not a judge. Nor a jury. And certainly not a gavel.

Magistrates, not judges, hear 95 per cent of criminal court cases in the United Kingdom, and these happen without a jury. The very few cases too serious for a magistrate are heard in the Crown Court, where juries may be present, but usually aren't. Fifty-nine per cent of all cases are settled by a plea of guilty, so a jury is unnecessary. Overall, juries decide only 12 per cent of all Crown Court charges.

Another thing you won't see in a British courtroom is a gavel.* Unlike American judges, who make frequent use of them, British judges have never used them.

To make an objection in a British court it's not necessary to jump out of one's seat and shout 'Objection!' at the judge. A British barrister will half-rise, cough discreetly or raise an eyebrow at the judge, and sit down again.

The modern way to restore order in a courtroom (as often happens at the International Criminal Court) is to switch off the witness's microphone.

In the nineteenth century, barring very rare specialist all-women juries, jurors were all male. Women did not sit on normal British juries until 1920. According to the *New York Times*, there was a murmur of astonishment in a Bristol court when the judge first said 'Ladies and Gentlemen of the jury' instead of the time-honoured 'Gentlemen of the jury'. Many British women couldn't sit on a jury until as recently as 1974. Jurors were required to own or lease a property, and most married women lived in a home held in their husband's name.

Juries weren't always expected to be impartial. They once investigated the facts of the case rather than merely listening to the evidence. It wasn't until the mid-eighteenth century that English law banned juries from bringing their own personal knowledge to bear on a case. Despite these improvements, a 2010 study of the justice system in England and Wales found that two-thirds of jurors didn't really understand the judge's legal directions.

In Australia a study of jury bias found that 60 per cent of people thought a defendant was guilty if they were sitting in a

---

* See also *The Discreetly Plumper Second Book of General Ignorance*, p. 133.

glass dock, compared with 36 per cent if they were sitting at an American-style table, even with identical evidence and witnesses. According to a 2011 Israeli study, judges are between two and six times more likely to release prisoners at the start of the day or immediately after a break.

So, if you're ever up before the beak, try to time it for after lunch.

What's the oldest profession?

Tool-making.

If you thought it was prostitution, Rudyard Kipling would have agreed with you. In his short story 'On the City Wall' (1888) he was one of the first to call it 'the most ancient profession in the world'. In fact, the oldest profession that we know about for certain is the production of stone tools, or 'flint-knapping'.

The ancestors of modern humans were turning lumps of flint into tools more than 2.5 million years ago – long before they discovered how to make fire or even how to speak. In fact, making tools may have helped them learn to talk. Modern research shows that the area of the brain used to make a stone tool is very close to that which controls language.

In *The Descent of Man* (1871) Charles Darwin wrote, 'To chip a flint into the rudest tool . . . demands the use of a perfect hand . . . the structure of the hand in this respect may be compared with that of the vocal organs.' Early attempts at language are likely to have been hand gestures reinforced by sound, so the flint-knappers, with their skilled hands, may have given mankind the tools to speak as well as those to survive.

Stone hand axes are by far the most popular tool ever made,

multipurpose objects that can be used for both bashing and cutting. They were virtually the only tools in use for the first 2.3 million years of human existence; all other implements have been made in the last 200,000 years. To make hand axes, hard 'hammerstones' were used to chip off flakes of stone into a basic shape. This was then refined with a softer hammer, such as a piece of antler.

How old is prostitution? Though we don't have any definite evidence that it pre-dates flint-knapping, it may in fact be older than humanity itself. When a group of capuchin monkeys at Yale University were given tokens that they could swap for treats, such as grapes, it didn't take long for one of the male monkeys to trade one of his tokens for sex. (Having obliged him, the female who took the token swapped it for grapes at the earliest opportunity.)

STEPHEN *Anyway. Moving on. What's the oldest profession?*
DAVID MITCHELL *Prostitute!*
KLAXON
DAVID *I'm just shouting prostitute like I usually do.*
ALAN *It must be 5 o'clock.*

Who first wore high heels?

Men. Soldiers, in fact.

High-heeled shoes were invented in the Middle East — probably in Persia, where they date back to the ninth century. They were designed for horsemen to keep their feet firmly in the stirrups and were so effective that riders could stand upright and fire a bow and arrow at the gallop. (American cowboys still wear boots with raised heels.)

Heels made their way to Europe in the sixteenth century, when men started to wear them as fashion statements. Louis XIV wore shoes with 4-inch heels to look chic and to boost his height. To show they were manly, he had them decorated with battle scenes. His courtiers were allowed to wear high-heeled shoes with red soles to show they belonged to the court – so heels became a status symbol. Charles II of England wore an enormous pair of heels to his coronation in 1661, despite being 6 feet tall.

Women only started wearing heels as part of a 1630s fashion for imitating men: they also cut their hair, took up smoking pipes and wore men's hats. Even children started wearing heels. In seventeenth-century Europe everyone was wearing them.

In the eighteenth century the Enlightenment declared that men were inherently rational, and so should wear rational clothing. By the 1730s they'd abandoned high heels, part of a fashion shift called the 'Great Male Renunciation'. They also stopped wearing make-up and lacy tops. Women hung on to their heels for another 50 years, but even they gave them up after the French Revolution. It wasn't until the advent of photography and the rise of the erotic postcard that heels came back into fashion again.

Platform shoes are even older than high heels. They have been traced back to ancient Greece, where the goddess Aphrodite often clumped about in them. In Renaissance Venice women wore 'chopines' – platform shoes several inches high. They needed two servants to prop them up to walk in the street.

Wildly impractical shoes signify wealth and privilege. If you're wearing 6-inch stilettos, there's no way you could work in the fields – so the fact you are wearing them shows you're not expected to.

Name a traditional Italian bread

Grissini, Altamura or piadina – but not ciabatta.

Ciabatta was invented in 1982. The first citation for it in the *Oxford English Dictionary* is from 1985, the year it was introduced to Britain by Marks & Spencer. And the reason it was invented was to spite the French.

In 1982 French baguette imports were flooding Italy's sandwich market and robbing the locals of trade. A group of Italian millers met and discussed how to create an equally tempting product. They spent weeks testing new batches of loaves until one of them, Arnaldo Cavallari, came up with 'ciabatta'.

Ciabatta is Italian for 'slipper'. Cavallari called it that because he thought it looked like one. Luckily for Italy, the bread became hugely popular – as did Cavallari himself. Not only was he the saviour of his country's bread, he was a four-time national rally champion. The title of his autobiography gives a sense of his style: *A Life in the Sun: The Rally, the Bread, the Women*.

French bread only took on its long thin shape in the nineteenth century, and even this wasn't popular in the provinces until the twentieth. The baguette look was seen as a fancy metropolitan fad, pandering to the effete Parisian fondness for crusts.

The French bakers' lobby – the delightfully named 'Observatoire du Pain' – claims the French eat a sixth as much bread as they did a century ago. In 2013 this prompted them to launch a nationwide poster campaign reminding people, '*Coucou, tu as pris le pain?*' ('Hey, have you picked up the bread?') Even so, the French still get through 10 billion baguettes a year, and France has the world's highest concentration of independent bakeries.

Ciabatta is relatively new to Britain, but bread has been baked here since 3500 BC. Lumps of burned Neolithic bread were found in Oxfordshire in 1999.

Bread is 80 per cent gas – mainly bubbles of carbon dioxide produced by the yeast as the dough rises.

Who first ate frogs' legs?

The English.

The earliest record of a frog or toad being cooked anywhere in the world comes from a Mesolithic site a mile from Stonehenge in Wiltshire, where in 2013 archaeologists found the remains of a three-course meal. The charred amphibian's leg appears to have been a starter, followed by a fish course and finally blackberries for pudding. The site is dated to around 7000 BC – some 8,000 years before the first evidence of frogs being eaten in France.

Frogs were a nutritious snack for Stone Age Britons – easy to cook and with lots of protein. They had long been eaten in

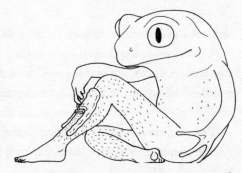

China and were independently popular in the Aztec Empire too. It wasn't until the twelfth century that French monks, banned from eating meat, managed to get frogs designated as fish, thus kick-starting a national delicacy.

Edible frogs are now a protected species in France after the frog population plummeted: so they're imported, mainly from Indonesia and Bangladesh. The French get through three to four thousand tons of legs a year, which is about 70 million frogs' worth. In Asia they're even more popular. It's believed that a billion frogs are taken from the wild and end up on human plates each year, raising the risk that they may soon become seriously endangered.

The great French chef Escoffier thought the British aversion to eating frogs stemmed from the fact that the word 'frog' itself isn't particularly appetising. He had more success after renaming them 'dawn-nymphs'. On Chinese menus they're delicately described as 'field chickens'. Two hundred years before Escoffier, *The Accomplisht Cook* by Robert May offered this exciting recipe: a pie made with live frogs that would 'cause much delight' and cause any ladies at the table to 'skip and shreek'.

What happens to most of the world's liquorice?

It's not in Liquorice Allsorts; it's in cigarettes.

Most liquorice isn't used in sweets but to flavour and moisten tobacco. A 2011 report by the world's largest liquorice producer stated that almost two-thirds of their sales were to the tobacco industry.

Liquorice belongs to the pea family and grows to over 2 metres (6 feet 6 inches) tall with attractive purple flowers. But farmers are only interested in the rhizome – the part of the stem growing under the soil. The word 'liquorice' is from the Greek *glycyrrhiza*, which means 'sweet root'. A little goes a long way – the extract of the root, glycyrrhizin, is 50 times sweeter than cane sugar. Liquorice is also an important ingredient in shoe polish and soap and helps produce the foam in fire extinguishers.

Liquorice's first documented appearance in England was in 1579, but monks may have grown it in their herb gardens before then. Until the nineteenth century it was mostly used as a medicine – even the classic liquorice sweet known as 'Pontefract cake' was designed as a pastille to be dissolved in water and drunk to aid digestion. It was also used to treat wounds, asthma, eczema and urinary problems and to ease the pain 'of disenchanted relationships'.

On the down side, glycyrrhizic acid, also found in the roots, inhibits the production of testosterone, and liquorice eaten by people over the age of 40 can cause irregular heart rhythms – although you'd have to eat over 55 grams (2 ounces) a day for at least a fortnight.

It wasn't until the late nineteenth century that liquorice was widely used for sweets. Some had grim names and shapes: 'Kelly-in-a-Coffin' was a sugar baby in a tiny casket, and another from 1895 was called a 'Hangman's Noose'.

Liquorice Allsorts are made by Bassett's of Sheffield at the rate of 14 million a day. They also make Jelly Babies, originally named 'Peace Babies' to mark the armistice at the end of the First World War. But they were modelled on sweets made in 1864 by the Lancashire confectioner Fryer's, under the slightly alarming name 'Unclaimed Babies'.

Name the most important vow taken by Trappist monks

Sshhhhh! Don't say that! Trappists have never taken a vow of silence.

The official Trappist website says monks may speak for three reasons: 'functional communication at work or in community dialogues; spiritual exchange on different aspects of one's personal life; and spontaneous conversation on special occasions'. Another website adds, 'Trappists enjoy friendly conversations with each other in a conversation room.'

Trappist monks are definitely quiet, which is encouraged as it creates more time for silent prayer. Until the 1960s many monks were so keen to keep quiet they communicated using sign language. One old text gave signs for 127 words and phrases, including, 'I would like a sacramental wafer', 'I would like fish' and 'I need a whip'. Older monks still remember the signs to this day.

The three vows Trappist monks do take are: a vow of stability (promising to live with one monastic community for the rest of their lives); a vow of obedience to a particular abbot; and a vow of 'conversion of manners', a promise to live the monastic life in all its parts.

The Trappists began in 1664 as a reform movement within the Cistercians, who had themselves begun as a reaction to the perceived laxness of the Benedictines. The Cistercians established themselves near Dijon in 1098 at Cîteaux (Cistercium in Latin).

The Trappist movement was led by Armand Jean le Bouthillier de Rancé (1626–1700), abbot of La Trappe Abbey in Normandy. He was concerned that the implementation of the Rule of St Benedict (the set of guidelines for the monastic life laid down in the sixth

century) had become too relaxed, and urged much stricter observance, involving silent prayer and agricultural work. In 1892 the pope granted the Trappists their own order, independent of the Cistercians. Today there are only about 3,900 of them worldwide. Trappist nuns are called Trappistines.

Despite their reputation for austerity, Trappists make some of the world's best beer. They are not required to abstain from alcohol and, because they sell it to support their community, they are simply obeying chapter 48 of St Benedict's Rule: 'for then are they monks in truth, if they live by the work of their hands'. Because their beer contains high residual sugar and live yeast, unlike most beers, it develops its flavour in the bottle. The Trappists of St Sixtus Abbey in Belgium brew Westvleteren XII, considered by many to be the world's best beer. When in 2012 they decided to make a small amount of it available, they got so many calls that the local telephone exchange crashed.

JIMMY CARR *The oldest joke I found that still sort of works is an old Greek joke, and it was: a barber says to a man, 'How do you want your hair cut?' And the man says, 'In silence.'*

Which town hanged a monkey thinking it was a French spy?

It didn't happen in Hartlepool, whatever the locals tell you.

It's a great story. During the Napoleonic Wars the people of Hartlepool spotted a French ship in trouble off the coast. As they watched nervously to see if any enemy sailors would come ashore, a lone figure washed up: the ship's monkey mascot, dressed in a military uniform. No one in Hartlepool had ever seen a monkey – but they had never seen a Frenchman either. So they assumed the short, hairy creature was a French sailor, did their patriotic duty and tried the creature as a spy. Unsurprisingly, it was unable to answer any of the court's questions and so was found guilty and hanged in the town square.

Today the local Rugby Union team Hartlepool Rovers is known as 'the Monkeyhangers' and, in 2002, 'H'angus the Monkey', the man who performed as Hartlepool United Football Club's mascot, was elected the town's mayor.

Some local historians think the people of Hartlepool may have actually hanged a boy rather than a monkey. Boys who worked on the gundecks of eighteenth-century warships fetching gunpowder were known as 'powder monkeys'. Perhaps one of these was the only survivor of the shipwreck.

In fact, the whole thing is a myth. The first known reference to the story is in an 1850s song by Ned Corvan (also known as Cat-cut Jim), a popular north-eastern music hall artist of the time. It seems he adapted a popular joke about monkeys and Frenchmen and attached it to Hartlepool.

There's no mention of the event in the extremely thorough *History of Hartlepool* written in 1816, a year after the war ended – and none in the local press cuttings from the time. Furthermore, exactly the same story is told of Boddam, Cullen and Greenock in Scotland and Mevagissey in Cornwall.

ALAN *When the monkey was in the dock, it was very evasive. Didn't give a straight answer to any question.*
CLIVE ANDERSON *'This is a kangaroo court,' he said.*

What's the northernmost place on mainland Britain?

Surely it's John o'Groats?

Not so. John o'Groats is the most north-easterly point of Britain, but a place called Dunnet Head is even further north. There isn't a great deal to see in the village of John o'Groats, but there's only a lighthouse at Dunnet Head.

John o'Groats isn't even the furthest point from Land's End. There's an uninhabited spot called Duncansby Head, which is a few miles further away – though not as far north as Dunnet Head and not as far east as John o'Groats. At the other end of the country, Gwennap Head is further from Duncansby Head than Land's End.

Until recently John o'Groats was very run down: the Scottish magazine *Urban Realm* pronounced it 'the most dismal place in

Scotland', adding, 'The overriding temptation upon reaching the famous northerly cliffs is to chuck oneself off them.' Until 2013 you had to pay £10 to have your photograph taken next to the signpost pointing to other parts of the UK – though you could personalise it to add your hometown. But the village has now been spruced up – and there's a sign you can photograph for free.

The original John o'Groats was a fifteenth-century Dutch ferryman called Jan de Groot. His tomb is in the church in the nearby hamlet of Canisbay.

It's about 600 miles as the crow flies from John o'Groats to Land's End, but well over 800 miles by road. The record for running the route is nine days and two hours. In 2005 a golfer named David Sullivan hit a golf ball the whole way: it took him three months, 247,000 shots and about 300 balls. In 2008 an enterprising pensioner made the journey using his free bus pass and did it in just over a week.

The first attempt to walk the distance was described in the book *From John O'Groat's [sic] to Land's End, or 1372 miles on Foot.* It was written by two brothers, Robert and John Naylor, who made the trip in 1871 and simply seemed to fancy a really long walk. They went a very circuitous route to see as much as they could, refused all offers of lifts, didn't allow themselves to drink or smoke, and had to visit at least two religious services every Sunday.

STEPHEN *In 2005 a golfer named David Sullivan hit a golf ball all the way from John o'Groats to Land's End. It took him three months.*

CAL WILSON *And did he mean to do it? Did he mean to do it? Or was he just trying to get it in the hole, you know?*

Which country do missionaries go to more than any other?

America.

In 2010 32,400 missionaries travelled to the USA from other nations – more than to any other country. These 'reverse' missionaries from Asia, Africa and Latin America give two main reasons for going there. The first is that America is the modern 'Rome'. It's the world's largest Christian country, as well as the wealthiest, the most powerful and the one with the best education system. To base a Christian mission in the USA gives a movement global legitimacy and prestige. The second reason is that many see the USA as a Christian nation in trouble. Although the proportion of churchgoers in the USA is four times greater than in Britain and 71 per cent of Americans still call themselves Christian, this has dropped by 15 per cent since 1990. In addition, the country's status as a 'beacon of light' has been tarnished by the rise of consumerism and sexual immorality. To preserve Christianity as the world's biggest religion, particularly in the face of a militant Islam, America can't be allowed to fail and follow Europe's lead into secularism.

At present America also produces more missionaries than any other nation – in 2010 they exported 127,000 of them. Most go to Christian countries – the top nine destinations contain a third of the world's

Christians, and only 3.5 per cent of the world's non-Christians. This is largely because many non-Christian countries restrict or deny missionary access: people suspected of working as Christian missionaries in Muslim countries such as Saudi Arabia, Somalia and Northern Nigeria face arrest and imprisonment.

Early missionaries made it a lot further and a lot faster than many people realise. There were Christian monasteries in China in the sixth century and, in the eleventh century, a third of the world's Christians were living in Asia.

One of the most famous American missionaries was Lottie Moon (1840–1912). Born into a devout Southern Baptist family in Virginia, she was one of the first women to receive a degree at a Southern university. Fluent in five languages, including Hebrew, she left teaching in her early thirties to become a missionary in northern China. To be a single, female missionary at that time was almost unheard of and she campaigned tirelessly to win equality for women in the Baptist Church. She also set remarkable personal standards, sharing all she had with the Chinese people around her, many of whom were starving to death. She herself died of malnutrition on her way back to America, aged 72. A legendary symbol of the American missionary movement, the Lottie Moon Christmas Offering for Missions has since raised a total of $1.5 billion.

Where did the *Mayflower* land in America?

Every American schoolchild knows the answer is 'Plymouth Rock', but that's wrong.

Plymouth, Massachusetts, today is a popular tourist area and Plymouth Rock is the 'most visited rock in New England',

with over a million visits each year. It has come to symbolise the pilgrims' courage and steadfastness. But it's almost certainly not where they landed.

In 1620 102 men, women and children set off from Plymouth, England, to settle in North America, where they would be free to practise their religion as they wished. Today they are called Puritans, but at the time they were known as Separatists. ('Puritans' were those who stayed behind and tried to purify the old Church.) The hired crew of the *Mayflower* called them neither; they referred to them as 'Psalm-singing puke stockings'.

The *Mayflower* first made landfall at the tip of Cape Cod, but the colonists eventually settled by a small hill, coincidentally already called Plymouth, just like their port of departure from England. With their ship anchored nearby, the colonists set up their new town. While their anchorage was supposedly at Plymouth Rock, there's almost no evidence for this. The whole story rests on the testimony of a man in his nineties, writing more than 120 years after the event. So he wasn't an eyewitness, and recent research has shown he probably misremembered.

The man in question, Thomas Faunce, was the son of one of the Pilgrim Fathers. At the age of 94 he decided he wanted to see the area one last time. He was carried for more than 3 miles on his chair to the shore, where he saw the boulder and began to weep. He claimed his relatives had landed right there. With nobody left alive to contradict him, the myth of Plymouth Rock was born. No first-hand accounts of the landing mention any rocks at all, and the captain of the *Mayflower* would have been mad to try and tie up to a large rock in a heaving December swell when a convenient inlet lay close by.

In 1774 some of Plymouth's patriotic citizens decided to move the boulder from the shore to the front of the town's meeting-house. Twenty teams of oxen were brought in for the job, but as the men loaded the rock on to a carriage, it split in two. Now in much more manageable pieces, the bottom half was left where it lay, while the top half was taken into town.

Fifty years later the rock was moved again, this time to the front of a new museum. Again it fell from the cart and split. Worse still, locals swarmed over it with hammers and chisels and grabbed their own little splinters of history. The bottom half of the stone that remained on the shore didn't fare much better. In the 1860s, it was trimmed to fit inside a monument, and a bit left over was used as a doorstep.

Today visitors often comment that what remains of Plymouth Rock is a little underwhelming. This is hardly surprising: it's barely a third of its original size, and only a third of that is visible. The rest is buried below the sand.

HENNING WEHN *Puritans, they regarded luxury as sinful, didn't they?*

STEPHEN *Yes, they did.*

HENNING *So some of them set off to America and the others opened B&Bs in Britain.*

What was the date of the American Declaration of Independence?

2 July 1776.

In 1776 the Continental Congress voted to declare the 13 US colonies 'Free and Independent States' not on the 4th but on the 2nd of July. John Adams, later the second president, excitedly wrote to his wife telling her that in the future, 2 July 1776 would be seen as 'the most memorable epoch in the history of America' and that it would be celebrated with 'shows, games, sports, guns, bells, bonfires, and illuminations from one end of this continent to the other'. As we know, he was wrong.

So how did the Fourth of July become Independence Day? After the vote, Congress decided to inform the public by issuing an explanatory document – essentially, a press release. But they took two days to approve the final wording and it wasn't until 4 July that the Declaration of Independence acquired its first two signatures: John Hancock and Charles Thomson. Copies were distributed across the nation with '4th July' printed on them, and that became the date we're all familiar with. The British government didn't find out that America had declared independence until 10 August.

So how did the new country celebrate the first anniversary of the momentous 2 July vote? They didn't. By then, the 4th – the date on the document – had become the one that everyone remembered.

Famous people born on 2 July include the German novelist Hermann Hesse, the former first lady of the Philippines, Imelda Marcos, and the American actress Lindsay Lohan.

STEPHEN *I happened to be at a 4th of July party the American ambassador was holding at his house in Regent's Park, and . . .*
PHILL JUPITUS *Stephen, you've got to tell us, was it Ferrero Rocher as far as the eye can see?*

When should you take down your Christmas decorations?

February.

Taking down decorations on Twelfth Night (5 or 6 January) is a modern superstition. For many centuries they were kept up until Candlemas Eve, 1 February. Candlemas celebrates Mary and Joseph taking the baby Jesus to the Temple at Jerusalem and presenting him to the Lord. According to St Luke's gospel they had to sacrifice two pigeons to do so.

Early Christmas decorations consisted mainly of greenery, which kept the house looking cheerful even when the weather outside was miserable. Some people clung to older, pre-Christian beliefs about these – namely that they contained woodland spirits who, if you left the decorations up, would cause mischief in your house. Careful householders took them down and burned them just to make sure.

In North America Candlemas is celebrated as Groundhog Day. Groundhogs are large rodents related to squirrels and, according to folklore, if it's cloudy when a groundhog emerges from its burrow on this day, spring will come early. If it's sunny, the winter weather will persist for six more weeks.

Of course, the groundhog has no interest in weather forecasting: he's looking for a mate. Recent statistics, released by the USA's National Climatic Data Center, 'show no predictive skill for the groundhog'. Groundhog Day comes from an older medieval European tradition of the Candlemas Bear, where people watched for a hibernating bear as it awoke to get a similar weather prediction. The rarity of bears in France meant that this duty eventually had to be taken over by a man in a bear costume. A similar tradition in Germany is called *Dachstag* ('Badger Day'), and in Ireland they use a hedgehog.

Until the seventeenth century 'Christmas' lasted almost three months, from the Feast of St Martin on 11 November to Candlemas on 2 February. Although today it doesn't officially begin until Advent (the fourth Sunday before Christmas), the shops make it seem as if it's starting earlier and earlier – a process known as 'Christmas Creep'. This is getting faster, and it's not just retailers. Analysis of Internet searches in 2007 found people started looking for 'Santa Claus', 'elf' and 'presents' on 11 November. By 2013 they started on 25 August.

Which holiday is celebrated on 26 December every year?

It's not Boxing Day.

Boxing Day in Britain is defined as 'the first working day after Christmas', so it's not always on 26 December.

For example, if Christmas Day falls on a Friday, Boxing Day is on Monday the 28th, because the Saturday and Sunday aren't working days. When Christmas falls on a Saturday, Boxing Day is on Monday the 27th (the next working day) and, to make up for Christmas Day being on a weekend, the Christmas Bank Holiday moves to Tuesday the 28th – so that, in one sense, Boxing Day

sometimes comes before Christmas.

But there is a holiday that always takes place on 26 December: the Feast of St Stephen. Appropriately for someone whose feast day comes the day after Christmas, St Stephen is the patron saint of headaches. He also looks after deacons, horses and coffin makers, and is the patron saint of stone workers – which is grimly ironic as he was the first Christian martyr to be stoned to death.

St Stephen's Day is celebrated as an official public holiday throughout most of Europe; only Commonwealth countries celebrate Boxing Day instead. The name comes from the British tradition of giving small 'Christmas boxes', containing money or treats, to workers for their service throughout the year.

In Scotland Boxing Day was once known as 'Sweetie Scone Day', when the lords and ladies of great estates would make cakes with dried fruit and spices to distribute among the poor.

In Ireland Boxing Day is sometimes called 'Wren Day', after a tradition that continued till the early twentieth century. Children hunted and killed a wren and took it from door to door, offering its feathers in exchange for money.

Boxing Day in Wales was even grislier: female servants who were caught oversleeping were traditionally whipped with holly branches.

Which seasonal event was 'Jingle Bells' written for?

Thanksgiving.

'Jingle Bells' is the only Christmas song that doesn't mention Christmas, Jesus or the Nativity. That's because it was written to celebrate Thanksgiving.

Originally entitled 'The One-Horse Open Sleigh', 'Jingle Bells' was the work of American composer James Lord Pierpont (1822–93), uncle of the financier J. P. Morgan. Pierpont's father commissioned it for a Thanksgiving service.

Pierpont led a wild life – at 14 he ran away to sea and joined a whaling ship. At 27 he left his wife and children in Boston to join the California gold rush. After re-inventing himself as a photographer, he lost all his possessions in a fire and moved to Savannah, Georgia, where he joined the Confederate army during the Civil War. Throughout this period he continued to write songs, ballads and dance tunes, including Confederate battle hymns and 'minstrel' songs for performance by white people with blacked-up faces. Some of his less festive tunes include 'We Conquer or Die' and 'Strike for the South'.

The states of Massachusetts and Georgia both claim Pierpont was there when he wrote 'Jingle Bells' in 1857. Wherever he was, he made very little money out of it and never lived to see his song's enormous popularity.

'Jingle Bells' was the first tune played live in space. On 16 December 1965, as US astronauts Wally Schirra and Tom Stafford were preparing to re-enter the Earth's atmosphere in *Gemini VI*, Stafford contacted Mission Control to report a UFO. 'We have an object, looks like a satellite going from north to south, probably in polar orbit . . . Looks like he might be going to re-enter soon . . . I see a command module and eight smaller modules in front. The pilot of the command module is wearing a red suit.' Before Houston could respond, Schirra began playing 'Jingle Bells' on a harmonica he'd smuggled aboard in his spacesuit. He was accompanied by Stafford on sleigh bells.

'Rudolph the Red-nosed Reindeer' started life as a colouring book devised by US advertising copywriter Robert May in 1939. His reindeer was originally called 'Reginald' but he changed his mind at the last minute and the book sold 2½ million copies in its first Christmas alone. The song was written a decade later by May's brother-in-law Johnny Marks, who also wrote 'Rockin' Around the Christmas Tree'. Marks was Jewish, joining a tradition of Jewish songwriters behind classic Christmas songs, including 'White Christmas' (Irving Berlin), 'Let It Snow' (Sammy Cahn) and 'Santa Baby' (Joan Javits).

The story of 'Winter Wonderland' (1934) is a sad one. The lyrics were inspired by watching children playing in the snow outside the sanatorium where songwriter Dick Smith was dying of tuberculosis. He died the following year but, unlike Pierpont, at least saw his song – performed by Guy Lombardo and His Royal Canadians – reach number 2 in the US *Billboard* charts.

Who should you visit on Mothering Sunday?

The vicar.

Rather than being a day for visiting your mum, Mothering Sunday was originally the day everyone returned once a year to their 'mother church' – the main church or cathedral in the area – for a special celebratory service in the middle of Lent. As on other important religious occasions, whole families went together. Mothering Sunday was widely observed until Victorian times, when Advent and Christmas overtook Lent and Easter as

the principal events of the religious year.

There had long been a tradition for people to give their mothers gifts on Mothering Sunday – partly because people made the wrong word association, and partly because it was often the only day in the year servants got time off to visit their mothers. But, as it fell into disuse in Britain, a new version sprang up in America.

In 1908 a woman called Anna Jarvis held a memorial service in West Virginia to honour her mother, who had died a few years earlier, and also to remember all the other mothers belonging to her church.

The event was a huge success, and Anna spent the next six years tirelessly promoting the idea. It caught on so successfully that in 1914 President Woodrow Wilson proclaimed Mother's Day a national holiday. Anna Jarvis always insisted the apostrophe in 'Mother's' should come between the 'r' and the 's', to make it clear that each family was honouring one particular mother. She never became a mother herself.

When America joined the Second World War, its servicemen brought Mother's Day to Britain, and it very quickly took hold. For convenience, it was arranged to take place on the same day as Mothering Sunday (which remained in the Church of England calendar, even if it wasn't often observed).

Jarvis fought a desperate campaign to keep Mother's Day non-commercial. When she saw card manufacturers, florists and confectioners using it for profit she was livid, and later fought to have the holiday abolished – organising boycotts, threatening lawsuits and even getting herself arrested in the process. She described the Mother's Day industry as 'charlatans, bandits, pirates, racketeers, kidnappers and termites that would undermine with their greed one of the finest, noblest and truest movements and celebrations'.

Despite this, it looks as though it's here to stay: more than 20 million Mother's Day cards are sent in the UK every year. Anna Jarvis wouldn't have approved. As she wrote, 'A printed card means nothing, except that you are too lazy to write to the woman who has done more for you than anyone in the world.'

STEPHEN *But it's actually nothing to do with your biological mother, it's to do with your mother church.*
SARA PASCOE *Do you think that excuse is going to hold up next year for any of us?*

How old would Jesus have been in the year AD 2000?

Not 2,000 – you have the Pope's word for it.

In 2012 Pope Benedict XVI released the final volume of his trilogy *Jesus of Nazareth*, which debunked much of the story of Jesus' birth. He pointed out that, contrary to popular belief, there were no oxen, asses or any other beasts at the Nativity.* He also said that Jesus' birthdate – and therefore the whole BC/AD system – was several years out, thanks to a 1,500-year-old mistake

---

* See also *The Book of General Ignorance (the Noticeably Stouter Edition)*, p. 333.

by a Romanian monk called Dionysius Exiguus or 'Dennis the Small'.

The error began in the sixth century with Pope Gelasius I. He was a very well-organised man, having worked as a secretary to two earlier popes, and set about putting the Catholic Church in order. One of his first tasks was to come up with a reliable method of finding the correct date for Easter, and he asked the learned Dennis the Small to do it. In doing so, Dennis came up with the dating system we use today, based on the birth of Christ. (He never actually used the labels BC and AD, though. That took 200 years to catch on.)

We don't know how he made his calculations – the Bible doesn't give a date or a year for Jesus' birth – but he was a skilled mathematician and astronomer, as well as being well versed in the Holy Scriptures. His final calculation wasn't bad, given that he was writing 500 years after the event. But better dating methods have shown he was wrong by at least four years: in particular, we know that King Herod, who was alive when Jesus was born, died in 4 BC. Other estimates for Jesus' actual birth date vary between 7 BC and 2 BC.

In his book Pope Benedict declines to give an exact date for Jesus' birth, instead simply writing that Dennis 'made a mistake in his calculations by several years'.

Benedict also pointed out that the notion of Jesus being born on 25 December has no historical basis. We don't even know which season he was born in; the whole idea of celebrating his birth at the end of the year is probably linked to pagan traditions and the winter solstice.

In the Gregorian calendar – the one we still use today – there is no year 0. It goes straight from 1 BC to AD 1.

What would Jesus' mum have called him?

Several possibilities, but not Jesus.

For a start, when Jesus lived in Galilee, the letter 'J' didn't exist. In Hebrew, his name was Yeshua or Yehoshua – from which we get the name Joshua. In Aramaic (the language he probably spoke at home) it was Isho or Yeshu.

When the Gospels were translated from Hebrew into Greek, Yeshua became Iesous. When the Greek was rendered into Latin, it became Iesus. Joshua and Jesus were once the same name.

Classical Latin had no letter J – Caesar was Iulius, not Julius. Except for a handful of borrowed foreign words, modern Italian still has no J. The letter J wasn't really in common use until the seventeenth century, at first to distinguish between words with 'i' as a consonant, pronounced as 'y' in 'iest' (jest) and the short vowel sound 'i', as in 'it' or 'inch'. J wasn't used in English until around 1630, so Shakespeare never used it either – he wrote *Romeo and Iuliet*, *King Iohn* and, like Caesar himself, *Iulius Caesar*. In time, J came to be spoken in English like the Old English 'dj' sound, as in 'hedge', while in Spanish J still has a 'Y' sound' and in French it's halfway between the two.

In Hebrew Jesus' father's name was Yusuf, not Joseph, and Jesus would have been Yeshua ben Yusuf ('Joshua, son of Joseph'). It's possible neither of them were carpenters. The Hebrew word used to describe what they did is *naggara* (*tekton* in Greek). It only comes up twice in the New Testament and other possible meanings are 'architect', 'stone mason' and 'builder' — so Jesus may have been a brickie rather than a chippie.

In 2012 more than 4,000 American children were given the first name Jesus. There were also 800 Messiahs, and 29 Christs.

STEPHEN *What did Jesus' mum call him?*
ALAN *Jo Junior.*

What was the name of the saint from Assisi?

John.

The man we know as St Francis of Assisi (about 1181–1226) was baptised Giovanni (after John the Baptist) by his mother, while his father was away in France. When his father got back, he changed it to 'Francesco' ('Frenchman') because he didn't much care for John the Baptist, but he loved France.

In English Francesco became Francis and, as far as we know, the saint was the first person to be called that. But it didn't become a popular name in Britain until the sixteenth century, when it hit a sudden vogue because of the great Basque missionary, St Francis Xavier. He was co-founder of the Jesuit order and took Christianity deep into Asia, establishing missions in India, Japan and Borneo. Francis Bacon (1561–1626) and Sir Francis Drake (1540–95) were both born at the height of his popularity. Today he is patron saint of China, India, Indonesia and Pakistan, and the patron saint of Asia overall.

Three hundred years earlier, the original St Francis had grown up a wealthy playboy before renouncing his worldly possessions to become a beggar and a preacher. According to Christian tradition, he was the first person to miraculously receive the stigmata – the wounds of Jesus – on his own body. He is now most famous for preaching to a group of birds, which stopped singing to listen to him. Thanks to this miracle, he is the patron saint of animals and ecology. He is also one of two patron saints of Italy (the other is St Catherine of Siena) and the patron saint of merchants, lacemakers, tapestry makers and of not dying alone. He was awarded this last distinction because, in his view, we are never alone – the Sun, the Moon, birds, animals and insects are just as much our companions as people.

Francis is not the only Catholic saint from Assisi. In fact, he's not even its patron saint: that's St Rufinus of Assisi. Other local saints include Vitalis of Assisi, Clare of Assisi and Agnes of Assisi.

Clare and Agnes of Assisi were sisters, and among the first followers of St Francis. St Clare is the patron saint of television, because she had a vision of a Mass taking place on the other side of the city which was projected onto the wall of her room like a TV outside broadcast.

St Vitalis of Assisi was not quite so lucky when the titles were being handed out: he is the patron saint of diseases of the genitals.

When was the name 'Wendy' first used?

It wasn't in *Peter Pan*.

J. M. Barrie didn't invent the name 'Wendy', as is often claimed. It occasionally appears on nineteenth-century censuses both in England and the USA. But it wasn't restricted to girls: in

1797 there was a boy called Wendy born in Gloucestershire. And if alternative spellings are permitted, the earliest known Wendi lived over 2,000 years ago – the great emperor Wendi of the Han dynasty who ruled China in the second century BC.

What Barrie's 1904 play *Peter Pan* unquestionably did was to make the name Wendy popular. It also invented the Wendy House, which is the small shelter the Lost Boys build for Wendy when she first arrives on their island. Barrie inadvertently came up with the name for Quality Street chocolates. Decades after it was written, the name and characters from his 1901 play *Quality Street* were used in the product's advertising and packaging.

Most Barrie scholars now think he got the idea for the name 'Wendy' from five-year-old Margaret Henley, who tried to call him 'friendy' but mispronounced it 'fwendy'. Margaret was the daughter of the one-legged poet William Ernest Henley, who wrote Nelson Mandela's favourite poem 'Invictus'. The character of Long John Silver in Robert Louis Stevenson's *Treasure Island* was based on Henley – so Long John Silver was Wendy Darling's father.

Peter Pan was named after Pan, the Greek god who was abandoned by his mother as a child. The title of the first Peter Pan book (1902) was initially going to be *The Boy Who Hated Mothers*, and in the play Barrie intended Peter to be 'a demon boy, the villain of the story'. He was very disappointed with the statue of Peter Pan in Kensington Gardens, saying, 'It doesn't show the devil in Peter.'

Barrie was very well connected. In 1890 he formed a cricket team of his famous friends that remained active until 1913. Its members included Rudyard Kipling, H. G. Wells, Arthur Conan Doyle, P. G. Wodehouse, G. K. Chesterton, Jerome K. Jerome and A. A. Milne. The team was called the Allahakbarries, from the mistaken belief that *Allah akbar* meant 'Heaven help us' in

Arabic – rather than its actual meaning 'God is great'.

During rehearsals for *Peter Pan* Barrie ordered Brussels sprouts every day for lunch, but never ate them. When his friend William Nicholson asked him why, Barrie said, 'I cannot resist ordering them. The words are so lovely to say.'

What kind of reasoning did Sherlock Holmes use?

Holmes used abduction – not deduction – to crack his cases.

Deductive reasoning is when a conclusion is certain, provided the facts are true. For example: all men are mortal, Watson is a man. Deduction: Watson is mortal. Holmes, however, more often used *abductive* reasoning, which works by drawing the *most likely* conclusion from the available evidence. In essence, it's an educated guess – though Holmes would have hated this description. In *The Sign of the Four* he says, 'I never guess. It is a shocking habit – destructive to the logical faculty.'

The use of deductive reasoning isn't the only misconception about Holmes. He never wore a deerstalker and never smoked a calabash (the curly pipe he's often shown with). The hat was added by illustrator Sidney Paget and the pipe appeared in later stage adaptations. Fans concerned that Holmes is single often claim Irene Adler as a potential love interest for him. But she only appears in one of Conan Doyle's stories, 'A Scandal in Bohemia', and there's no indication he finds her attractive.

A recent BBC *Sherlock* episode has Holmes using a 'mind palace' memory technique, something else he never did in the books. This involves taking a walk through an imaginary house or 'palace' and putting each thing you want to remember in a specific place. By retracing the journey, the brain is able to recall vast amounts of information. The mind palace technique is first recorded in ancient Greece and is credited to the Greek poet Simonides of Ceos (556–468 BC). He first demonstrated it when he was the sole survivor of a dinner party after the roof collapsed. He was able to identify the bodies by remembering who had been sitting where at the table. Sherlock Holmes describes the inside of his head not as a palace but a 'brain-attic'.

Arthur Conan Doyle (1859–1930) found his creation a terrible burden in later life. He once said, 'If I had never touched Holmes, who has tended to obscure my higher work, my position in literature would at the present moment be a more commanding one.' He complained to a friend, 'I feel towards him as I do towards pâté de foie gras, of which I once ate too much, so that the name of it gives me a sickly sweet feeling to this day.' His public didn't agree with him. After he killed off his detective by having Sherlock and Moriarty wrestle each other to death in a plunge from the Reichenbach Falls, he suffered a deluge of protest, and a woman picketed his home with a sign that read 'murderer'. As a result, he reluctantly brought Holmes back from the dead for 13 new stories called *The Return of Sherlock Holmes*, published in serial form in 1903–4.

The enduring appeal of his most famous work might have been enough, but Conan Doyle achieved much else besides his writing. A qualified doctor, he served as ship's surgeon on a whaling vessel, before settling down as a GP near Portsmouth. In 1884 he was one of the founders (and the first goalkeeper) of Portsmouth Football Club. He also played for Marylebone Cricket Club and once bowled out W. G. Grace. In 1893 he introduced skis (or 'snow shoes', as he called them) to Switzerland for the first time – he'd learned to use them in Norway. In 1911 he drove from London to Hamburg, the first time British and German cars had competed against each other, and a precursor of the German Grand Prix of 1926. In his latter years, he became a committed spiritualist. At his memorial service, an empty chair was reserved for him in case he decided to attend.

STEPHEN *No. Not deduction. The word is actually 'abductio'. Abduction. It does have a different meaning.*
JACK WHITEHALL *Yeah, you abduct people, they give you information.*

What was the name of the cabin boy in *Captain Pugwash*?

Tom.

The widespread idea that the characters in *Captain Pugwash* had obscene names like Seaman Staines, Master Bates and Roger the Cabin Boy is a perfect example of the urban myth. In 1991 *Pugwash*'s creator, John Ryan, won legal cases against the now defunct *Sunday Correspondent* and the *Guardian* after they wrote that the BBC had pulled the programme due to the rude names. At the time the show was still going strong and the characters had perfectly acceptable names such as Tom the Cabin Boy,

Barnabas, and Cut-throat Jake. There was a Master Mates and a pirate called Willy, but that's about as risqué as it got.

Captain Pugwash – or, to give it its full title, 'Captain Pugwash, the Story of a Bad Buccaneer and of the many Sticky Ends which nearly befell him' – made its debut as a comic strip in the first issue of the *Eagle* comic in 1950. In 1957 *Pugwash* appeared on television for the first time, and three years later the strip moved to *Radio Times*, where it ran for eight years and 400 editions. In 1974–5 30 episodes were made in colour. The series was revived in 1997 by HIT Entertainment for a further 26 programmes. The jaunty theme tune, 'The Trumpet Hornpipe', dates from the mid-nineteenth century and is played on an accordion.

Ryan developed Pugwash's iconic animation style himself. He put cardboard cut-outs of the characters on backgrounds, controlling their movements with cardboard levers. Scenes were shot in real time with each episode taking two to three weeks to create. Peter Hawkins – who also voiced Bill and Ben, and the Daleks and the Cybermen from *Doctor Who* – provided the voices. Ryan attributed Pugwash's success to his two competing qualities – greed and cowardice. He said, 'It may be that the Captain is popular because we all have something in common with him. What would you do if you saw a delicious toffee on the nose of a crocodile?'

After the Second World War a group of scientists, including Albert Einstein and Bertrand Russell, published the Russell–Einstein Manifesto calling for nuclear disarmament. Looking for a place to discuss the issues away from government scrutiny, Canadian businessman Cyrus Eaton offered to fund it if they chose his house in Pugwash, Nova Scotia. They called themselves the Pugwash Conferences on Science and World Affairs.

In 1995 Pugwash won the Nobel Peace Prize.

Name a piece of music written by Henry VIII

'Greensleeves'? Nay.

Despite the persistent myth, there's no evidence Henry VIII wrote it. The first known reference to it was in 1580, more than 30 years after his death, when Richard Jones registered a ballad called 'A Newe Northen Dittye of ye Ladye Greene Sleves' at the London Stationer's Company. The song is a folk melody in a musical style called *romanesca* in which four chords are played over a simple repeating bass line. Originating in Spain, the style was popular with Italian composers but didn't reach England until the reign of Elizabeth I.

But Henry VIII is credited with at least 20 songs and 13 instrumental pieces. They were gathered together in a 1518 manuscript now known as 'The Henry VIII Songbook'. Among the tunes attributed to him are the merry 'Pastyme with good companye' (which lists the many good things a prince was able to enjoy) and the rather less merry 'Whereto should I express my inward heaviness?'

Some historians are sceptical about the king's gifts as a composer. They claim his works were largely arrangements of existing pieces and that giving him the credit had more to do with court flattery than musical ability. But there's no doubting his enthusiasm. He set up his own 50-strong choir, which followed him around singing as he visited his various palaces. He even stole singers from Cardinal Wolsey's choir to improve his own. All manner of foreign musicians attended his court, including a Venetian organist who would play for the king for up to four hours at a time. When his father, Henry VII, died, the court had just 15 official musicians; when Henry VIII died, it had 58.

Henry VIII played the lute and the organ, as well as a now obsolete instrument called the virginal. At his death he owned five sets of bagpipes, 19 viols, 26 lutes, 65 flutes and 154 recorders. Music wasn't his only diversion. He owned the first recorded pair of football boots, commissioned in 1526 from the Great Wardrobe so he could play in the notoriously violent Shrove Tuesday match with a group of young courtiers known as 'the henchmen'. He was also a keen jouster and pharmacist, personally making ointments from ingredients such as ground pearls and white lead to treat his wounds.

But, for all his many talents, writing 'Greensleeves' wasn't one of them.

What was the main event in a medieval tournament?

It wasn't jousting.

The centrepiece of the early medieval tournament was the mêlée. Rather than two knights charging each other with lances, this involved hundreds of knights on horseback slamming into each other in formation. The aim was to hold the line and turn as one and then select individual knights to capture. This act of turning is how the 'tournament' got its name – it literally means 'to turn around' in Old French. Knights that were captured were then ransomed, often for huge sums of money. Jousting did take place but it was strictly a side event.

The word mêlée comes from the French *mesler*, meaning 'to mix', and the modern sense of a confused brawl dates back to these extremely violent medieval events. To capture an opposing knight you were allowed to batter him so fiercely he had to surrender and follow you off the field of combat, or else you could simply drag him off. Mêlées were often fought over several square miles of ground and serious injuries were common. In fact, the only difference between a mêlée and a real battle was that both sides had 'safety zones', and rules were agreed on before combat was joined. Knights blunted their swords before taking part, but it wasn't until the 1300s that crossbows were banned from mêlées. The one thing that stopped them tipping over into real battles was the money that could be earned through ransoms. The mêlée was the first European team sport and, like football today, a talented player could transform his standing by earning the equivalent of millions of pounds.

One of the most famous tournament performers was William Marshal (1147–1219) an English knight who, at over 6 feet tall, was regarded as a giant. He was so successful he attracted the patronage of Henry the Young King, son of Henry II, and ended up as the First Earl of Pembroke and one of the country's richest and most powerful men. Even in his seventies, 'the Marshal' led the army that defeated invading French forces at the Battle of Lincoln in 1217.

By the mid-fourteenth century the mêlée had fallen out of fashion in favour of the more genteel sport of jousting. This was much cheaper for the barons, who only had to kit out themselves rather than a whole squadron of knights. Also, tournaments were increasingly held for female spectators, whose champions were easier to identify in a joust than in the blood-spattered chaos of a mêlée.

Why was the Colosseum called the Colosseum?

Not because of its size.

Although it was big enough to hold 80,000 spectators, the Romans called it the 'Flavian Amphitheatre'. Nobody called  it the 'Colosseum' until AD 1000, long after the Roman Empire was gone. The word 'colossal' comes from the Greek *kolossos*, which means a larger-than-life statue. Until the early Middle Ages, one of these, a 100-foot bronze statue of the Emperor Nero stood outside the stadium, and it's from this that the Colosseum got its name.

The Colosseum has had a varied career. In the sixth century it was used as a church and a cemetery. Then it became a quarry, a rubbish pit and an early form of shopping mall, where cobblers and blacksmiths plied their trade. From AD 800 until 1349 monks used it as an apartment block and as the home of a religious order. Pope Sixtus V (1521–90) tried to convert it into a wool factory to provide honest work for Rome's prostitutes. In 1671 a Catholic cardinal failed to turn it into a bullring. Four years later Pope Clement X dedicated it to the Christian martyrs and in 1749 Pope Benedict XIV installed a massive cross in the middle of the arena. Catholic ceremonies are still held in the Colosseum today, but there are no contemporary records of any Christians being put to death there.

Some Roman prisoners were punished by being torn apart – *damnatio ad bestias* meant being condemned to confront wild animals – and big cats frequently stalked the Colosseum: rolling ivory barriers had to be installed to stop them climbing into the cheap seats. But stories of martyrs being murdered to entertain the mob were largely made up by early Christian commentators and collected together in the *Acts of the Martyrs*. These claimed to be records of the trials, but most were embellished to exaggerate the Romans' treatment of early Christians. Written primarily to inspire the faithful, they were gory enough to work as entertainment.

Despite the lack of evidence, this association of the Colosseum with Christian martyrdom is what has ensured its survival. Pope Benedict XIV declared the building a sacred site and dedicated it to the Passion of Christ and the blood of the martyrs who probably didn't die there.

What is the name of the Queen's official residence?

It's not Buckingham Palace.

The monarch has lived in Buckingham Palace since Queen Victoria's time, but the official royal residence is a few doors down, at St James's Palace.

Henry VIII built St James's Palace on the site of a leper hospital. Anne Boleyn stayed there the night after her coronation; Mary Tudor signed away Calais there, and Charles II and James II were both born and baptised there. In 1941 the allied governments met at St James's Palace to agree the treaty that created the United Nations.

Today St James's is the senior royal palace in the United Kingdom. Following the death of the sovereign, the Accession Council meets there and announces the successor from the Proclamation Gallery overlooking the public courtyard. In addition, all ambassadors to the UK get their official certification from the Court of St James's. It is currently the London residence of the Princess Royal, Princesses Beatrice and Eugenie of York, and Princess Alexandra, cousin to the Queen.

The marshy countryside on which Buckingham Palace was built had a long association with royalty. Before the Conquest it belonged to King Edward the Confessor and supported a small village called Eye Cross. After the Norman invasion it fell under William the Conqueror's control and was bequeathed to the monks of Westminster Abbey. Five hundred years later, in 1531, Henry VIII reclaimed it as a royal residence. By the early seventeenth century the village had gone, and James I planted a mulberry garden to rear silkworms. Unfortunately it was the wrong species of mulberry, and silk production was abandoned in favour of property speculation.

The core of the building, Buckingham House, was built in 1703 as the country home of Tory politician and poet John Sheffield, First Duke of Buckingham and Normanby. In 1820 the architect John Nash set out to upgrade it to palace status, but he overspent wildly and was fired. William IV briefly considered turning the expensive white elephant into the new Houses of Parliament after they burned down in 1834. It wasn't until the accession of Victoria three years later that it was used as a regular home for the British monarch.

Victoria and Albert loathed the place. Lazy, insolent staff; no bathrooms; fires that smoked so badly they had to be kept very low: the royal couple found it cold, malodorous and unwelcoming. They began a decade-long improvement programme which included building the east wing – the one with the famous balcony, first used for a royal wave at the opening of the Great Exhibition in 1851. Marble Arch, formerly the entrance to the palace, was moved to the north-east corner of Hyde Park, where it is today.

In 2009 the *Sydney Morning Herald*'s travel blog listed Buckingham Palace as the most disappointing of British tourist attractions – a rating repeated in other surveys. They dismissed it as 'just a big grey building'.

The Union Flag is flown over Buckingham Palace when the Queen is out, not (as many people assume) when she's in. When she's at home, the Royal Standard is flown. A flag sergeant has the role of raising and lowering the right flag as the Queen arrives at or departs from the Palace.

How many English kings named Henry have there been?

Nine.

Though the last King Henry to reign was Henry VIII, nine Henrys have been crowned king of England.

The ninth was known as 'Henry the Young King'. He was the second of the five sons of Henry II and Eleanor of Aquitaine and was crowned and anointed king beside his father when he was 15 years old.

Crowning an heir apparent was a common practice in medieval France because it reduced the risk of disputed succession, but this was the only time after the Norman conquest that it happened in England. Henry ruled as 'associate king', and the only reason he isn't counted in the line of English monarchs is that he died before his father. Henry II was succeeded by his third son, Richard I.

The young King Henry was apparently very good-looking, with the reddish hair and blue eyes characteristic of his family. He wasn't much interested in ruling, though, and spent his time indulging his hobbies – raiding monasteries for money, throwing tournaments and hosting lavish banquets. He once held a dinner exclusively for a hundred knights all called William. According to the historian W. L. Warren, he was the only popular member of his family, but was also 'the only one who gave no evidence of political sagacity, military skill, or even ordinary intelligence'.

At 18 young King Henry left court to rebel against his father, because the old king had given land to his younger brother instead of him. But the two kings made peace a year later thanks to a gift of two castles in return for the young king's promise to behave. He died of dysentery aged just 28.

The custom of primogeniture, whereby the eldest son inherits all the family's property, came to Britain with William the Conqueror. Before that Anglo-Saxons bequeathed their estates to a variety of heirs. Some parts of England practised 'ultimogeniture', where the youngest son or daughter inherited everything. The law of primogeniture in England was only abolished in 1925.

Queen Elizabeth II was christened Elizabeth Alexandra Mary of York, but was under no obligation to be called 'Queen Elizabeth'; the monarch can choose whatever name they wish when they accede to the throne. Queen Victoria was originally called Princess Alexandrina of Kent and Edward VIII was Prince David, Prince of Wales. It's been suggested that when Prince Charles becomes king, he will be crowned as King George, to avoid sharing a name with Charles I, the only English monarch to be executed.

The sovereign of Great Britain never dies. Of course, individual kings and queens do die, but at the very same instant, the crown passes to the next in line.

What dynasty did Henry VII and Henry VIII belong to?

The Richmonds.

We call them Tudors, but they'd have hated that. Henry VII was Earl of Richmond, one of the most important titles in England. His son, Henry VIII, was 'the embodiment of the union of the families of Lancaster and York'.

The name 'Tudor' reminded the family of their humble Welsh origins. Henry VII, the last king of England to win his crown on the field of battle, was the grandson of the founder of the dynasty, Owen Tudor, a poor squire of great ambition who had a risky affair with the wife of Henry V. His Welsh name was Owain ap Maredudd ap Tudur ('Owen son of Meredith son of Tudor') but he used his grandfather's surname, rather than his father's. If he'd been more conventional, we might now be watching a TV series called *The Merediths*.

There were five Tudor monarchs (six if you count Lady Jane Grey), but the name was never used in official publications. Henry VIII was so embarrassed by it that he allowed Owen Tudor's tomb to be discreetly swept away in the Dissolution of the Monasteries. The word Tudor is virtually unused in any documents until the time of James I – and he wasn't a Tudor but a Stuart.

We use the surname Tudor today because of the historian and philosopher David Hume (1711–76), who devoted a whole volume of his *History of England* to 'the Tudors'. The book was a best-seller, despite – or perhaps because of – causing outrage among his contemporaries. Hume was a royalist and a conservative who enjoyed annoying the ruling liberal elite of his day. His main contention was that the hated Stuarts had been no worse than the Tudors who preceded them, describing Elizabeth I as 'particularly obnoxious' and suggesting Mary, Queen of Scots, was responsible for the murder of her husband. Thomas Jefferson, author of the Declaration of Independence and third president of the USA, called the book 'poison'.

Hume believed the Tudors were the enemies of liberty and destroyers of ancient constitutions and religions. But he could hardly have had a lower opinion of their name than the Tudors themselves.

Which king of Scotland succeeded Macbeth?

Lulach the Idiot.

If you've seen the play, you'd think it was Malcolm. But Shakespeare ignored large chunks of Scottish history for the sake of the story. For the same reason he also gave Macbeth rather a raw deal.

King Lulach the Idiot was Macbeth's stepson, and the son of Lady Macbeth – whose actual name was Gruoch. (Macbeth's real name was Mac Bethad mac Findláich.)

Shakespeare's Scottish play correctly says that Macbeth killed King Duncan, but it was in battle, not as Duncan slept – and far from being old, as the play suggests, Duncan was a mere 39. Furthermore, Duncan had started a military campaign against Macbeth in the first place, so it was at least partly his fault. Macbeth became king of Scotland by defeating Duncan in 1040, but he had a good claim to the throne on his mother's side anyway, which Shakespeare also neglects to mention.

Another Shakespearean misconception is that Macbeth was only king for a year or so – in fact he ruled for 17 years, nearly three times as long as Duncan. He even went on a pilgrimage to Rome, which suggests his rule was a secure one.

Eventually Duncan's son, Malcolm III, nicknamed Canmore (Scots for 'big head'), beat Macbeth in battle. But Macbeth managed to hang on to power for another three years until he was finally killed in 1057. Even then Malcolm didn't become king – Macbeth's stepson Lulach did. Some historians think this was his reward for secretly siding with Malcolm against his stepfather. If so, it was short-lived. Lulach reigned for just eight months before Malcolm had him murdered and took the throne for himself.

Despite the liberties he took with history, Shakespeare certainly captured the precariousness of life for the nobility in eleventh-century Scotland: Macbeth's father had been murdered, as had Lady Macbeth's grandfather.

The 'curse' of Macbeth is a recent fabrication. One version dates from 1896; another was made up by the theatre critic Max Beerbohm in 1898 because he was bored by the play and wanted to spice it up.

But the play has caused real violence on at least one occasion. In New York in 1849 two versions of Macbeth were put on at different theatres just a few blocks apart – one featured the

English tragedian William Charles Macready and the other the popular American stage star Edwin Forrest. The rivalry between them, fuelled by patriotic working-class support for Forrest and Macready's white-gloved, upper-class Anglophile audience, boiled over into a full-scale riot in which troops opened fire on the crowd leaving 25 people dead and hundreds injured.

Macbeth is the only Shakespeare play that contains the word 'rhinoceros' (Act 3, scene 4). The first living rhino didn't arrive in England until 1684, but Shakespeare would have been familiar with Dürer's famous woodcut, engraved in 1515, of the one belonging to the king of Portugal.

STEPHEN *There is a tradition, is there not, that the very saying of the name Macbeth in a theatre is bad luck.*
SUE PERKINS *You have to sleep with all your co-stars immediately.*
STEPHEN *Is that what you were told?*
SUE *Yes! Why?*
STEPHEN *How interesting.*

Which dog stood by his master's grave for 14 years?

The story of Greyfriars Bobby turns out to have been a publicity stunt.

The Greyfriars Bobby monument in Edinburgh was erected in 1873 and paid for by Baroness Burdett-Coutts, grand-daughter of banker Thomas Coutts and, after Queen Victoria, the richest and best-connected woman in Britain. The statue stands at the corner of Candlemaker Row and the George IV Bridge and was originally a drinking fountain with one level for humans and a lower level for dogs. It served as such until 1957, when the water supply was cut off for health reasons. It's the smallest listed building in Edinburgh.

According to legend, Greyfriars Bobby was a Skye terrier that kept a loyal vigil from 1858 to 1872 by the graveside of his master, police night watchman John Gray.

The historian Jan Bondeson has collated contemporary accounts and pieced together the real story. Bobby was two different dogs and they weren't even the same breed. The first Bobby was a mongrel dumped over the wall into Greyfriars churchyard in Edinburgh by a gardener at a nearby hospital who wanted to get rid of him. The graveyard keeper, James Brown, fed the dog, so of course he stuck around, but there was no buried master. That dog died in 1867 and was replaced by a younger model, a Skye terrier like the one in the statue, to keep attracting visitors to the by now famous site. This explains his unusually long lifespan – Bobby lived outdoors in the graveyard for 14 years. Even today a well-pampered indoor Skye terrier only lives for 12 years.

The 'Faithful Hound' is an enduring legend. In the *Odyssey* Homer writes of Odysseus' devoted dog Argus, who waits 20 years for his master to return, clinging to life to see him once more before he dies.

There is at least one true story of a faithful dog: Hachiko, a Japanese Akita belonging to Professor Hidesaburo Ueno of the University of Tokyo. Every day, when Ueno returned from work, Hachiko would meet him at the local railway station. When the professor suffered a brain haemorrhage at work and died in 1925, Hachiko waited at the railway station every day for nine years (no doubt helped by locals feeding him). Hachiko's stuffed remains are now on display at the National Museum of Nature and Science in Tokyo. In 1994 a recording of his bark was lifted from an old broken record and broadcast on national radio. Millions of listeners tuned in to hear the bark of a dog that had died 59 years earlier.

How did Pavlov get dogs to salivate?

Not by ringing a bell.

The Russian physiologist Ivan Pavlov (1849–1936) showed that dogs could be made to salivate by training them to associate a stimulus with food. He used a metronome, a buzzer, a harmonium, even electric shocks, but he never used a bell. Other scientists in the same field did use bells, but not Pavlov.

Pavlov wanted to understand the physical effects of mental stimuli. He had noticed his dogs salivated at the sight of a lab coat, because they knew an assistant was coming to feed them. He later showed they could discriminate between rhythms of 96 and 104 beats per minute, or between ascending and descending musical scales, and dribble or not accordingly. He called this a 'conditioned' response, and he was the first person to prove it scientifically.

It made him famous. The British philosopher Bertrand Russell hailed his work as essential to our understanding of the philosophy of mind, and Aldous Huxley used it as a major theme in *Brave New World*. Perhaps because he is mainly associated with slobbering dogs, Pavlov's reputation has suffered in recent years. But he was a brilliant and versatile scientist and Russia's first Nobel Laureate, winning the prize in Physiology or Medicine in 1904 for his analysis of gastric juices in dogs. This was well before his work on conditioning.

Dog drool repaid him in other ways. His experiments produced large amounts of gastric juice from the dogs he was observing about 2 pints a day from a large dog). This was collected by placing the dogs in restraining harnesses in front of a bowl of mince, which they could see and smell but not reach. A tube then drained the juice produced by their stomachs, which was then sold as a popular treatment for indigestion. By 1904 he was selling 3,000 flagons of canine gastric juice a year, raising nearly half his annual research budget.

Pavlov was an early pioneer of behaviourism (the theory that people have no free will and what they do is dictated solely by what happens to them). But his ultimate aim was much more ambitious: to discover 'the mechanism and vital meaning of our consciousness and its torments'. In trying to unite psychology and physiology, the more data he gathered, the more unsure he became. His experiments with pigs failed miserably, and he was forced to conclude that his work had raised more questions than it answered. Towards the end of his long life he wrote, 'We are surrounded – nay crushed – by a mass of details demanding explanation.' Today most neuroscientists would say we still are.

Why should you rely on the 'wisdom of crowds'?

You shouldn't.

The growing consensus among mathematicians and statisticians is that the 'wisdom of crowds' – the idea that lots of people can produce a better answer than a few people – is a myth.

Charles Darwin's cousin Francis Galton carried out the archetypal wisdom-of-crowds experiment in 1906 . He went to a village fair and offered a prize to whoever could guess the weight of an ox. No one, including the experienced farmers, came close individually but the average of all 787 submitted guesses was exactly the beast's actual weight.

This now appears to have had more to do with luck than any underlying principle. Crowds regularly get things wrong. People are often swayed by each other's guesses (experts, for instance), leading towards a misplaced bias. For example, if someone before you guesses there are 500 Smarties in a jar, you're unlikely to guess there are 10 million. If the first guesser was way off, the final 'crowd' guess will almost certainly be wrong. Where there isn't a 'correct' answer – e.g. financial crises or politics generally – this 'herding' effect can have disastrous consequences.

Crowd judgments can be improved by diversity. A 2004 study showed that a varied group of problem-solvers made a better collective guess than a group of like-minded 'experts'. It seems that if you want to improve the accuracy of a crowd's estimate, add individuals who hold opinions that are actively opposed to the general consensus.

It's possible that the statisticians currently debunking the 'wisdom of crowds' are themselves a crowd whose judgments are suspect because they listen to each other. Though, paradoxically, that would be an argument both for and against the concept . . .

Why should you avoid feral pigeons?

Don't bother – they're not as germy as you think.

Despite much scaremongering about pigeons, there's almost nothing you can catch from them. Pigeons do carry diseases – like cats, dogs and every other animal on Earth – but cases of them infecting humans are extremely rare.

In 2004 a comprehensive study found 176 cases of pigeon-to-human disease transmission between 1941 and 2003 – less than three a year. (Lightning, by comparison, kills up to 24,000 people a year.)

The report concluded, 'Although feral pigeons pose sporadic health risks to humans, the risk is very low, even for humans involved in occupations that bring them into close contact with nesting sites.' If your immune system is unusually weak, the risk is higher, but for most people the risk is infinitesimally small.

Feral pigeons are the ruffianly descendants of doves kept by humans in centuries past. They're properly known as 'domestic rock doves'. Feral pigeons, tame pigeons and rock doves are the same species, no matter how battered and deformed the city variety looks. Pigeons were the first bird to be domesticated and have remained man's best (feathered) friend for millennia. They provided guano for fertiliser and, before chickens became popular, they were widely eaten as food.

But their real talent was carrying messages. Pigeons have been delivering letters for 5,000 years. The Swiss army's 30,000-strong pigeon messenger service lasted until 1995. Even as recently as 2009 a pigeon took a 4GB memory stick across 50 miles of South Africa far faster than the country's biggest Internet company could transfer the data online.

In the Second World War 250,000 pigeons carried vital military information in pouches on their legs. In coastal areas of England, birds of prey were culled to allow pigeons to bring their messages home unharmed. On a long journey, flying hundreds of miles at

40 miles an hour, a pigeon could lose a fifth of its weight. On short-haul flights they might manage 60 miles an hour.

All RAF bombers carried a pigeon on board. Thousands of airmen in crashed planes were saved from drowning by releasing a pigeon with their location attached to alert rescuers. Pigeons served on ships and submarines, and some paratroopers carried pigeons too, in a special sling on their chests. In 1944 thousands of pigeons were dropped on France by parachute so that French citizens could send back details of German troop movements.

Medal-winning pigeons in the Second World War included Winkie, Tyke, Gustav, Paddy, Billy, Mary, Princess, Commando, Scotch Lass and William of Orange.

STEPHEN *Pigeons don't really spread that much disease, though they do obviously leave a fair amount of poo. But then so do humans, don't we. We've just got a better way of dealing with it, perhaps.*
SEAN LOCK *I tend not to leave it on people's shoulders.*
STEPHEN *That's the difference.*
SEAN *I mean I wouldn't say I was well brought up, but there's a few benchmarks we tried to set early on in the toilet training.*

How hot does water have to be to wash the bacteria off your hands?

Cold water is just as effective as hot.

The most important ingredient when washing your hands is soap. The temperature of the water makes almost no difference. While bacteria can be killed by hot water, it would need to be almost boiling. If you're washing your hands in boiling water, bacteria will be the least of your worries. Even chilled water works fine, provided you scrub, rinse and dry properly.

Washing with unnecessarily warm water wastes a lot of energy. Hands are washed 150 billion times every year, and heating the water for them pumps as much carbon dioxide into the atmosphere as 250,000 cars.

Not that washing hands isn't important. If everybody in the world washed their hands properly, a million deaths a year could be prevented. But a 2013 study showed that only one in 20 Britons washes their hands correctly. The biggest errors are not washing for long enough (you're supposed to lather for 15–30 seconds each time) and not drying thoroughly (germs can get back onto your hands much more quickly if they're wet). As a result, at any given time, there are faecal bacteria present on one in five pairs of British hands.

We aren't just bad at washing our hands; we lie about it too. People coming out of the toilet at motorway service stations were asked whether or not they had washed their hands. Ninety-nine per cent claimed they had, but electronic recording devices showed only 32 per cent of men and 64 per cent of women were telling the truth.

Soap was invented in Mesopotamia 5,000 years ago. The ancient Romans preferred the Greek approach to cleanliness: anointing the body with oil and then removing it with a metal scraper known as a strigil; Cleopatra liked to rub herself with fine white sand. According to Roman legend, soap came from Mount Sapo (*sapo* is Latin for soap). Animals were sacrificed there as burnt offerings. When rain mixed with the animal fats and wood ash from the fires, soap was the result. Unfortunately there is no record of a 'Mount Sapo'. Soap arrived in Rome as a result of the conquest of northern Europe. The best soap was German; the second best from Gaul. The Gauls used it to dye their hair.

Soap didn't catch on in Britain until the twelfth century, and producing it was a closely guarded secret – as it remains for some to this day.

RICHARD OSMAN *You know when you leave a fiver in your pocket when you put it in the wash?*
STEPHEN *Yes.*
RICHARD *It would be awful if you left some Cup-a-Soup in your jeans.*
STEPHEN *The whole wash would come back as consommé. Most unfortunate.*

What would happen if the world suddenly stopped spinning?

You won't be thrown into space.

The Earth spins at just over 1,000 miles an hour (at the equator, that is – it's slightly slower at the poles), and we stay on it because the force caused by the spin is not enough to overcome the effect of gravity. Even if the Earth suddenly stopped spinning, there still isn't enough forward momentum to fling us off the planet's surface into space. For that to happen, the Earth would need to have been travelling 17 times faster.

If that sounds like good news, think again. Although the planet may have stopped, we won't have. We – and everything else not bolted down – will continue moving at the usual speed until we're stopped by something solid. Worse still, the air that surrounds us will also keep moving, creating a supersonic wind travelling at twice the speed of the fastest tornado. It will destroy all man-made structures, uproot forests, create massive ocean waves and generally scour the planet's surface of everything that isn't solid rock. Although friction will slow the wind speed down within minutes, the damage will already have been done and most of the animal life on the planet wiped out.

If you somehow manage to survive the original event (perhaps by being underground or lurking at the poles), you will emerge into a very different world. The Sun will move much more slowly across the sky, so a day and night will each last six months. On the dark side of the planet, temperatures will plunge; on the bright side, everything will bake in the constant sunlight.

And if that sounds inhospitable, the planet will also have lost its magnetic field, something that was created – like in an electric motor – by its rapid rotation around its axis. This will leave survivors with no protection from the Sun's harmful ultraviolet rays, making even limited exposure to sunlight lethal.

The Earth is actually slowing down, but only by 0.02 seconds per century. This very slight drag is caused by the Moon, which is held in orbit by the Earth's gravity, causing the planet a tiny loss of forward momentum. To keep our clocks correct, we adjust for this slowing by occasionally adding a leap second at the end of a year, but the overall effect is that every single day is very slightly longer than the one before.

It means that today really is the longest day of your life.

STEPHEN *What would happen if the Earth suddenly stopped spinning?*
ALAN *Well, half of the world would be plunged into eternal darkness. All the moths would have to go that way. The butterflies would have to go that way. The moles would be really confused.*

What is the deepest canyon in the USA?

It's not the Grand Canyon.

At its deepest, the Grand Canyon is 6,000 feet deep, but at least two other canyons in the USA are deeper: King's Canyon in California and Hell's Canyon on the Idaho–Oregon border. The record probably goes to King's Canyon, which for a short stretch reaches a depth of 8,200 feet (2,500 metres).

Nonetheless the Grand Canyon is impressively big – 277 miles long, up to 18 miles wide and a mile deep on average. It was completed 6 million years ago, but some sections are up to 70 million years old. Dinosaurs may have roamed inside it. The oldest exposed rock is 2 billion years old. The canyon was formed, very slowly, by the 300-foot-wide Colorado River, which flows through it at 4 miles an hour.

The Grand Canyon is in Arizona, not Colorado. In 1999 the US Postal Service got it wrong and printed 100 million stamps saying 'Grand Canyon, Colorado'. They all had to be destroyed, at a cost of $500,000. The Colorado River flows through the canyon, but the canyon itself is definitely in Arizona.

It stayed unexplored for a long time. The first recorded boat trip through it was in 1869, led by John Wesley Powell (1834–1902), a one-armed geologist and American national hero. It was he who fixed the name as the Grand Canyon (previously it was the Big Canyon or Great Canyon). His four boats were called *Maid of the Canyon*, *Emma Dean*, *Kitty Clyde's Sister* and *No Name*.

The 1,000-mile trip was nerve-wracking. The ten men of the expedition had no idea if they would be swept over a huge waterfall as they rounded each bend in the river. Four of them died and the rest nearly went mad. To lighten the boats they threw away huge amounts of food (225 kilograms or 500 pounds) of bacon on the first day alone) and by the end they'd run out of provisions and survived by eating stale flour.

The longest canyon on Earth is 2 miles under the ice of Greenland – it's 460 miles long, half as long again as the Grand Canyon. It was discovered only in 2013, by scientists studying airborne radar images.

Earth's canyons pale in comparison with Mars's largest canyon system, the Mariner Valleys. Thought to have been caused by volcanic magma tearing through the planet's thin crust, they extend almost 2,500 miles across a fifth of Mars's surface, equivalent to the distance from London to Toronto. Some of the chasms are the largest canyons yet discovered – 4 miles deep and up to 125 miles wide. Among them are the exotically named Abyss of Ophir and Labyrinth of the Night.

Where is the world's tallest statue of Jesus Christ?

The one in Rio doesn't even make the top three.

The tallest is Christ the King in Swiebodzin, a small town in western Poland. The statue itself is 108 feet tall (33 metres, one for each year of Jesus' life) making it 10 feet taller than Christ the Redeemer in Brazil. But if you include Christ the King's gilded crown and base, it's taller still: a total of 172 feet.

The statue took five years to erect and was completed in 2010. It began as a 'small garden structure', but ambitions soared as the local authorities realised it could make Swiebodzin a site of pilgrimage for Polish Catholics. For others, the whole project was a folly. When a crane collapsed during building works, crushing a labourer's foot, some saw it as a sign of disapproval from God.

Rio de Janeiro's Christ the Redeemer was finished in 1930. The statue's face was sculpted by Romanian artist Gheorghe Leonida,

previously best known for his work *Le Diable* ('The Devil'). At the opening ceremony the floodlights were turned on by the radio pioneer Guglielmo Marconi, more than 5,000 miles away in Rome. It was the tallest statue of Jesus in the world for more than 50 years, until Cristo de la Concordia was built in 1987 in Cochabamba, Bolivia. This statue is currently the second tallest Jesus in the world, and would be the tallest if they hadn't put a crown on the Polish one. The third tallest is in Vietnam, the Vung Tau Christ, completed in 1993.

As impressive as these giant Jesuses are, they are dwarfed by the world's largest Buddhas. Many of these are modern, but it's an old tradition. In 1588 the Japanese ruler Toyotomi Hideyoshi took all the swords in the country and melted them down to make a huge Buddha, which was destroyed in an earthquake ten years later. The giant Buddhas of Bamiyan, destroyed by the Taliban in 2001, were more than 1,500 years old. In the world today, the tallest statue of any kind is the Spring Temple Buddha in Zhaocun, China, completed in 2008. It is more than 200 metres tall – a height equivalent to sticking the Angel of the North on top of the Gherkin in the City of London.

What species of tree is the tallest ever?

It's neither a giant redwood nor a sequoia.

The tallest tree ever measured was a eucalyptus found in Australia in 1871. It had fallen over, but was measured with surveyor's tape and found to be 433 feet tall – taller than the Statue of Liberty or Big Ben.

As well as growing to an enormous size, eucalyptus trees can tell you where to dig for gold. They absorb gold from deposits up to 130 feet deep in the soil, and traces appear in their leaves and bark – though you'd need the contents of 500 trees to make one gold ring.

The tallest living tree is Hyperion, a coastal redwood in California's Redwood National Park. It's 379 feet tall; the park managers refuse to reveal its precise location to prevent vandalism.

The world's *largest* tree is also in California – it's called General Sherman. It stands tall at 275 feet – the same size as a 27-storey building – has a volume of 52,478 cubic feet and weighs about 2,000 tons – as much as six blue whales. It's at least 2,000 years old.

The world's oldest individual tree is yet another Californian: Methuselah, a bristlecone pine. At 4,765 years old it is older than Stonehenge or the Giza pyramids. But some trees grow by cloning, allowing themselves to die and regrow many times over. One such, recently discovered in Sweden, has roots that are 9,550 years old. It gets its name, Old Tjikko, from the deceased dog of the geologist who discovered it.

Giant trees need a lot of water – a mature sequoia uses up to 500 gallons a day. The moist, humid climate of the northern California coast is ideal for them. Heavy rain sweeps in from the Pacific and there are regular marine fogs, which trap moisture in the soil and the tree canopy by preventing evaporation.

In 1964 Donald Currey was a student taking samples from a very elderly tree, Prometheus, when two of his boring tools broke inside the tree. He asked for permission from the US Forest Service to cut it down, which they granted. When he examined his newly felled tree, it turned out to be almost 5,000 years old – the oldest non-clonal tree that had then been discovered.

Currey switched to studying lakes.

Which way do sunflowers face?

Fully grown sunflowers don't face towards the Sun.

The idea that sunflowers are heliotropic – that they move to track the movement of the Sun – isn't strictly true. They stop following the Sun as soon as they begin to bud. After this point, they remain fixed in one position – usually facing east to avoid being overheated as the afternoon Sun sinks westwards.

A single sunflower isn't one flower but hundreds clustered together. Each tiny flower has both male and female components. After pollination they all produce seeds. Jerusalem artichokes aren't artichokes but sunflowers – they once grew wild on the Great Plains of the USA and Canada and were first brought to Europe by the Spanish in the early sixteenth century. The name 'Jerusalem' is a mishearing of *girasole* ('turn-to-the-sun'), the Italian word for sunflower. Jerusalem artichokes and the other sunflowers are almost the only food plants to have originated in North America (as opposed to Central or South America).

The protein-rich oil from sunflower seeds was well known to Native American tribes. In Europe the plants were grown principally for their ornamental value until the late seventeenth century when Peter the Great of Russia brought some home from a trip to Holland. The discovery of the oil produced by crushing the large seeds coincided with the Russian Orthodox Church's ban on traditional Russian cooking oils during Lent and on fast days. Russian farmers were quick to exploit the loophole and took to planting and milling them on an industrial scale, covering over 2 million acres by the 1830s. Ironically, it was Russian immigrants to the USA and Canada who re-introduced the sunflower as a commercial crop. One of the most popular North American varieties was an import: the Mammoth Russian. There are more than 70 recorded varieties, including the swamp sunflower, the giant sunflower, the slender sunflower, the cheerful sunflower, the neglected sunflower, the showy sunflower and the hairy sunflower.

The two series of sunflowers painted by Vincent Van Gogh in Paris and then Arles in 1887–8 are now among the most famous paintings in the world. He had painted them in part as an attempt to woo fellow artist Paul Gauguin into establishing an artists' community with him in Arles in the south of France. He was pleased with his work, and so was Gauguin at first. Van Gogh later wrote to his brother Theo in January 1889, 'Gauguin likes them extraordinarily.'

Unfortunately, Gauguin and Van Gogh agreed on very little else, and during one argument in December 1888 Van Gogh ran at Gauguin with an open razor. Gauguin escaped injury but, later that night, Van Gogh cut off his own ear and took it to the local brothel, where he asked a prostitute to 'look after it carefully'. Van Gogh was sectioned and Gauguin left Arles, just two months after he had arrived. He never saw Van Gogh again. Less than 18 months later, Van Gogh died from complications caused by a self-inflicted gunshot wound to the chest.

In 1987 *Still Life: A Vase with Fifteen Sunflowers*, painted by Van Gogh in Arles, sold for almost $40 million, nearly four times the previous record paid for a painting.

STEPHEN *Thanks to our friends from the Dutch version of 'QI',
we were able to give you the correct pronunciation of Van Gogh,
the great man's name. It sounds like an outbreak of pneumonia in a
frog pond.*

What colour is a robin's breast?

Look carefully: it's orange, not red.

Robins got the name 'redbreast' in the 1400s. It was the best
anyone could do, because English had no word for orange. The
word 'orange' (meaning the fruit) entered English around 1400 –
but it wasn't used as the name of a colour until the 1540s. Until
then what we see as orange was called red.

Robins were called 'ruddocks' in Anglo-Saxon times. Elsewhere
in Europe they also have nicknames with the word 'red': *rougegorge*
(red throat) in French, *pettirosso* (red chest) in Italian, and in
German, *Rotkehlchen* (little red throat).

Despite their jolly appearance and their use as a symbol
of peace, robins are viciously
territorial. A tenth of robins
die of fractured skulls caused
by fighting other robins.
Three-quarters of robins don't
make it to their first birthday.

Robins defend their
territory throughout the year,
not just during the breeding
season. They fight most in the

early winter because that's when they're first establishing their boundaries. Robins are so aggressive they will even attack stuffed robins or tufts of red feathers. Curiously, they will relent and share their territory when conditions are especially harsh. A robin's heart beats very fast – a thousand times per minute.

Robins are much tamer in Britain than in the rest of Europe, and the British have traditionally had a taboo on killing them (although at the end of the Victorian era there was a brief fashion for using their feathers to adorn ladies' hats). In Europe they have been trapped and eaten for centuries: in Cyprus about a million are illegally killed each year for food.

Other 'reds' from the animal kingdom that are actually orange include the red kangaroo, the red panda, the red squirrel and the red kite.

In medieval times red kites were protected by law; as scavengers, they helped to keep cities clean. In later centuries the opposite applied. Wrongly blamed for killing lambs, they were considered vermin and had a bounty put on them. By the 1960s there were only a handful of pairs left in the UK.

Conservationists began concerted re-introductions in the 1990s and as a result there are now too many for ornithologists to survey accurately – perhaps as many as 1,800 breeding pairs.

Not everyone's happy about this. Some schoolchildren have been banned from eating their lunch in Oxfordshire playgrounds because of the risk of being injured by kites as they swoop to steal their food.

Even the most aggressive robin wouldn't do that.

Could you beat the king of dinosaurs at an arm wrestle?

Not a chance.

Tyrannosaurus rex's arms have been unfairly ridiculed over the years. They might look tiny, but that's just in comparison with the rest of its body. Compared to a human, *T. rex* had plenty of upper body strength. By looking at the size of their fossilised arm bones and analysing the spots where the muscles were attached, scientists estimate they would have been able to lift more than 181 kilograms (400 pounds). The average untrained man would find it hard to lift more than 68 kilograms (150 pounds).

Nevertheless, no one's quite sure what the *T. rex*'s arms were used *for*. They might have been to hold prey, to grip mates during sex, for balance, or to wave to other dinosaurs. Because soft tissue doesn't survive in the fossil record, it's unlikely we will ever know for sure. It may be that, had the species lasted a million years longer, its arms might have withered away completely. The real strength of *T. rex* was in its bite. It had the strongest bite of any land animal, exerting more than 57,000 newtons of downward pressure – roughly the same force that you would feel if you were sat on by an elephant.

Of the 50 *T. rex* fossils that have ever been found, the largest is called Sue. While the skeleton (officially known by the much less catchy name of FMNH PR 2081) is usually referred to as a 'she', nobody knows if Sue was male or female. 'She' is named after Sue Hendrickson, the palaeontologist who found her on a Sioux reservation in 1990. This led to a lawsuit over who owned the bones – in other words, the Sioux sued Sue over Sue. In 1997, with ownership agreed, Sue was sold for $8.36 million, making her the world's most expensive dinosaur. She is 4 metres (13 feet) tall, the height of a large elephant, died at the age of 28 and, judging by the eroded bones in her small but powerful forearms, probably suffered from gout.

We don't know what Sue did with her arms, and we don't know how she had sex either. Did she, like most birds, use the 'cloacal kiss' (pressing bottoms together)? Or, like snakes and lizards, did her partner have a phallus that 'everted' (popped out)? What we do know is the name of her closest living relative. In 2003 the 68-million-year-old femur of a *T. rex* was found in the Rocky Mountains. When its DNA was sequenced, its closest match was found to be that of an ordinary chicken.

It seems that dinosaurs still roam the Earth. There are at least 19 billion of them at any one time and they all go 'cluck'.

STEPHEN *A T. rex turd was found in Saskatchewan in 1998. And it was 17 inches long and 6 inches thick.*

ALAN *How did they know? Was there a dead T. rex next to it that had pooed itself to death?*

JOHNNY VEGAS *No, it was found reaching for the toilet roll with its tiny claws.*

Which animal has the most teeth?

It's not the shark, or the crocodile – and it's certainly not the blue whale. The animal with the most teeth is the slug.

Crocodiles have between 60 and 80 teeth. Sharks, who continually shed and replace their teeth, can get through 50,000 in a lifetime. But slugs easily outstrip either of them. One species of umbrella slug, *Umbraculum*, can have up to ¾ million teeth.

Gastropod molluscs (slugs and snails) need so many teeth – technically known as 'denticles' – because of their unique eating style. Their teeth are arranged on a tongue-like ribbon called a radula (from the Latin *radere*, to scrape). Instead of chewing their food, they use this like a circular saw, buzzing over vegetation and filing it to pulp it as they go.

Not all slugs and snails are vegetarian. The eyeless nocturnal ghost slug, first found in Wales, is the stuff of nightmares for earthworms. *Selenochlamys ysbryda* ('moon-cloak ghost' in Greek and Welsh) eats worms by shredding them alive and then sucking up the remains like spaghetti.

The radula has evolved in different ways in different molluscs. The highly venomous cone snail uses it as a hypodermic needle to inject its prey with poison. Many snails use their radula to clean dried mucus off their shells. You can even hear them doing this if you listen closely. The teeth on a limpet's radula are the hardest known substance in biology. They are made of a type of iron called goethite, and limpets use them to cling to rocks with a vice-like grip and excavate them like a tiny JCB.

Johann Georg Lenz (1748–1832) of the University of Jena discovered goethite in 1806. He named it after his friend, the writer and philosopher Johann Wolfgang von Goethe (1749–1832). Goethe had become obsessed with mineralogy in his twenties, as a result of his plan to re-open a medieval silver mine in the Harz mountains. By the time he died, he had amassed 17,800 samples – the largest private collection of rocks and minerals in Europe.

Blue whales, by the way, don't have any teeth at all.

STEPHEN *George Washington had hippopotamus tusk teeth.*
LINDA SMITH *He must have had quite an overbite.*

How many claws does a lobster have?

It's six, not two.

All true lobsters belong to the family *Nephropidae* (which means 'kidney-eyed'). They have ten legs, the first three pairs of which also have claws. Admittedly, the first pair is much larger and more obvious than the others, but the other four are definitely there.

Lobsters are born ambidextrous but start to develop 'handedness' quickly – they use one claw to slowly crush hard objects and the other to grab and tear soft flesh.

The crusher is always the dominant claw; female lobsters are highly attracted to the large crushers of males. Whether the left or right claw becomes the crusher is determined simply by which a young lobster uses most. Once it's established, the crusher/gripper preference is fixed for life. The claws of an adult male lobster can make up 50 per cent of its weight.

Lobsters can swim backwards but not forwards. They listen with their legs and taste with their feet. Their gills are on their upper thigh and their brains (no bigger than the tip of a ballpoint pen) are in their throats. Their kidneys and bladders are in their heads and their teeth are in their stomachs.

Their sex lives are pretty interesting too. Female lobsters can take a male's sperm and wait for more than a year before using it. Older females can use one deposit of sperm to lay two completely different sets of eggs.

Lobsters moult 25 times in their first five years, growing a bigger shell each time. This means having to go on a starvation diet first, to make sure they can squeeze backwards out of the old one. As soon as they're out, they bulk up by binge eating and filling their bodies with water, so their shell will grow back bigger. Sometimes they even eat their old shell.

Lobsters aren't the only animals with one dominant claw. Male fiddler crabs have two claws, one normal sized and one massively enlarged. They use the large one to fight other males or wave them to attract females. If they lose their fighting claw, they can grow back another one. This is just as big but much lighter and with no serrated teeth. Although useless for fighting, the male still waves it about to attract a female. Despite their tiny brains, even crustaceans can learn how to bluff . . .

How do crickets make their chirps?

Not by rubbing their legs together.

It's been known since at least the time of Pliny the Elder (AD 23–79) that crickets make noise by rubbing their wings together. They have a large vein along the bottom of each one covered with comb-like 'teeth'. They chirp by scraping the top of one wing over the bottom of the other at high speed.

Rubbing body parts to make a sound is called 'stridulation'. No insects do it just with their legs, though some grasshoppers rub their legs on their abdomens, and some spiders (which are arachnids, rather than insects, of course) do it by rubbing their front two legs against their next two.

Only male crickets chirp. They have four songs: one to attract a distant female; one to court a nearby female; one to warn off another male; and one to celebrate a successful mating session. Female crickets usually won't mate with males unless they perform a courtship song. They hear this with their legs – crickets' ears are located on their front legs, just below the knees. Although tiny, they work just like our own ears. Their eardrums capture sound, the vibrations are amplified by a fluid-filled organ called the auditory vesicle and the information is sent via the nervous system to the brain.

Some Hawaiian crickets cannot chirp. This allows them to escape detection by the tachinid fly, which locates crickets by their chirps and deposits deadly parasitic larvae on their bodies. Fortunately for these mute male crickets, the females agree to mate with them without the traditional courtship song.

Most crickets chirp more when it's hot. If you count the number of chirps made by a snowy tree cricket in 14 seconds and add 40, you'll get the temperature in Fahrenheit. This is called Dolbear's Law, published in 1897 in an article, 'The

Cricket as a Thermometer', by physicist Amos Dolbear. The snowy tree cricket is one of the most widespread US species and has a particularly clear and regular call. The novelist Nathaniel Hawthorne once wrote, 'If moonlight could be heard, it would sound just like that.'

Bush crickets, or katydids, can be masters of disguise. One Australian species, the Spotted katydid, provides the first documented case of 'acoustic mimicry used in an aggressive manner'. It can imitate 22 different species of cicada in order to lure and eat them.

In 2012 scientists at the University of Leicester studied the fossil of a long-extinct, prehistoric bush cricket. By assessing the spacing of the rasp-like teeth along the wing edge they were able to recreate its exact mating call – a sound last heard 165 million years ago.

How do cuckoos raise their young?

Mostly, they do it themselves.

There are over 140 species of cuckoo, but fewer than 60 lay their eggs in other birds' nests. We only think of cuckoos as parasites because of the behaviour of the common cuckoo (*Cuculus canorus*) which is widespread across Europe and was once common in Britain.

A common cuckoo mother can land in another bird's nest, remove an egg, lay her own egg and leave within ten seconds. Some are so bold they turn up while the host bird is present and lay their egg regardless. Common cuckoos spend summer in Europe and winter in Africa, with the result that the parents never meet their offspring. Before scientists worked this out by tracking them, many people thought cuckoos in winter turned into sparrowhawks (they look vaguely similar).

Once they have laid their single egg, female common cuckoos often return to check whether it's been accepted. If the host bird has pushed the foreign egg out, the cuckoo will destroy the host's nest. The unlucky hosts quickly learn their lesson, and the next time a cuckoo lays an egg they tolerate it.

Until the early twentieth century, many ornithologists – known as 'the regurgitators' – believed cuckoos laid an egg, swallowed it and then spat it into the host's nest. In 1922 a Birmingham businessman, champion egg-collector and cuckoo-obsessive, Edgar Chance, finally proved what really happened. Together with Oliver Pike, one of the pioneers of natural history film-making, he made a film called *The Cuckoo's Secret*, which showed the female swiftly laying its egg while the host birds weren't looking, and followed the chick's growth and ejection of its nest mates. The film ends with the host 'mother' feeding the chick, now five times bigger than herself.

Having a cuckoo in the nest can be good for the host bird. Crows' nests with cuckoos in them are more likely to produce at least one crow fledgling than nests without cuckoos. When threatened, cuckoo chicks excrete a vile-smelling, burning fluid that deters predators seeking to prey on baby crows.

Other birds use cuckoo tactics. The South American screaming cowbird (*Molothrus rufoaxillaris*) dumps its eggs in the nests of bay-winged cowbirds (*Agelaioides badius*). Unlike cuckoos, but luckily for the screaming cowbirds, their chicks are identical. The whydahs or indigobirds of the African Viduidae family lay eggs in the nests of finches. The whydah chicks grow up peacefully with their nest mates and make no attempt to evict them.

There are also several thousand species of cuckoo bees, which lay eggs in other bees' brood cells. These are even more badly behaved than common cuckoos: when the cuckoo bee hatches, it eats the food prepared for the host's offspring and then the offspring themselves.

How clever are dolphins?

Not especially.

At least, that's the view gaining ground among marine scientists. Since the 1950s dolphins have been seen as a particularly intelligent species – closer in their mental powers to humans than our nearest relatives, the chimpanzees.

The myth of the 'super-dolphin' was mostly the work of a neuroscientist called John C. Lilly (1915–2001) whose books *Man and Dolphin* (1961) and *The Mind of a Dolphin* (1967) captured the public imagination. Although some of Lilly's research was sound and led to the establishment of the US Marine Mammal Protection Act of 1972, many of his experiments were dubious. In one, he shared LSD with his 'pet' dolphin, Peter, in the hope they might be able to talk to each other. He also claimed dolphins were spiritually enlightened and that they communicated in holographic images. With his friends Allen Ginsberg and Timothy Leary, Lilly is now regarded more as a counter-culture guru or crank than as a serious scientist.

Leading the charge against the 'hyperintelligence' of dolphins is animal behaviourist Justin Gregg, who points out that many of their 'special' abilities are shared by other animals. Dolphins can distinguish between the ideas of 'many' and 'few' – but so can mealworms. Dolphins can be trained to interpret symbols – so can parrots and sea lions. Dolphins use complex signals to communicate – so do bees. Dolphins use tools – so do crows and crabs. Dolphins may be able to recognise themselves in the mirror – but so can magpies.

Even goldfish may be smarter than dolphins. Goldfish will try to leap out of a bowl to escape, something that never occurs to dolphins hemmed in by nets.

Those arguing in favour of dolphins point to the facts that they can learn dozens of human words, use highly complicated whistles and team up to hunt fish or protect their partners. Captive dolphins have been taught to collect litter that falls into their pool so they can exchange it for fish later. Some even tear up big bits of litter to blag more fishy rewards out of their human trainers. The US Navy uses them to detect mines. Their brains can be larger than human ones, but this may be merely to insulate them from cold water.

'Intelligence' is a complicated and multifaceted idea, especially when applied to animals. Rather than a ladder with man at the top and dolphins and chimps just behind, Gregg's argument is that we should marvel at the skills we don't share with dolphins (like echolocation) and stop 'looking at them through the narrow lens of the human condition'.

Which animal has the most genes?

It's not people, or the blue whale, but the tiny water flea.

DNA carries the code for every life form. A long stretch forms a single gene, and about a thousand genes make up a chromosome. The human body has 23 pairs of chromosomes, all of which are present in every single cell.

You'd think more complicated or bigger animals have more genes, but it's not that simple. The largest known animal genome belongs to the water flea *Daphnia pulex*. It has 31,000 genes, compared to the 20–25,000 of a human. Water fleas are crustaceans found in ponds and marshes all over America, Europe and Australia but, despite the size of their genome, adults are no larger than a hyphen (-).

Water fleas have a huge genome because they can multiply and copy their genes much faster than other species, often in response to stress. The threat of a predator can lead them to rapidly develop spines, helmets or even teeth on their necks. This ability for genes to respond to the environment is at the centre of a new field of study called epigenetics. This argues that our genetic code is less like a computer program and more like a musical score. Different organisms in different environments have different ways of expressing the information locked in their DNA.

Given its extraordinary genome, the water flea is one of the star organisms of epigenetics. But it's of more than just academic interest. By studying how water fleas change on a genetic level, we are learning more about how the environment can affect our own genome, giving us vital knowledge in the fight against hereditary diseases such as cancer.

As the water flea shows, there's no way of telling how much DNA a species has based on its appearance. A raspberry, as you might expect, has less than 10 per cent of the genetic material of a human, but an onion has 12 times as much. And some amoebas (100 trillion times smaller than a person) have genomes a hundred times larger.

STEPHEN *Which animal has the most genes?*
ALAN *Jeremy Clarkson.*

What is junk DNA good for?

Quite a lot, actually.

Only 2 per cent of our DNA is actively involved in overseeing the production of the proteins which make new cells. The remaining 98 per cent was once thought to be useless, random, genetic soup – the dark matter of the human genome, dubbed 'junk DNA' by Japanese-American geneticist Susumu Ohno in 1972.

Nowadays it's called 'non-coding' DNA: it doesn't tell the body how to make proteins, but it does decide how much gets made and which bits should be turned on and off. For example, non-coding DNA tells the cells in the liver they should produce liver enzymes, and hair cells that they should make the protein keratin, from which hair is made. Without the non-coding DNA, much of the coding DNA would be like a motorway without any signs.

There is still a lot to learn about DNA and how it works – there are long stretches of code that are highly repetitive and serve no obvious function. These are known as 'pseudogenes'. Nevertheless, the idea that only 2 per cent of human DNA is useful is clearly wrong.

Barring mature red blood cells, and a few other cells in the skin, hair and nails, each and every cell in your body contains two metres of DNA. As there are 37 trillion cells in your body that makes 45 billion miles of DNA – enough to reach to Neptune and back eight times over.

DNA is long but very thin. Bundled together, 25,000 strands would be no thicker than a single human hair.

Who discovered DNA?

Not Crick or Watson or Rosalind Franklin, but Johannes Friedrich Miescher.

Swiss biologist Miescher (1844–95) discovered DNA in 1869, 84 years before Crick, Watson and Franklin worked out its shape.

Trying to understand the nucleus of cells, Miescher took bandages soaked in blood and pus from Prussian soldiers in a local hospital, and mixed them with enzymes from a pig's stomach he'd got from a butcher. This produced a grey goo he assumed was a protein, but it didn't act like one. He called it 'nuclein'.

Miescher's boss, the eminent German chemist Felix Hoppe-Seyler, was not impressed. Even when Miescher replicated his experiment and showed he'd found an entirely new substance in human cells, Hoppe-Seyler offered the distinctly back-handed compliment that Miescher had merely 'enhanced our understanding of pus'. Perhaps due to this lack of encouragement, Miescher didn't go on to identify DNA as the building block of life. He did wonder if nuclein might be involved in heredity, but soon discounted it. He couldn't believe a single molecule could account for all the variation seen within species.

It was more than 60 years before anyone proved DNA communicated genetic information, and 25 more before Crick and Watson won the 1962 Nobel Prize in Physiology or Medicine for identifying the shape of its molecule. They discovered DNA is double-helix-shaped, like two interlocking spiral staircases.

Rosalind Franklin, who produced the first images of DNA, was supposedly snubbed by the Nobel Prize Committee when they awarded the prize to Crick and Watson in 1962. In fact, Franklin died of cancer in 1958 and was ineligible for the prize, which is never given posthumously. It was shared by Crick and Watson – and Maurice Wilkins, who'd worked with Franklin on the images.

The science of DNA has moved on to such an extent you can now extract your own. Swish salt water around your cheeks, spit into a glass containing more salt water and a teaspoon of washing-up liquid and mix for a minute or so. Then get someone over the age of 18 to pour some ice-cold vodka very slowly into the glass, so it forms a layer on top of the salt water. In a couple of minutes you'll see white strings start to form. These are strands of your own DNA, without a pig's stomach or a pus-soaked bandage in sight.

STEPHEN *About 1 to 4 per cent of our DNA is Neanderthal, so we cross-bred.*
JACK DEE *So were there ever, for instance, Homo sapiens who married Neanderthals? You imagine a wedding like that.*
JIMMY CARR *There's going to be a punch-up in a car park, isn't there.*

Who invented the hovercraft?

The British inventor Christopher Cockerell usually gets the credit, but there are several earlier claimants.

A Russian inventor called Vladimir Levkov and a Finn

called Toivo Kaario both built prototype hovercrafts in the 1930s. Levkov was working on a 'hovertank' when the Russian authorities cancelled his research at the start of the Second World War and destroyed the evidence. Cockerell's hovercraft didn't get off the ground until 1956, the year he filed his patent.

In 1916, well before even Levkov and Kaario, the Austrian inventor Dagobert Müller von Thomamuehl successfully built a vehicle that hovered on a cushion of air. But this (and Levkov's machine) had to be moving forward in order to work, so are not considered 'true' hovercraft. (The technical definition of a 'true' hovercraft is one that can hover when stationary.)

Hovercrafts are wonderfully odd. They travel on a 3-foot cushion of air, which is pumped downwards and trapped inside a rubber curtain. Cockerell made one early demonstration model by putting a cat-food tin inside a coffee tin and pumping air into the gap to create the cushion of air. The air cushion was patented as early as the 1870s, but engines weren't powerful enough to make a viable vehicle.

The hovercraft never became the revolutionary technology Cockerell hoped for – he wanted to see fleets of them crossing the Atlantic at 100 miles per hour. The last cross-Channel hovercraft ended operations in 2000. These days, the only one you can travel on as a passenger in Britain runs between Southsea and the Isle of Wight.

The problem with hovercraft is that they are so expensive to run. They use a huge amount of fuel and the rubber skirting has to be replaced frequently as it takes so much punishment from the pressure of the air inside.

Why was the dishwasher invented?

Not to wash dishes faster, but more carefully.

Patents for dishwashers exist from before the 1880s, but none of them worked as well as that designed by Josephine Garis Cochran (1839–1913) of Shelbyville, Illinois, in 1886. A wealthy socialite, she had so much time on her hands that she spent it fretting about the state of her china. One night she got so irritated by the clumsiness of her maids that she did the washing-up on her own. She found out how difficult it was to avoid chipping cups and plates and vowed to invent a machine that could do the job without causing so much damage.

Cochran's invention was crude and cumbersome but effective. There was a small pedal-driven version and a larger steam-powered one. The latter, which could wash and dry 200 dishes in just two minutes, was the sensation of the 1893 World's Fair in Chicago. (Other exhibits at the same fair included a 10-ton Canadian cheese, a 38-foot-high, 13-ton temple crafted completely from chocolate and the world's first Ferris wheel.)

The washing machine won first prize in its category, but at $250 each (about $6,600 today) they were too expensive for home use. Instead Josephine targeted hotels and restaurants, and she sold enough to keep Cochran's Crescent Washing Machine Company in business until her death in 1913. The company finally became part of the Whirlpool Corporation.

Dishwashers were revolutionary for hoteliers, and also for revolutionaries. The Russian anarchist Peter Kropotkin (1842–1921) was excited by their potential to free workers from oppression. Americans were less enthusiastic. Servants complained it would take away their jobs; clergymen considered them immoral as they would allow women to shirk their God-given labour.

Dishwashers are still a luxury in the UK today. Fewer than half of households own one, and many believe they use more water than washing up by hand. (In fact, they use less than a sixth as much.) But a recent survey in America found people who think washing machines an unnecessary luxury may well be right: more than three-quarters of people who owned one admitted to restarting the cycle just to avoid unloading it.

When was the selfie invented?

1839.

Robert Cornelius, an American chemist, silversmith and lamp manufacturer, took the first photographic self-portrait. He is glaring past the camera with tousled hair and his arms folded. Due to long exposure times, he would have had to stay in position for a full minute.

Photographic 'selfies' were common in the early days – photographers often acted as their own models. If you count drawings and sculptures, the oldest selfie is much older. Artists have been putting themselves into pictures for millennia. There is a stone selfie in ancient Egypt, carved by a sculptor called Bak in 1365 BC. According to the ancient Greek writer Plutarch, the

sculptor Phidias put his own face onto the shield of his bronze statue of the goddess Athena in the Parthenon – an outrage that got him sent to prison.

The oldest ever *drawing* of a face might be a 27,000-year-old cave painting at Vilhonneur in France. It's hard to be sure, but the impressionistic lines seem to show an eye, nose and mouth.

The first known photograph was taken in 1826. It was a rather dull view from outside the workshop of the French inventor Joseph Nicéphore Niépce (1765–1833). The exposure period took so many hours that, in the final photograph, the sun appears to be shining on two sides of a courtyard at once. Later on, Victorian exposure times were cut down to 30 seconds. Because this is too long to hold a convincing smile, it has given us the unfair impression that the Victorians were humourless.

In photographs of babies, Victorian mothers were sometimes behind them, covered in cloth so they could not be seen holding the child still while its picture was taken. At the other end of things, many Victorians had photos taken of their relatives after death – until the 1880s photographers' adverts often said they were ready 'to make pictures from corpses if desired'.

Photography gave a boost to pornography – but it began mildly. In 1893 there were press reports in Britain about young men reportedly forming a 'Vigilance Association', whose purpose was 'thrashing the cads with cameras who go about at seaside places taking snapshots of ladies emerging from the deep'.

When was 'OMG' first used?

Earlier than you think.

The first time anyone used 'OMG' to mean 'Oh My God' was in 1917, in a letter to Winston Churchill. The letter was from John Arbuthnot Fisher, former British admiral and First Sea Lord (the highest rank in the Royal Navy). His exact words were: 'I hear that a new order of Knighthood is on the tapis [tablecloth] – O. M. G. (Oh! My! God!) – Shower it on the Admiralty!'

Fisher's naval career spanned 60 years, and he is often recognised as England's greatest admiral since Lord Nelson. In 1911 he predicted war with Germany would break out in October 1914. He was only two months out – it was actually August. Popular with sailors for replacing weevil-infested hard biscuits with freshly baked bread, Fisher was also the driving force behind the production of the first modern battleship, HMS *Dreadnought*. He resigned his naval post in 1915 after quarrelling with Churchill over Gallipoli.

OMG isn't the only modern abbreviation with old roots. IOU first appeared in 1618. The *Oxford English Dictionary*'s (*OED*) 2009 'Word of the Year' was 'unfriend', which dates back to 1659, when Thomas Fuller wrote to fellow theologist John Heylyn, 'I Hope, Sir, that we are not mutually Un-friended by this Difference which hath happened betwixt us.'

And text-speak dates back a lot further than text messaging. In 1711, for example, Joseph Addison complained about the way words were being 'miserably curtailed' – he mentioned pos (itive) and incog (nito). Jonathan Swift thought that abbreviating words was a 'barbarous custom'. Eric Partridge's *Dictionary of Abbreviations* (1942) contains dozens of SMS-friendly examples, such as agn (again), mth (month) and gd (good).

LOL was first used in the 1960s, when it was doctors' slang for 'little old lady'. Sometimes doctors extended it to LOLINAD (Little Old Lady In No Apparent Distress). NASA's *Apollo* mission computers in the 1960s and 1970s used 'LOL memory'; this was named after the little old ladies – former textile workers – who literally wove the software together out of copper wire.

Both LOL and OMG entered the *OED* in 2011. BFF (Best

Friends Forever) made it in the same year, as well as 'heart' as a verb meaning 'to love', which was first seen in a 1984 car bumper sticker reading 'I heart my dogs [*sic*] head'. Some newspapers claimed the heart logo had been included in the dictionary entry, thus making it the first symbol defined in the *OED*, but this didn't happen.

Ancient Romans often started letters with SVBEEV, an abbreviation of '*Si vales, bene est, ego valeo*', or 'If you're well, that's good – I'm well'. From 80 BC they used SPQR as a shortened version of '*Senatus Populusque Romanus*' – 'the Senate and People of Rome'. It appeared on shields, coins and buildings at the time. This is the oldest acronym still in use: as part of his attempt to forge a new Roman Empire, Mussolini had SPQR emblazoned on sewer drain covers across Rome, where they remain to this day.

Who wrote the first English dictionary?

Robert Cawdrey. Or Richard Mulcaster. Either way, it wasn't Dr Johnson.

In 1582 a schoolteacher called Richard Mulcaster published a list of 8,000 English words. It was an attempt to impose some rules on the buccaneering, 'make-it-up-as-you-go' world of sixteenth-century English. But it was very basic – the words had no definitions – and most literary historians don't think it counts as a dictionary. The first undisputed dictionary was *Robert Cawdrey's Table Alphabeticall*, which listed 3,000 'Hard Words' with definitions attached. It came out in 1604, beating Samuel Johnson's dictionary by 150 years.

Although Johnson's dictionary of 1755 had 42,773 entries, it was far from comprehensive. At the time, English had between 250,000 and 300,000 words. Among many others, Johnson left out 'nemesis', 'bank note', 'virus', 'zinc', 'athlete', 'malaria', 'irritable', 'underdone', 'anus' and 'euphemism'.

Johnson disapproved of French words so he ignored 'cutlet', 'bourgeois' and 'champagne'. Oddly, he seemed to have no problem with 'escargatoire', which he defined as 'a nursery of snails'. There were no entries for the letter X (in fairness, previous dictionaries had included about 20, but they were hopelessly obscure). Rude words in Johnson's dictionary include 'bum', 'arse', 'piss', 'fart' and 'turd'. The word 'pissburnt' was defined as 'stained with urine'. Many definitions include dubious information – such as that female elephants lie on their backs to have sex (they don't) or that whole millipedes make a good laxative when swallowed.

Words that are in Johnson's dictionary but have since fallen out of fashion include 'deosculation', defined as 'the act of kissing', and 'mouth-friend' ('one who professes friendship without intending it'). Other words have changed their meanings. A 'urinator' was 'someone who dived', and a 'lavatory' was 'something in which parts diseased are washed'. Some definitions are half-hearted: a 'sock' is 'something put between the shoe and foot', 'lunch' is 'as much food as one's hand can hold', and a 'crab' is 'a crustaceous fish'.

Johnson was a physically imposing man, though half-deaf, blind in one eye, scarred by scrofula and possibly afflicted by Tourette's. He wasn't a doctor until ten years after the dictionary was published. He hadn't even claimed his degree from Oxford because of money troubles, and his college only gave him a Master's in 1755 because the dictionary was about to be published.

The dictionary catapulted him into the front rank of famous men of the age. It was funded by subscription and the money pledged totalled £1,575, worth about £190,000 today. Johnson planned to complete the project in three years. In the end it took him nine (most of it pulled together in the last 18 months). In the painfully slow world of lexicography, this is astonishingly quick: there were 44 years between the publication of the first and last volumes of the *Oxford English Dictionary*, and its Swedish equivalent, *Svenska Akademiens Ordbok*, is still being written. The Swedes started in 1884 and expect to finish in 2017.

STEPHEN *Can you remember who wrote the first dictionary in English?*

ALAN *Baldrick.*

What is literally the most misused word in the English language?

The word 'literally' has been used to mean its opposite for over 200 years.

In 2011 the *Oxford English Dictionary* added an extra definition for 'literally': 'Used to indicate that some metaphorical or hyperbolical expression is to be taken in the strongest admissible sense.' It included a disclaimer that, while widespread, this usage is considered 'irregular' by many, as it's the exact opposite of its literal meaning – which is 'not figuratively or metaphorically'. The oldest known use of a non-literal 'literally' occurs in *The History of Emily Montague* (1769) by Frances Brooke (1724–89). Written by an Englishwoman living in Canada, and the first novel ever set in North America, it contains the line, 'He is a fortunate man to be introduced to such a party of fine women at

his arrival; it is literally to feed among the lilies.'

Much outrage over the new definition stems from confusion about the role of the *OED*. Dictionaries are descriptive, not prescriptive. Entries are not rules but records of how words are used. Great care is taken over which words are allowed into the *OED*, and once a word is added it is never removed.

Words proposed but rejected for addition to the *OED* are stored in a secret vault. They include 'nonversation', a conversation that isn't going anywhere; 'furgling', fumbling in your pocket for keys or change; and 'stealth-geek', someone who hides their niche interests. The awkward sidestepping dance you find yourself doing when you meet someone walking towards you is a 'polkadodge'. If words aren't immediately accepted for publication, it doesn't mean they will never be. 'Earworm' – the name for a catchy song that gets stuck in your head – was once in the vault. It was added to the *OED* in 2011.

'Literally' isn't the only word to have changed its meaning. It once wasn't nice to call someone 'nice' – it meant 'foolish'. 'Bully' meant 'darling'; 'silly' meant 'worthy'; 'resentment' meant 'gratitude'; and a 'clue' was 'a ball of wool'.

A 2009 survey found that the most misused phrase in English was 'damp squid'. It should be 'damp squib': a squib is a small explosive which must be kept dry to work. But words and meanings evolve through usage. Each time anyone says 'damp squid', it's one step closer to a place in the *OED*.

What does a cowboy call his rope?

A rope.

Although films and books call them 'lassos', the people who use them never call them that. To a cowboy, the term 'lasso' is strictly for soft-handed city folk.

Nobody knows why they don't like the word. Maybe because it's Spanish: it comes from *lazo* (meaning 'snare') and early mentions refer to it as being from 'Spanish America'. One of the earliest of these is in Washington Irving's *A Tour of the Prairies* (1835): 'The coil of cordage is called a lariat, and answers to the laso of South America.' A lariat is another word for a lasso, as are 'riata' and 'reata' – all three are also Spanish in origin. Whether or not it's anti-Hispanic prejudice, American cowboys like to call a rope a rope, and the act of using a rope to catch an animal they call 'roping'.

Lassos weren't invented in the Wild West. The ancient Egyptians used them to capture antelopes and wild oxen. Unlike cowboys, they didn't do so from horseback – they hid behind a bush and sprang out to ambush them. Just like modern cattle, they were rounded up and branded – but with a hieroglyph rather than initials.

NASA are planning to lasso an asteroid. They hope to do this using a robot-controlled rocket fitted with a kind of giant drawstring bag. Once bagged, the rock would be brought back to Earth and examined to assess the potential of mining asteroids for rare minerals, as well as learning more about the origins of the Solar System. If it sounds simple it isn't: even a small asteroid 25 feet across, weighs 500 tons and travels at 55,000 miles an hour. The $100 million mission is set to launch in 2019.

Another commercial use for the lasso is in the oil industry. Marine haulage companies lasso icebergs that threaten oil rigs and tow them out to sea.

Even animals use lassos. Velvet worms ensnare their prey by spitting a string of glue a distance of up to 3 feet. The bolas spider doesn't bother to spin a whole web – it dangles a single thread with a blob of silk on the end into a gap where a moth might fly. It then releases chemicals that resemble a male moth's sex pheromones and jiggles the line so that the blob on the end looks like the fluttering of a female moth. When a male flies over to investigate he becomes entangled and the spider pulls him in and eats him. Bolas spiders can even alter the proportions of pheromones they produce to lure different species of moths at different times of night.

STEPHEN *What does goulash mean, do you know?*
ROB BRYDON *It actually means cowboy. I learned this while I was there.*
STEPHEN *Cowboy, you're right. Goulash means cowboy.*
ROB *Ride 'em goulash.*

What kind of hat did they wear in the Wild West?

Bowler hats.

Cowboys rarely wore 'cowboy hats'. They wore whatever came to hand – a sea captain's cap or a straw hat, but especially the bowler or 'derby'.

The bowler was designed by London hat makers Thomas and William Bowler in 1849. It was a tough, low-rise hat specifically designed to protect the heads of mounted gamekeepers from low-hanging branches, but its practicality and strength made it particularly popular among cowboys.

The idea that cowboys mainly wore Stetsons began with the artist Frederic Remington (1861–1909). A cousin of the famous gunmaker, he specialised in paintings of nineteenth-century America and always drew cowboys wearing them.

Not all cowboys were white, either. Half of them were black or Mexican. They had segregated rodeos and tougher lives than their white counterparts, but generally faced much less discrimination than minorities in the rest of the USA.

Calling Stetsons '10-gallon hats' probably began with Mexican cowboys, from the Spanish *galón*, or galloon, a type of narrow braided trimming around the crown. The alternative theory – that it was used to carry water – is much less likely: a Stetson can only hold around three-quarters of a gallon. It was invented in 1865 by John B. Stetson, who went on to become the world's largest hat maker, turning out 3,300,000 hats a year from a 9-acre factory in Philadelphia. The Stetson became known as the 'derby' after an outlaw called 'the Derby Kid'.

The other staple of frontier mythology is the bank robbery, but historians at the University of Dayton, who looked at 15 states over the 40 years of the period, found evidence of only eight bank heists. These days, America has more than 5,000 bank robberies a year.

There were also fewer guns in those days. The second most common cause of arrest was for carrying a firearm illegally. In the 1880s guns were banned in Dodge City – if you entered town with one you had to hand it over to the sheriff and get a ticket in exchange. The gun laws in the 'Wild' West were much tougher than they are in America today.

STEPHEN *What kind of hat did they wear in the Wild West?*
SHAPPI KHORSANDI *Ten-gallon hat.*
ROSS NOBLE *Oh no, of course, because now it's litres, isn't it. So . . .*
ALAN *Forty-five-litre hat.*

Where is Harris Tweed made?

Not on the Isle of Harris, but on the Isle of Lewis.

The 'Isle' of Lewis and the 'Isle' of Harris are actually one island joined by a narrow strip towards the southern end, Lewis being the larger northern bit. Together they make up the largest of the British Isles other than the British mainland and Ireland. The only remaining 'Harris Tweed' mills are on Lewis, not Harris – so it should really be called 'Lewis Tweed'.

Whatever it's called, it's the only commercial hand-woven tweed in the world. The Harris Tweed Act of 1993 says the cloth must be 'hand-woven by the islanders at their homes in the Outer Hebrides, finished in the Outer Hebrides, and made from pure virgin wool dyed and spun in the Outer Hebrides'.

Spinning and dyeing the wool takes place in one of the three mills on Lewis. The wool then goes to the weavers' homes to be turned into cloth, and the cloth goes back to the mills for the finishing processes. The final touch is the addition of the Harris Tweed Authority's orb symbol – guaranteeing it's the genuine article. The authority's pattern book has over 4,000 colour/pattern combinations. In 2014 Heriot-Watt University created a tweed that smells of whisky. The scent is built into the fabric's layers to make it last.

'Tweed' only accidentally shares a name with the Scottish river.

Like denim, serge, chino, gabardine and drill, it has a herringbone pattern, known as 'twill'. In 1831 James Locke, a London hat maker, took a delivery of 'tweel' from Hawick in the Borders. Misreading the writing on the parcel as 'tweed' (and assuming it was named after the river), he sold it as that, and the name stuck.

As well as tweed, Lewis is famous for the discovery (also in 1831) of the Lewis Chessmen. Made of whales' teeth and walrus ivory, the 93 chess pieces date to the twelfth century. A peasant found them buried on the beach and ran for his life, fearing he had disturbed a conference of elves. More recently, NASA used 'knotted wrack', a remarkable seaweed from Lewis, to fireproof their astronauts' notebooks.

Unlike the weaving of Harris Tweed, Fair Isle knitting is not a protected craft. Anybody can use the name. If you want a genuine, hand-made Fair Isle jumper you'll have to be quick. Fair Isle is a tiny island between the Shetlands and the Orkneys and has 70 inhabitants, only four of whom can knit. The moment the first boat load of visitors arrives each year, the island's shop immediately sells out of Fair Isle jumpers, hats and scarves.

Which bone of a whale is used for whalebone corsets?

'Whalebone' isn't bone.

'Whalebone' is baleen, a substance found at the back of a whale's mouth that filters plankton and enables it to eat. It looks like bone, but isn't: it's actually keratin, the same stuff that makes up your hair and fingernails, or the horn of a rhinoceros. The word comes from the Latin *balaena*, 'a whale', which in turn derives from the Greek *phallaina*, which is related to *phallos* ('swollen penis'), presumably because of the whale's shape.

A blue whale has 320 pairs of baleen plates in its mouth, each a metre long. Its strength, lightness and flexibility made it the plastic of the nineteenth century. A Boston merchant published an inventory of 54 'whalebone' products, including whips, parasols, umbrellas, divining rods, back supporters, busks, corsets, tongue scrapers, shoehorns, suspenders, policemen's clubs, canes, riding crops, billiard cushion springs, fishing rods and shavings to stuff mattresses. Most 'whalebone' has now been replaced by plastic or fibreglass.

At the end of the nineteenth century many doctors thought women's skeletons and respiratory systems differed naturally from men's. In fact, almost a hundred years of wearing corsets had deformed the average woman's shape. Even a well-fitting 1880s corset could inflict severe pain on the lower ribs and cause indigestion, constipation and weakened back muscles. But women of the time didn't have ribs removed so they could squeeze into one. Given the dangers of going under the knife in those days, that would have been a terrible idea.

Despite the down sides, wearing a corset was probably better than not wearing one. Clothes in the nineteenth century were heavy and multilayered, and the corset offered useful back support for overdressed ladies. Orthopaedic corsets have been used in this way for centuries and are still prescribed for both men and women. After he was shot in 1968, Andy Warhol wore a corset permanently to ease the strain on his weakened spine.

What's the loudest animal for its size?

It lives in water, but it isn't what Alan Davies might think.

The loudest animal on Earth relative to its size is a tiny member of the water boatman family, *Micronecta scholtzi*, an insect that lives in your local pond. Scientists have recorded it 'singing' at up to 99.2 decibels – equivalent to the noise made by a loud orchestra heard from the front row. The male lesser water boatman makes music rather like a violinist but, instead of a fiddle and bow, he rubs ridges on his abdomen with his penis. This is only 50 micrometres across, roughly the width of a human hair, and scientists are mystified by how such a minute creature – nicknamed the 'singing penis' – can produce such extraordinary amplification. Although we don't know how they do it, we do know why – it's to attract a mate by out-singing the competition. Most of its volume is lost moving from the water into the air, but it's still clearly audible to anyone standing by the side of the pond.

The loudest individual animal regardless of its size is the blue whale. Its call measures 188 decibels – louder than a lion's roar, a howler monkey's bark or the 140 decibels made by a jet taking off. It's called a 'whistle' but it's actually more of a rumble, with a sound so low that it's felt rather than heard. Other whales can sense the vibrations from thousands of miles away. At 20 hertz, it's the deepest sound the human ear can hear.

A single whale of unknown species sings at a much higher frequency than any other. Known as the '52-hertz whale', it is heard in the northern Pacific every autumn before swimming south to the Californian coast. Perhaps because its call is too high-pitched to be heard, no other whale has ever replied, so it has earned the nickname 'the loneliest whale in the world'. Some marine scientists think it might be the offspring of a blue whale that has crossbred with another species; others think it may be deaf.

One creature that is very far from deaf is the greater wax moth. It can hear sounds at a frequency of 300 kilohertz, far higher than any other animal can hear and, even more mysteriously, far higher than any animal can make. Moths need to be able to hear in ultrasound to evade bats, their main predators. But the highest frequency ever produced by a bat is only 212 kilohertz. No one knows how or why the greater wax moth acquired its unique ability.

STEPHEN *What is the longest animal in the world?*

ALAN *I think that even the longest snake wouldn't be as long as a really really long sea animal like a whale . . .*

KLAXON

STEPHEN *Oh dear, oh dear. It's not the blue whale.*

ALAN *It's not the blue whale?*

STEPHEN *Bill?*

BILL BAILEY *The common or garden domestic cat.*

ALAN *It's about that long though?* (DEMONSTRATES BY HOLDING OUT HIS ARMS)

BILL *Yes. But when you stretch them out . . . Have you ever held a cat up under its arms like that, they're massive.*

Where do fish live?

Not necessarily in water.

The Pacific leaping blenny, also known as the leaping rockskipper, is a tropical fish that lives on several Pacific islands, including Guam. Although very much a fish, it is officially classified as a land animal as it lives there permanently.

Blennies have given up on the sea. They hop between rocks on the shoreline, using their tails as springs. Their enlarged fins help them cling on to wet rocks. They have to stay damp, so they live by the sea's edge, but they jump out of the way of big waves to avoid being swept away. They even reproduce on land. Zoologists believe blennies are a classic example of what happened when the first animals moved from the sea onto land.

It turns out that *lots* of fish can survive out of water. Nearly 50 different families of fish can breathe air. Chinese snakehead fish do, and survive for several days out of water if kept wet. Some snakeheads can even flop their way across muddy ground. Mudskippers can walk on land. Mangrove killifish can live in logs for months on end during dry spells. Climbing perch can walk, though they can't actually climb. They're so called because they're sometimes found in trees, but it turns out to be because birds have carried them up there.

Animals first left the sea about 400 million years ago. Scientists at McGill University have recently studied an ancient species of walking, air-breathing African fish called the bichir (*Polypterus senagalus*) to see how this might have happened. By raising bichirs out of water (but keeping them moist with puddles and mist sprays) they found that within a year they were able to lift their heads higher, keep their fins tucked further in beneath them, take faster steps and undulate their tails less frequently. They had even grown the beginnings of a neck. This rapid adaptation shows it may not have been as difficult as once thought for marine animals to leave the sea and live on land.

Some fish can drown. Gars are an American fish that breathe air thanks to a gas bladder, which they use as a lung. They surface, gulp air in through their mouths and push it into their bladders. This allows them to swim in water with low oxygen content, but the flipside is that they're dangerously dependent on them. If they get trapped in a net under water, they can easily drown.

Where do penguins live?

Only two of the 19 species of penguin live in Antarctica.

One species, the Galapagos Island penguin, lives on Isabella Island, which isn't even in the southern hemisphere. The island is just north of the equator and land temperatures there can reach close to 30 °C, which sounds much too hot for a penguin. Fortunately, the Humboldt Current sweeps cold water from the Antarctic up past the islands. This not only cools the sea, but brings huge shoals of ocean fish that the penguins live on.

All other wild penguins live in the southern hemisphere, but most don't live in Antarctica. The two species that do are emperor penguins and Adélies. Penguins like a range of climates. Adélies, chinstrap penguins and gentoos prefer ice; rockhoppers live on cliff edges and shorelines, and South American Magellanic penguins inhabit burrows.

Given that they mostly live at opposite ends of the world, you might think penguins are safe from polar bears. But Humboldt penguins from Peru have been spotted all the way up the west coast of North America, some making it as far as the Gulf of Alaska, which is perilously close to the Arctic domains of the polar bear. It's thought the penguins got there on boats (it's too far to swim) after being adopted as pets by passing sailors.

Alaskan penguins aren't the only birds to find themselves in an unusual place. The UK has a wild parakeet population which is growing by 30 per cent each year. It currently numbers about 50,000 birds living in parks all across London and south-east England. Some believe they're descended from a pair that Jimi Hendrix released in the 1960s; or that they escaped from Shepperton Studios during the filming of *The African Queen* in 1950. The most likely explanation is more mundane: some private pets or aviary specimens got loose in the mid-1990s and, finding no natural predators and plenty of food, have bred unchecked. They're originally from the Himalayas.

In 2012 three British holidaymakers in Australia were charged with stealing a protected animal after they got drunk and broke into SeaWorld. They had planned to swim with the dolphins and leave, but when they woke up the next morning they found a fairy penguin named Dirk in their apartment. You should always resist the urge to pick up a penguin – they have very delicate bones. Rescue centres will only handle the birds if they need medical attention.

STEPHEN *It's actually very hard to sex a penguin, by which I mean to determine its gender.*
SANDI TOKSVIG *Not for them, presumably.*

Where did the camel get its hump?

The Arctic.

In 2006 we revealed that camels came from North America,* but we didn't realise how far north. Since then, scientists have found fragments of a camel's leg bone from over 3.5 million years ago in the Canadian Arctic. These early camels were nearly twice the size they are now – over 3 metres (11 feet) tall – and they evolved their fat-filled hump to help them survive the cold.

The Arctic was warmer back then and forested with conifer and birch. As the Ice Age came, the camels moved south to escape the cold. On reaching the deserts they found themselves surprisingly suited to their new environment. Their big flat feet, which evolved for spreading their weight over snow, now helped them to walk on sand. The thick fur on their backs, originally developed to keep them warm, now shielded them from the heat of the Sun. And their three eyelids, once so effective against snowstorms, now protected their eyes from wind-blown sand.

The camel's hump is just as useful in the desert as it once was in the frozen north. Almost all its fat is stored there, rather than being evenly distributed over its body, so it stays cool in warm environments. The hump isn't rigid: if a camel uses up its supply of fat, the hump shrinks and flops over to one side. Once the camel has fed and slept properly, it returns to its original position. Baby camels don't have humps – they only start growing them when they begin eating solid food.

The two main species of camel are Bactrians and dromedaries. Bactrians have two humps and dromedaries one. An easy way to remember this is to take the first letter of their names and turn it on its side. Wild Bactrians are critically endangered – with fewer than 800 left, they are rarer than pandas.

* *The Book of General Ignorance (the Noticeably Stouter Edition)*, p. 131.

What is Antarctica's largest native land animal?

A 6-millimetre-long (¼-inch) midge.

Belgica antarctica is a tiny, flightless insect and the only animal to
live all year round in Antarctica. Penguins visit to lay eggs, but
they don't stay all year.

The midges are incredibly tough. A *B. antarctica* larva can
survive at −15 °C and dehydrate itself to a third of its original
weight. They do this to save themselves from being killed by the
water in their own bodies. If the water freezes into ice, the midge
will die.

B. antarctica have no wings, which prevents them being blown
into the sea by the biting winds, and they spend a lot of time
covered in penguin excrement. This contains no oxygen – so the
midges have adapted to survive without it for as long as a month.
They spend two years as larvae, building up enough energy for
reproduction. The adults live for only a week, just enough time
to mate, lay eggs and die.

The only other permanent animal life on Antarctica is a few
mites, but there are 100 species of moss and up to 400 lichens,
as well as algae that grows in little pools or in the microscopic
spaces between particles of quartz rock.

Some humans live in Antarctica all year round, but they're
not native. Their research bases are heated, but life is tough for

them too: fresh water is in such short supply that showers can be limited to three minutes every third day. People staying with the British Antarctic Survey over winter must have a blood type matching that of a colleague, in case they need a transfusion.

If an animal dies in Antarctica, it is freeze-dried by the cold and wind. A corpse can be 300 years old and look like it died only a few weeks earlier.

STEPHEN *George Murray Levick was the naturalist on Scott's ill-fated expedition. And he discovered what he called 'the astonishing depravity of penguin behaviour'.*
SANDI TOKSVIG *Be fair, it's Antarctica, there's nothing else to do.*
JOHNNY VEGAS *And on their night off they dress as pandas. Which just muddies the water.*

How high could a flea jump if it was the size of a human?

Not as high as you'd think.

The world high jump record is held by Cuban Javier Sotomayor. In 1993 he cleared an 8-foot bar, or 1.25 times his own height. The common flea can jump 100 times its own height. Some species can get up to 200 times higher.

It is often said that if a flea were scaled up to the size of a human, it could jump 1,200 feet in the air – higher than London's Shard or the Empire State Building in New York. But the laws of physics would prevent this happening. The strength of muscles depends on their cross-sectional area. When an animal increases in size, this area increases, but the animal's weight increases much more: the smaller the animal, the greater its strength-to-weight ratio.

While human-sized fleas couldn't jump over skyscrapers, ordinary fleas are remarkable jumpers. They store energy in a substance called resilin, which is made up of thousands of tiny protein springs that can stretch to three times their length and return to their initial shape without losing any elasticity. If we had resilin in our limbs, we'd do a lot better at the high jump than we do now.

Fleas aren't the champion jumpers in the animal kingdom. That honour goes to the froghopper, or spittlebug, best known for covering garden foliage with 'cuckoo spit' – an anal secretion that protects up to 100 eggs and developing larvae, and tastes so bad nothing will eat them. A froghopper can jump about as high as a flea can, but is around 60 times heavier, making it a much greater athlete. When jumping, the froghopper experiences a force of 400 g, well over 100 times that which an astronaut experiences re-entering Earth's atmosphere. To a predator, the froghopper must seem to vanish into thin air.

JOHN SERGEANT *Here is a very old joke. How do you build a flea circus? You have to start from scratch.*

What would happen if the population of China all jumped at once?

Nothing.

It's not true that if all the Chinese (1.3 billion people and rising) jumped into the air simultaneously it would knock the

Earth into a different orbit.

Nothing of the sort would happen. It's a basic principle of physics that every action has an equal and opposite reaction. If the population of China jumped up in the air, it would push the Earth away from them slightly; as they fell back the force of gravity would attract the Earth slightly towards them – the planet and the Chinese would be back where they started, with no harm done.

Even if the population of China could be organised to jump at once, it's been calculated that the resulting thud would equate to only 500 tons of TNT, 40 times smaller than the force of the atom bomb dropped on Hiroshima and nowhere near enough to displace Earth from its orbit. Even if the entire human race (whose estimated weight in 2012 was 316 million tons) stood in a single spot and jumped, the world would move less than the width of a single atom.

Compared to humanity, the Earth weighs a really gigantic amount. It has a mass of about 6,000,000,000,000,000,000,000,000 tons. Although 40,000 tons of space dust falls on the Earth every year, the planet's mass decreases annually by 50,000 tons. This is because 3 kilograms of hydrogen and helium atoms leaves the atmosphere for space every second. Gravity can't hold them: Earth's magnetic field is 100 times weaker than a fridge magnet.

Which island could the whole population of the world stand on?

The Isle of Wight isn't big enough any more.

In 1950 it was worked out that the population of the Earth, then around 2.5 billion, could fit onto the island, which has an area of 147 square miles. Even then it would have been a squeeze, with little more than a square foot of space for each person. Now, with Earth's population at well over 7 billion, there's no way we'd all fit on.

In his 1968 novel about overpopulation, *Stand on Zanzibar*, John Brunner correctly predicted that by 2010 world population would have reached 7 billion, and that we would need a bigger island. As he said, Zanzibar, off the east coast of Africa, is big enough at 640 square miles – although the Isle of Skye would be closer in size.

Stand on Zanzibar is prescient in other areas too. It foresaw the rise of China and the creation of the EU, as well as laser printing, electric cars, in-flight movies and satellite television. It predicted computer viruses and coined the term 'worm' for them. It has a character called President Obomi, and even pre-empted what you're reading now. *Stand on Zanzibar* has a book-within-a-book that pokes holes in common wisdom called *You're an Ignorant Idiot*.

Contrary to claims that the UK is overcrowded, if all the land in the country was shared equally between every man, woman and child, we'd each have an acre. And, if we all lay down next to one another, we could fit 90 billion people into the UK: that's 12 times the total population of the Earth, and equal to the total number of humans who have ever lived.

Where is Krakatoa?

If you've heard of the 1969 movie *Krakatoa: East of Java*, you probably think you've a pretty good idea.

But Krakatoa is actually west of Java. The film's director, Bernard L. Kowalski, knew this perfectly well, but stuck with 'east' as it sounded more exotic.

When Krakatoa erupted up in 1883, it was the loudest sound ever caught on recording equipment. Two thousand miles away, in Western Australia, it sounded like artillery fire – the equivalent of hearing an explosion in the Canary Islands from London. The captain of a ship 40 miles from Krakatoa wrote, 'I am convinced that the Day of Judgment has come,' and reported that the eardrums of half of his crew had shattered.

Another Indonesian volcano actually is east of Java – the much bigger Mount Tambora. Kowalski could have called his film *Tambora: East of Java*: its eruption in 1815 was even more spectacular.

Krakatoa threw 6 cubic miles of debris into the sky, but Tambora generated 38 cubic miles of it, darkening the sky so much that the following year was known as 'the year without a summer'. Crops failed, and the global climate changed so rapidly that a new strain of cholera evolved, claiming hundreds of thousands of lives around the world. Tambora's eruption also led, indirectly, to the writing of *Frankenstein* – Mary Shelley was on holiday with her husband and Lord Byron near Lake Geneva. If the weather had been nicer, they might have spent the time going on bracing walks. As it was, they were forced to stay inside and think up ghost stories.

But Krakatoa and Tambora both pale into insignificance beside the most violent of all volcanic eruptions: Lake Toba in Sumatra (also west of Java). It happened 70,000 years ago, when

Homo sapiens had just emerged out of Africa. The eruption ejected nearly 700 cubic miles of debris into the sky – the equivalent of 19 million Empire State Buildings.

Toba's eruption appears to have had a devastating effect on the human race. Genetic analysis shows the population fell to no more than 10,000 and, according to some estimates, as few as 40 breeding couples. There is no definite proof the two are linked, but it seems likely that Toba came very close to wiping out all human life on the planet.

What's the world's largest body of dead water?

Not the Dead Sea but the Black Sea.

'Dead water' lacks oxygen – the technical term is anoxic – and so it can't sustain complex life like fish and plants, only single-celled organisms like bacteria. The Black Sea is nearly 90 per cent anoxic, and it's also huge – 700 miles long, 1½ miles deep, with a surface area larger than Iraq and a volume of 132,000 cubic miles.

The Black Sea is bordered by six countries: Turkey, Romania, Bulgaria, Ukraine, Russia and Georgia. Four major rivers pour into it: the Dniester, the Don, the Dnieper – and the Danube, which contains half of Europe's fresh water. Oddly, the top layer of the Black Sea, which is connected to the Mediterranean, has plenty of oxygen and teems with life. The dead zone begins 300 feet down. It is a gloomy, anoxic, stagnant pond that stretches all the way to the bottom, a mile below.

The two layers don't mix because they have different densities. The lower layer is choked with vast colonies of algae that feed on nutrient-rich fertiliser running into the sea from the surrounding farms. In the process the algae starve larger organisms of oxygen and when they die, they are eaten by bacteria, using up yet more oxygen.

Worse still, the sea has been invaded by an American species of comb jelly, probably brought in with the bilge water of foreign vessels. Comb jellies can eat ten times their own weight in food every day and at one point there were a billion tons of them in there – ten times the weight of all the fish caught in the world each year. As a result, the Black Sea's once thriving fishing industry has been brought to the edge of collapse.

The Dead Sea, by comparison, at 32 cubic miles, is not even a sea, it's a saltwater lake. It's not the saltiest body of water in the world either – that honour goes to Don Juan Pond in the Antarctic.*

Ninety-seven per cent of the world's water is salt water. If all the salt in the oceans were extracted and spread over the United States, it would make a layer a mile deep.

STEPHEN *What these jellyfish do is they keep the circulation of the water extremely healthy. And they also mix the cold with the deep warm water at the surface.*

ROSS NOBLE *I've got one I put in the bath so I don't have to do that.*

---

* See also *The Discreetly Plumper Second Book of General Ignorance*, p. 14.

How many American Great Lakes are there?

Not five but four.

Two of the 'smaller' ones, Lake Michigan and Lake Huron, are actually a single body of water connected by the Straits of Mackinac. Their levels fall and rise together, and geologists call the whole system 'Michigan–Huron'. This combined lake is not only larger than Lake Superior (making it the largest of the Great Lakes), it's also the largest freshwater lake in the world.

In fact all America's great lakes are connected to each other to some extent. You could theoretically paddle a canoe from Duluth, Minnesota, on the far west coast of Lake Superior, through Huron–Michigan, Erie and Ontario, and on down the St Lawrence river into the Atlantic Ocean, a journey of 2,300 miles. Only Michigan–Huron, however, has the same water level. To pass between the others you must traverse a system of canals and locks.

In 1998 the five (or four) traditional 'Great Lakes' were joined by a sixth (or fifth): Lake Champlain. For just over a fortnight it became a Great Lake – despite being 15 times smaller than the smallest of the others, Lake Ontario.

It acquired this status as part of Senate Bill 927, signed by President Clinton, who probably had other things on his mind. The object was to enable Vermont to claim federal grants to study the lake's ecology, something that was only open to the eight 'Great Lake States'. These other states weren't at all pleased about this. Ohio representative Steven C. LaTourette called for the lake's name to be changed from Champlain to 'plain shame' and after just 18 days it was downgraded again. So today there are only four Great Lakes: Erie, Ontario, Superior and Michigan–Huron.

What are deserts made from?

Rocks, mostly. Or shingle. Or salt. Or snow.

Most deserts aren't sandy. Deserts are defined not by what's on the ground but by how much rain they get – a desert is somewhere that gets less than 10 inches of rain each year.

The world's sandiest desert is Australia's 'Great Sandy' – and even that is only 50 per cent sand. The Sahara is 15 per cent sand, and only 2 per cent of the North American desert is sand. Taking the world as a whole, only 20 per cent of deserts are made of sand. Nearly half is pebbles and cobbles: the finer grains have blown away.

Large expanses of sandy desert are known as 'ergs'. The world's largest erg is Saudi Arabia's Empty Quarter, with 250,000 square miles of sand.

In American deserts more people drown than die of thirst. Desert storms are often very violent and, after a sudden rainstorm, normally dry stream channels can fill up extremely rapidly and result in dangerous flash floods.

Around the world about a billion sand particles a second are formed from the erosion of rocks. This sand is extremely mobile. More than 27.7 million tons of sand and dust travel every year from the Sahara to South America, giving the Amazon rain forest the nutrients it needs to flourish.

China's Gobi and Taklamakan deserts have been growing rapidly in recent years and the resulting storms often cover Beijing in dust. To counteract this, the Chinese have been planting a 'Great Green Wall' across northern China. When completed in 2050, it will contain over 100 billion trees in a belt nearly 3,000 miles long, covering more than a tenth of the country.

Not all beach sand is made the same way. Coral sand, for instance – the extra-fine white stuff you get on Caribbean beaches – is mostly the excrement of parrotfish. One parrotfish can produce a ton of soft white sand every year.

Nor is the sand we see always new. There are grains of sand in the Namib Sand Sea in Namibia that are at least a million years old.

STEPHEN *Where is the driest place on Earth?*
CLIVE ANDERSON *It's a couple of counties in North Wales. Especially on a Sunday, you can't get a thing.*

What is the ozone layer made of?

Very, very little of it is ozone.

If you took a random selection of a million gas molecules from the ozone layer, 999,985 of them would not be ozone. Ozone is extremely rare. The only reason the 'ozone layer' gets its name is that 15 molecules in a million is a much higher concentration than in the rest of the atmosphere.

If you could stack all the air in the atmosphere at the same density as it is at sea level and at 0 °C, it would form a layer 5 miles thick. If you took all the ozone and arranged it in the same way, it would be a tenth of an inch thick.

Ozone is a paradox. It's only 0.00006 per cent of the atmosphere but weighs 3 billion tons. It's essential for our survival in one way and very bad for us in another. Despite its low concentrations, the ozone in the ozone layer absorbs 99 per cent of the Sun's ultraviolet light, which is harmful to all living things. Outside the ozone layer, however, it can have serious effects on your health, triggering asthma attacks and severely irritating the lungs.

Fridges and aerosols used to contain chemicals called chlorofluorocarbons (CFCs). These were banned in the late 1990s when it was discovered that a single molecule of CFC could destroy 100,000 molecules of ozone. Despite the ban, a recent study by NASA found that the hole in the ozone layer won't be completely patched up until around 2070.

Ozone is created when ultraviolet light from the Sun hits oxygen in the stratosphere. The solar radiation has enough energy to split oxygen (O_2), a molecule made of two oxygen atoms, into its constituent parts. These free atoms then collide with standard oxygen molecules to form ozone (O_3).

A similar chemical reaction occurs when lightning strikes. The world's biggest ozone generator is a semi-permanent electrical storm over Venezuela's Lake Maracaibo. The warm, methane-rich air rises from the marshes around the lake to meet the cold, dry winds sweeping down from the Andes, and the lightning arcs 280 times an hour, 10 hours a night, up to 260 days a year. Meteorologists still don't really know what causes it.

Used by generations of seamen arriving at the Gulf of Venezuela and known as 'the Maracaibo Lighthouse', the phenomenon has been going on for hundreds of years and was first recorded in 1597. The Spanish playwright Lope de Vega wrote about it in a poem in which he told how Sir Francis Drake's attempt to sack the Maracaibo garrison in 1596 was foiled when the regular lightning flashes revealed his ships to a Spanish watchman. It was Drake's last mission. He died the following January and was buried at sea.

Does the air get warmer or cooler the higher you get?

Oddly, the answer is both.

The lowest layer of Earth's atmosphere is called the troposphere. It's where we live and where most 'weather' happens. The higher you go in it the colder it gets, which is obvious to anyone who's climbed a mountain or seen ice on the outside of an aeroplane window. Air temperature depends on the speed at which air molecules move: the slower they go, the colder it gets. As you go up, air pressure decreases: there's more space for the molecules to move in, so they spread out and slow down. We experience this as a drop in temperature.

Beyond the troposphere, though, everything changes. In the next layer up, the stratosphere, the temperature increases with height. Starting at a low of −51 °C (only 10 °C warmer than the surface of Mars), it rises to a relatively balmy −3 °C, perfectly bearable with a coat on. The heat in the stratosphere comes from the ozone layer buried in the middle of it. This absorbs most of the Sun's ultraviolet light, which generates heat as it converts the oxygen in the air (O_2) into ozone (O_3).

Air at the top of the stratosphere is a thousand times thinner than at sea level. Above the stratosphere are the mesosphere and the thermosphere, where it gets thinner still. At sea level, an air molecule will bump into another one after moving just a millionth of an inch.

In the thermosphere it would have to travel 3 miles.

Last there's the exosphere – the region where air molecules escape Earth's gravity and start floating off into space. This stretches from 600 miles to 120,000 miles above the Earth's surface. The outer limit of the exosphere is where interplanetary space officially starts.

By this definition – it's about halfway to the Moon – Yuri Gagarin didn't make it to space in 1961, and the International Space Station, which orbits at about 250 miles up, isn't in space either.

Which humans have been closest to the Sun?

Not astronauts, but Africans.

The Earth's path around the Solar System is more complicated than we're told at school. It doesn't move in a perfect circle around the Sun: its orbit is an ellipse, so it's always moving either closer to or further away from it.

The shape of this ellipse changes over time: it's closer to a circle now than at any time in the last 100,000 years. At the moment, the difference between the furthest we get from the Sun and the closest we get to it is around 3 per cent. In the past it's been as much as 12 per cent.

The Earth is currently around 93 million miles from the Sun and the closest point in its orbit is known as perihelion. According to Stuart Eves of Surrey Satellite Technology, 70,000 years ago this distance shrank to 90.6 million miles. At that point, any of our earliest ancestors standing on the equator at noon would have unwittingly broken the record for being the human beings to get closest to the Sun. This record has never been beaten. The Earth is 224,000 miles from the Moon. The astronauts who went there were still more than 2 million miles further from the Sun than those unnamed Africans.

How close could humans get to the Sun? Current technology would allow an astronaut to get surprisingly near without burning up. To protect it on re-entry, a space shuttle's heat shield is designed to withstand temperatures of 4,700 °C. A spacecraft approaching the Sun wouldn't get that hot until it was 98 per cent of the way there, about 1.3 million miles away. On the other hand, no one would be alive to see it: cosmic radiation would have long since killed everyone aboard. For the time being, the safest way to travel through the universe is on Spaceship Earth.

STEPHEN *How many Earths could you fit in the Sun, were you able to do such a thing?*
ALAN *Four. Easily.*

How long does light from the centre of the Sun take to reach Earth?

A thousand centuries.

Light takes 8½ minutes to reach Earth from the Sun, but to get from the centre of the Sun to its surface it takes about 100,000 years.

The life of a tiny packet of light, or photon, begins as it forms in the Sun's core as a result of nuclear fusion. It's then almost immediately absorbed by an atom, before being emitted again in a random direction. After travelling for a millimetre (0.03 inch) or so, it finds another atom and is absorbed and then emitted, and this continues again and again until it reaches the surface of the Sun. As one NASA scientist puts it, 'Light travels through the Sun only slightly better than light travels through a rock.'

If the light travelled in a straight line, a photon would get to the Sun's surface in just a couple of seconds. But because it is constantly being spat out in random directions, it takes millennia. No one can say exactly how long each photon takes: estimates vary between 10,000 years and 170,000 years.

Also, it's a simplification to think of a single photon struggling all the way to the surface. These little lumps of energy are constantly splitting and reforming with one other. Some will get to the surface in a very short space of time, but most will be stuck inside for ages, ricocheting backwards and forwards.

Once it escapes from the Sun, the light travels through space at a much zippier 300,000 metres per second. Even so, it will still be 5½ hours before it reaches Pluto.

The surface of the Sun is about 5,000 °C but the temperature at its core is a staggering 13,600,000 °C. It's made of gas, but is almost as dense as lead. Every second, the Sun converts about 4 million tons of matter into energy, but it's so enormous that it still has several billion years of life left.

The Sun accounts for 99.8 per cent of the mass of the solar system. Earth could fit into it 1,300,000 times over. If you could stand on the Sun, you would weigh 28 times more than you do on Earth – although, if you were standing on the surface of the Sun, weight gain would be the least of your problems.

STEPHEN *What does it mean when a sunscreen is factor 50?*
ALAN *It means that if the Sun was so hot you were going to burn in one minute, if you put that on, you can stay 50 minutes.*
STEPHEN *Yes. That's right.*
BILL BAILEY *Or if you put it on in England, you could stay for a lifetime.*

How much does a shadow weigh?

Less than nothing.

Light doesn't have mass. So you might think a shadow, which is simply a lack of light, wouldn't weigh anything either. But it's more complicated than that.

Although light doesn't have mass, when it strikes a surface, it imparts a small force due to its momentum. So, if you block the light by standing in front of it and casting a shadow on the surface, that small force is now missing. If you cast a shadow onto a set of bathroom scales, the light's downward force is no longer there and you have created a negative weight.

Unfortunately, no scales are sensitive enough to register such a tiny negative weight. A shadow covering the whole of greater London would only have as much effect on the capital's mass as removing three Boris Johnsons.

Russian scientist Pyotr Lebedev (1866–1912) first proved light exerts a force on an object due to its momentum in 1898. He suspended a wafer-thin piece of platinum foil in a vacuum jar and saw it move (very slightly) when a lamp was shone on it.

Though the pressure exerted by light is imperceptible on Earth, one day it may be useful in space. A light-powered spacecraft

would start very slowly, but with nothing to slow it down in outer space, the pressure would build up until it reached a huge speed, propelled entirely by sunlight. This may solve the so far insurmountable problem of long-distance space travel – how to carry enough fuel.

In the meantime, it's the other way round. Space scientists have to calculate the pressure created by light from the Sun, which creates resistance to every rocket or shuttle that leaves the Earth. Unless it's allowed for, the sunlight on a spaceship heading to Mars will take it over 60 miles off course before it reaches its destination. The pressure of light also exerts a constant force on orbiting satellites, which spend half their time in sunlight and half in shade. These tiny changes in pressure add up, leading to inaccuracies in GPS.

So the next time your satnav goes wrong, blame it on a shadow that weighs less than nothing.

What is the strongest creature for its weight in the world?

It's not ants. It's gonorrhoea bacteria.

The gonorrhoea bacterium can pull with a force equal to 100,000 times its body weight. If a human could do this, a

12-stone man could comfortably pull the Eiffel Tower behind him.

The reason for its extraordinary strength is the tentacle-like structures called 'pili'. These can be up to ten times its body length: the bacteria use them like grappling hooks to crawl along surfaces and infect them.

Gonorrhoea is one of the very few diseases that's exclusive to people. But, as well as humans catching gonorrhoea, gonorrhoea can catch humans. The bacteria can be contaminated by fragments of human DNA.

Most people believe ants are the strongest animals for their size, and they certainly are extremely strong. A 2014 report in the *Journal of Biomechanics* revealed that the strongest part of an ant is its neck. To prove this the researchers used, in their own words, 'extreme and destructive measures'. They anaesthetised the ants and glued them by their heads to a centrifuge, spinning it faster and faster until their bodies flew off. The ants' necks survived forces 5,000 times their body weight.

Despite the strength of their necks, ants can't lift 5,000 times their own body weight – it's more like 20 to 100 times, depending on the species.

There is one animal that trounces ants at weight-lifting. The tiny oribatid mite, a member of the spider family as little as a fifth of a millimetre (0.007 inch) long, can resist a pull of 1,180 times its own weight. Alternatively known as moss mites or beetle mites, they can also pull something 530 times their own weight up a vertical surface, using only two of their eight legs.

To test this, researchers from the University of Tübingen fixed the mites to a pin with superglue and measured how much force it took to pull them off.

Isn't science fun!

STEPHEN *What would you say if I said to you that the British Empire was built on diarrhoea?*

RICH HALL *I'd say you were full of shit. Any word that ends in 'rhoea' is just bad news, isn't it? Diarrhoea, pyorrhoea, gonorrhoea. North Korea.*

What's the worst thing a swan can do to you?

A number of alarming things, but it can't break your arm.

Swans may make threatening noises but your arms are safe with them. A bird's bones are not only smaller and thinner than human ones; they're also hollow. Unless a person has very brittle bones due to illness or old age, even a whack from the angriest of swans will leave the bird much the worse off.

Perhaps because they know this, swan attacks are extremely rare. In spring, swans try to frighten people away from their nests by making themselves as big as possible and spitting and hissing, but they're bluffing. The Abbotsbury Swannery in Dorset has a thousand swans. In its 600-year history there have been no recorded attacks on humans.

Bones broken by swans usually turn out to be caused by people falling over in panic, rather than a blow from a wing.

One such case took place in Dublin in 2001, when Mrs Mary Ryan sued the council for failing to place a warning after a swan attacked her and she fell and cracked her wrist.

Two years earlier a man in East Sussex being chased by police ran into the River Ouse. This spooked a swan, which flapped and squawked towards him. The bird was so aggressive the man decided he'd rather take his chances with the law and gave himself up.

The law on swans goes back to the 1482 Act Concerning Swans, when killing and eating them was restricted to the monarch and certain royally approved institutions. Swan meat is said to be delicious, with a flavour somewhere between pork and beef.

The Queen has the right to ownership of all unmarked white mute swans in Britain, but she only exercises this on stretches of the Thames. The man responsible for recording and preserving British swans is David Barber, the Queen's Swan Marker. He thinks the myth of arm-breaking swans dates back to the twelfth century, when swans were valuable game birds. Gamekeepers might have spread the story to deter hungry poachers. It seems to have worked. More than half the mute swans in Europe now live in Britain.

Mute swans aren't mute. They make a variety of noises: 'heorr', 'yip', 'yap yap yap', 'glok glok' and a 'hoarse trumpeting call'. In flight, their wings make a 'wou wou wou' noise. They got their name because they're quieter than whooper swans – but they're certainly not silent. And – a far cry from arm-breaking – until 1785 they were called 'tame swans' because of their docile nature.

Name a monogamous bird

Neither swans nor penguins really 'mate for life'.

There are very few truly monogamous birds. While 90 per cent of bird species pair off for at least one breeding season, the vast majority are simultaneously cheating on the side.

Swans and penguins are often depicted as living in harmony with a single partner, but infidelity is rife. DNA tests have shown that, among black swans, one in six cygnets is the product of 'extra-pair copulations'. Even the supposedly loyal emperor penguins

acquire a new partner every year: hardly monogamy as we would know it. As for Adélie penguins, their promiscuity is notorious and can include bouts of necrophilia and paedophilia.

The first person to document their mating behaviour, George Murray Levick, was a scientist with the 1910–13 Scott Antarctic Expedition. He was so shocked by what he saw that he wrote his notes in ancient Greek – so only educated Englishmen would be able to understand them.

Nature loves a compromise. While infidelity produces a broader spread of genes and therefore healthier offspring, fidelity helps with rearing them and improves their chance of survival. Birds living in harsh weather conditions are more likely to cheat on their partners, because this increases the odds that at least one chick will be genetically suited to cope. As climate change bites, it's likely that birds will become less and less faithful.

Only 10 per cent of the animals said to 'mate for life' really do so. Some of them are birds, though. Puffins, for example, appear be completely faithful to their partners. And black vultures, which live in close family units, have virtually no record of infidelity. Scientists think this might be due to 'the prohibition of copulation in the presence of relatives'.

Elsewhere in the animal kingdom, wedding shrimps are truly monogamous; after copulation they move, as a pair, inside a sponge that can only fit two adult shrimps. Their offspring squeeze through holes to escape but the adults remain trapped inside.

The flatworm *Diplozoon paradoxum* goes even further to avoid adultery. When a male meets a female they fuse together to form a single organism – leaving them no choice but to remain faithful for the whole of the rest of their lives. Even death does not them part.

Name a non-venomous snake

There's no such thing: all snakes produce toxins.

Pythons and boa constrictors are traditionally called 'non-venomous' snakes because they crush their prey to death rather than using poison. But in 2013 Professor Bryan Fry of the University of Queensland showed that while their oral glands have been 'repurposed' by evolution to make mucus to lubricate the passage of the prey they swallow, this still contains small amounts of toxins. Fry comments, 'Their toxins are the equivalent of a kiwi's wing or the sightless eyes of blind cavefish – defunct remnants of a functional past.'

In 2009 Fry demonstrated that the world's largest lizard, the Komodo dragon, killed its prey with venom. He has since isolated venom from many apparently non-venomous species, and believes all snakes and most lizards descend from a common ancestor he calls *Toxicofera*. The first snakes were similar to today's large constrictors and his theory is that the original purpose of venom was defensive – to kill the bacteria that flourished during the slow digestion of prey. This eventually evolved to be an efficient form of attack: powerful toxins injected by their fangs allowed snakes to grow smaller and faster, enabling them to catch rodents and amphibians.

A snake that contains a little venom but not enough to harm

humans is known as 'clinically non-venomous'. Three-quarters of all snakes fit into this category.

If someone is bitten by a snake, don't try to suck out the poison. Not only will this make things worse for you – it can damage your throat and lungs, and if you have cuts in your mouth you could poison yourself – but it's also unlikely to help. Snake venom passes into the bloodstream too quickly to get it all out by sucking, and bacteria in your mouth could infect the wound.

Not all snakes transfer their venom by biting: African spitting cobras shoot it directly into their enemies' eyes. The jet is controlled by muscles around the venom glands, and directed by grooves in the snakes' fangs – so the liquid is 'rifled' like a spinning bullet. A spitting cobra hits its target's eyes at least 80 per cent of the time, and can tell the difference between a real face and a photograph.

There are many theories about how to tell a venomous snake from a clinically non-venomous one. Some say colourful snakes are more dangerous than drab ones; others that all venomous snakes have oval pupils or triangular heads. But there are plenty of exceptions. Black mambas, the most venomous snakes in Africa, are drab looking and have round pupils – and almost all snakes have more or less triangular heads.

The safest strategy is to leave all snakes to get on with their lives. Even the 'harmless' European grass snake (*Natrix natrix*) behaves like a mini cobra when annoyed, hissing and striking. Its small fangs are in the rear of its mouth and although not fatal to humans, its bite can sting and its venom leave raised and itchy puncture wounds. Interestingly, the grass snake is immune to the bite of the much more venomous adder.

Name a vertebrate with no backbone

Sharks.

None of the 470 species of shark contain any bones whatsoever. Their whole skeleton is made of cartilage – the hard but flexible material that supports human joints and gives noses, ears and Adam's apples their shape. Essentially, sharks get about with a backbone made of nose gristle.

There are advantages to having no bones. Cartilage weighs half as much, so it makes sharks lighter and more buoyant, and its flexibility allows it to turn rapidly when hunting prey. Because it never stops growing, counting the rings in a shark's spinal cartilage reveals its age.

Sharks have evolved other tricks in the 400 million years of their existence. Their teeth are arranged in rows and are constantly replaced, with new teeth pushing forward, as on a conveyor belt. Some species get through 50,000 teeth in their lives. Shark skin is very rough when stroked in one direction but very smooth in the other, which reduces friction as they swim. Sharks are not 'aerodynamic' (as they don't move through air) but they are 'hydrodynamic'. They have huge livers that produce lightweight oils, again for buoyancy. Some sharks are a quarter liver by weight.

Due to a misconception that sharks don't get cancer, some people take shark cartilage supplements. This is wrong on two levels: first, there's no evidence that shark cartilage fights cancer in humans, and second,

Who are you calling chicken?

sharks *do* get cancer. This is not, however, the major cause of fatalities that it is in humans. Humans are. We kill 100 million sharks every year, while the average number of humans killed by sharks each year is six.

Another myth about sharks is that they must continually keep moving, or they will die. In fact, most sharks have evolved so their breathing organs constantly pump water through their gills, meaning they can happily stop and rest. Others can lie still, so long as there is a current passing over them.

Less famous species of shark include the epaulette shark, the Atlantic weasel shark, the milk shark, the lemon shark, the rusty carpet shark and the splendid lantern shark.

What kind of creature is a Portuguese man-o'-war?

It isn't a jellyfish. It isn't even a creature.

The Portuguese man-o'-war is a colony of thousands of different organisms, called polyps, all working together to create what looks like a single animal. As most of this is made up of long, stinging tubes, it's called a siphonophore, or 'tube bearer' (from Greek *siphon* 'tube' and *pherein* 'to carry').

A siphonophore has four kinds of polyp. Pneumatophores ('air carriers') form a purple, air-filled jelly that acts as a sail, reminding eighteenth-century sailors of the ship called a 'man-of-war'. Dactylozooids ('finger life forms'), responsible for defence, trail behind as long, poisonous tentacles. Gastrozooids ('stomach animals') do the eating and digesting. And gonozooids ('sex beasts') manage the reproduction, making new polyps which adapt to any of the four roles required to make a man-o'-war function.

The gonozooids can't eat, the gastrozooids can't reproduce, and neither can defend themselves. That's the job of the sexless, appetiteless dactylozooids. Each kind of polyp relies on the others for specialist abilities it does not itself possess, and none of them can live on their own.

Portuguese men-o'-war drift on the currents and the wind and clump together in herds of 1,000 or more. That's why the appearance of just one is enough to close a beach. It's unlikely a Portuguese man-o'-war could kill you but their sting is very painful, as 10,000 Australians find out every year. This comes in handy for one of their predators, the male blanket octopus, which tears the dactylozooid tentacles off the man-o'-war and uses them as a weapon.

How many legs does the average animal have?

About 0.01.

That's the number you get if you divide the total number of legs by the total number of animals. The vast majority of animals are nematodes, tiny legless worms which live everywhere, and they skew the figures because there are so many of them. There are around 10 billion trillion nematode worms – that's 10 followed by 22 zeros – a thousand times more than all the insects in the world (and there are 1.6 billion times as many insects as humans).

Most nematodes (from the Greek *nema*, meaning 'thread') are less than a millimetre (0.04 inch) in length and some contain fewer than 1,000 cells. Almost every square centimetre of the planet is crawling with them. Ninety per cent of all life forms on the ocean floor is nematodes, and in rich topsoil there can be as many as a trillion per square mile. We don't know much about them – science has described about 80,000 species but there could be up to a million. The smallest are 0.08 millimetres (0.003 inches) long, and the biggest measure over a metre.

Nematodes have no blood, no respiratory system and they don't have the muscles that earthworms contract to propel themselves forward. They move by swirling in S-shaped curves. Most nematodes are parasites and depend for food on their host organism, but some free-living species survive by eating algae, fungi and excrement. If it gets too hot, too cold or too dry, nematodes can go into a state of suspended animation, and wake themselves up again when conditions improve.

Almost all animals contain vast numbers of nematode worms, so much so that if all the humans in the world disappeared, we would leave behind ghostly images of ourselves made entirely of the nematodes that used to inhabit us.

How many legs does a kangaroo have?

Three. The kangaroo is the only animal with three legs.

This discovery was made in 2014 by a team from Canada's Simon Fraser University. They corralled red kangaroos through a chamber that measured the downward forces they exerted as they walked. When they aren't hopping, kangaroos walk by putting their arms on the ground and moving their back legs in front of them. As they do this, they push down with their tail to propel themselves forward. The tail exerts just as much force as any of the other limbs, making it effectively a third leg. Not only that, it's the most important of the three in terms of momentum. Kangaroos walk with their tails.

The ancestors of today's kangaroos were marsupials that lived in trees and used their tails for climbing and gripping. But after 15 million years living on the ground as grass-grazing ruminants, the kangaroo's tail has evolved into an extremely specialised limb. It contains almost as many vertebrae as we have in our entire spine, and is full of powerful muscles. When fighting, kangaroos lean on their tails, leaving their hands free to box. They can even be used as a weapon – a swipe from a 'roo's tail can break a man's leg.

There are other candidates for animals with an odd number of legs, but none are convincing. Most starfish have five limbs, but these are arms not legs because they're not used for locomotion. Snails and slugs are called 'gastropods' ('stomach feet') because they only have one 'foot' they crawl around on. But this is an integral part of their bodies and not a limb, so they don't count either. Finally, almost all the Japanese spider crabs that are caught have nine limbs, but this is because they've lost one: they're all born with ten.

The only known animal with a naturally odd number of legs is the kangaroo.

STEPHEN *The western grey kangaroo is the fastest of all the kangaroos, and amazingly smells of curry.*
ALAN *That's just an Australian who's had a curry the night before, done a particularly stinky fart and then tried to blame it on a passing kangaroo.*

How many knees does an elephant have?

Two.

There's a widespread Internet 'fact' which states the elephant is the only animal with four knees. It's not true. Elephants have two knees at the back and elbows and wrists at the front, exactly like us. Elephants, horses, dogs and all other quadruped mammals all have two knees and two elbows.

Mammals have the same basic skeletal structure because we're descended from a common ancestor. A human arm, a dog's front leg, a bat's wing and a whale's front flipper all have similar bones (humerus, radius and ulna) organised in a similar manner. (Yes, whales have elbows!) However, the bones aren't always the same length or spaced in the same way – horses and birds, for instance, walk around on the equivalent of fingers and toes. The bit in the middle of a horse's front leg gets called a knee, but it's actually a wrist.

There's also a misconception that birds' knees bend backwards. It does look like that, but what you're actually looking at is their ankles. Birds' knees are tucked up close to their bodies and hidden under their feathers. These 'real' knees bend exactly like ours do.

Even bees have knees. They have femurs and tibia – the bones either side of the knee – and they have a joint between the two. All they lack is kneecaps.

Pliny the Elder came up with the idea that elephants are afraid of mice. He claimed they 'hate mice and will refuse to eat food that has been touched by one'. The US TV show *Mythbusters* tested this theory by putting mice in holes in the ground, covering them with balls of dung, and uncovering them when an elephant approached. The elephants were sometimes stopped in their tracks, but this was probably because they're wary of any sudden movement near their feet (baby elephants can be killed if they're bitten by snakes). In captivity and at eye height, mice don't bother elephants – trainers who held mice and then suddenly showed them to elephants reported that they 'looked bored'.

What elephants really don't like are ants, which swarm up inside their trunks. Research from the Mpala Research Centre in Kenya and the University of Florida revealed that some species of acacia trees retain ant colonies as bodyguards to keep hungry elephants at bay.

How many sphincters do you have?

A lot more than you think.

A sphincter is a ring of muscle around an orifice or passage in the body that can contract or relax to control whatever flows through it. As well as in your bottom, there are sphincters in your gullet, stomach, small intestine, even the pupils of your eyes. Animals have them too: whales' blowholes are controlled by sphincters. So are elephants' trunks. And a snake is effectively one big sphincter.

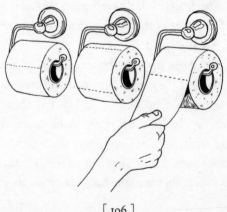

As for your anal sphincters, you have two not one. There's an outer sphincter, which operates voluntarily, and an inner one, which is involuntary. You also have a sphincter at the exit of your bladder. The sphincter at the opening of the bile duct is called the Sphincter of Oddi, after the man who identified it, the nineteenth-century Italian physiologist Ruggero Oddi. If it gets infected then you've come down with 'odditis'.

It's impossible to say exactly how many sphincters you have in your body. The tiny blood vessels that regulate blood flow into the capillaries have tiny 'pre-capillary sphincters' surrounding them. There are thousands of these.

The human body is full of extra parts you never knew you had. You have four jugular veins (an interior and an exterior one either side of your neck) and six eyelids: the upper and lower lids in each eye, and the little pink triangles in the corners, vestigial eyelids called the plica semilunaris or 'nictitating membrane' (from Latin *nictare*, 'to blink'). In many animals – such as cats, dogs, birds, reptiles and sharks – these still function, sweeping across the eyeball to clean and moisturise it without impairing vision.

Male readers may be surprised to discover they too have a vagina, the vagina masculina. In a female embryo, this grows into a sex organ. In male embryos, it remains undeveloped, a minute pouch hanging off the prostate gland.

For the first six weeks of our existence we are all female.

STEPHEN *LIGHTS DIM* *I'm going to ask Alan a very specific question now. Can you feel your sphincter relaxing?*
ALAN *I must say, I thought it was until you asked me.*

Which finger would you sacrifice first if you had to?

Not your pinkie!

After your thumb, your little finger is the one you can *least* afford to lose. According to hand surgeons, if a kidnapper asks you to give up a finger you should sacrifice the index finger on your non-writing hand. The rest of your fingers can compensate for the first finger quite well, but the little finger does a job that can't be easily replaced. Losing it halves your gripping strength.

As the medical reference book *Beasley's Surgery of the Hand* points out, 'Their value is generally underrated.' When we describe people as having 'opposable' thumbs, the main thing 'opposing' the thumb is the little finger. Try holding your knee and see how strongly your little finger can grip because of this. The index finger is better for delicate pinching and sudden grabbing. The middle finger can join either team as required.

The thumb accounts for 40 per cent of the hand's capabilities. If you lose a thumb doctors will sometimes replace it with one of your big toes, so you can keep gripping objects. Patients find that, despite the loss of a toe, their balance is generally fine afterwards.

If you're ever given the choice of losing a toe, it's probably better to lose the fourth one: the big toe is very strong and the little toe is important for balance. The oldest prosthetic item ever found was a wooden toe that was fitted to an Egyptian woman in about 1000 BC.

It's possible to regrow the tips of your fingers. Children below the age of ten can do this without any intervention, as long as the base of the fingernail is left. Recently, scientists have developed a miraculous powder made from a dried pig's bladder that will enable adults to do this too. In fact the substance – called 'extracellular matrix' – may one day allow us to regrow whole limbs.

After he got frostbite on an expedition to the North Pole, Sir Ranulph Fiennes cut off two of his fingertips with a Black and Decker microblade. He put them in a drawer as mementoes, but they have since gone missing.

If you lose a finger the best course of action is to put it in a sealed plastic bag and then put that into icy water. Don't put the finger on the ice itself: it might get frostbite and, the next thing you know, it'll go missing from the drawer . . .

STEPHEN *The fact is, pain is created by the brain. It's not a real thing . . . it's information.*

ROBERT WEBB *It doesn't help when you land a big mallet on your thumb going, 'It's just information! It's just information!'*

What happened to Walt Disney's body?

He wasn't cryogenically frozen.

For a start, there's no such thing as being 'cryogenically frozen'. Cryogenics is the scientific study of materials at low temperatures. Refrigerating the dead to bring them back to life later is called 'cryonics' or 'cryopreservation'. All three words come from the Greek root *kryos*, meaning 'icy cold'.

Second, in cryonic preservation the body isn't frozen. It is 'vitrified' (slowly cooled down) with chemicals being added to replace over 60 per cent of the water content of the body, specifically to prevent it from freezing. Freezing would cause irreversible damage to the body's cells.

Walt Disney died on 15 December 1966. He was cremated two days later and interred in the family plot in Glendale, California.

The tabloid *National Spotlight* later claimed a reporter had broken into the hospital where he died and had seen his body suspended in a metal cylinder. But Disney wasn't frozen (or even vitrified) —nor was he (as one conspiracy theory has it) stuffed and buried under the Pirates of the Caribbean ride at Disneyland. The first cryonically treated human being was James Bedford, who died a month after Disney.

In the USA it's illegal to begin the process of human cryonic preservation until the patient's heart has stopped beating. The patient's blood is then replaced with antifreeze, which is pumped around the body by a machine. The body is then carefully cooled to −196 °C and stored upside down in a cylindrical tank.

So far, nobody has ever been brought back to life from cryonic preservation, which may explain why only 200 or so people have signed up. (There's also the risk you'll be unceremoniously defrosted if your funds run out.) There are, however, cases of people being 'brought back from the dead' after suffering extreme hypothermia. In 1999 a Swedish skier was revived after being trapped with no heartbeat for over an hour in a frozen stream.

British inventor James Lovelock spent much of the 1950s reanimating frozen hamsters using hot spoons and a home-made microwave gun. The practical upshot of his research was that if you undergo a major heart operation, surgeons can now 'pause' your body at 18 °C while they work – a kind of controlled hibernation. NASA is studying hibernation in the animal kingdom in the hope of safely inducing 'hypersleep' in astronauts on long space voyages.

STEPHEN *Would you believe that they put a man on the Moon?*

ALAN *I kind of believe that they might have done some . . . some mocked-up fake photographs.*

STEPHEN *Really? Why?*

ALAN *Because someone convinced me of it, by talking about the angle of light and the shadows on the Moon and all that, but then I did an advert with Patrick Moore and I said, 'So, Patrick, did they land on the Moon?' and he looked so annoyed with me, and he explained to me how he had helped map the Moon for NASA and he'd spent years on the project, and the landing site was partly his idea and if I ever spoke to him again, he was going to be sick in my eyes.*

What happened to the *Mary Celeste*?

Nothing very mysterious.

The *Mary Celeste* was a real ship, found abandoned in the mid-Atlantic in 1872 with no apparent explanation for the crew's disappearance. It was carrying a large shipment of alcohol from New York to Genoa, with ten people aboard, including the captain, his wife and their two-year-old daughter. It was floating 600 miles off the coast of Portugal and described by the crew of the *Dei Gratia*, who found it, as 'a thoroughly wet mess'.

A lifeboat was missing, as was a sextant, and the ship's log suggested the captain thought he was nearer the mainland than he really was. It seems that, in a heavy storm with waterlogged pumps, they took to the lifeboat. But it was never found. A recent theory is that alcohol leaked from the hold and caused an explosion, but didn't set the ship on fire. This could have terrified the crew into abandoning ship without leaving a mark on the ship itself.

A survey of the ship found nothing unusual except for the fact that one of the barrels of alcohol had 'been started'. There were no signs of mutiny or piracy, no aliens, no spookily abandoned half-eaten meals. The newspapers called it a 'mystery' and some reported that bloodstains had been found in the captain's cabin, but the myth is mainly down to Sir Arthur Conan Doyle.

In 1884 he published a short story called 'J. Habakuk Jephson's Statement'. It was an anonymous, fictional account of an abandoned ship called *Marie Celeste*. Ten years later, ignoring the subtle difference in the ship's name, the *Boston Herald* printed the story as a true account and it's this version that has come to live in people's memories.

The real *Mary Celeste* was towed to Gibraltar and checked for evidence of wrongdoing, then set off again to Genoa with a fresh crew. She was later sold to an American con man called Gilman C. Parker. In 1885 he loaded her with a cargo of cheap rubber boots and cat food (fraudulently insured for $30,000) and sailed for Haiti. His plan was to sink her and claim the insurance, but she ran aground on the Rochelais reef of the Haitian coast. Gilman and his first mate were arrested and charged with attempted barratry, the illegal scuttling of a vessel (from the Old French *barat*, 'trickery'). Gilman was about to be found guilty but died in his cell before sentencing. His co-conspirator hanged himself and the *Mary Celeste* itself was burned and scuppered. Perhaps she really was cursed.

Who was the naturalist on board the *Beagle*?

Robert McCormick.

When Charles Darwin joined the *Beagle*'s voyage in 1831, he was not the ship's official naturalist. That post was held by the ship's surgeon, Robert McCormick, as was customary at the time. Darwin had been hired for two reasons: to provide the ship's captain, Robert Fitzroy, with a social equal during the voyage, and to make geological observations. Over the course of the trip he made four times as many notes on geology as he did on zoology.

Darwin almost didn't get the job. Fitzroy believed in physiognomy (the 'science' of judging people's character based on their physical appearance). He thought the shape of Darwin's nose indicated a lack of energy and determination. But once the voyage began he started to favour Darwin over McCormick, gave Darwin more opportunities to collect specimens on shore, and confined McCormick to the ship.

Darwin didn't think well of McCormick either. He wrote, 'My friend the Doctor is an ass, but we jog on very amicably: at present he is in great tribulation, whether his cabin shall be painted French Grey or a dead white – I hear little excepting this subject from him.' Eventually, frustrated and upstaged, McCormick went home in April 1832. From then until its return to England in October 1836, the *Beagle* was without its official naturalist.

Darwin had never planned to be a naturalist. He studied medicine at Edinburgh in the hope of becoming a doctor, but gave up after realising he hated the sight of blood, and left without a degree. His interests outside botany included backgammon, which he played twice every night with his wife, Emma – who was also his first cousin. Their son George became an academic and published a paper in the *Journal of the Statistical Society* titled 'Marriages between first cousins in England and their effects'.

Darwin was also passionate about earthworms. He had Emma play the piano to them, accompanied by his son on the bassoon, so he could study their response to music. The last book he published, just six months before he died in 1881, was titled *The Formation of Vegetable Mould through the Action of Worms, with Observations on their Habits*. Although he called it 'a small book of little moment' it was full of wonderfully clear and vivid writing about what *The Times* called in its review 'them of low degree'. It went on to outsell all the other books he'd published in his lifetime, including *On the Origin of Species*.

What bird did the Ancient Mariner shoot?

He didn't even see an albatross, let alone shoot one.

The Rime of the Ancient Mariner contains the line 'with my cross-bow / I shot the albatross', so you'd be forgiven for thinking he did shoot an albatross. But it seems to have been a case of mistaken identity.

Samuel Taylor Coleridge based his poem on a dream had by his friend John Cruickshank of Nether Stowey in Somerset. Cruikshank had been reading a book by George Shelvocke, a notorious British pirate, which described the shooting of a 'disconsolate black albatross' while rounding Cape Horn.

The only albatrosses found around Cape Horn are wandering albatrosses, which are white, not black. Black albatrosses live in the northern Pacific. But there is a black-coloured bird that's common around Cape Horn: the giant petrel, which looks like a rather mournful albatross (it's also known as the 'stinker' or 'glutton' because of its smell and uncouth table manners). It's almost certain that the 'albatross' reported by Shelvocke, dreamt about by Cruikshank and written about by Coleridge, was actually one of these.

From this misidentification comes the idea that killing an albatross is bad luck, and the use of the word 'albatross' to mean a jinx. Before Coleridge's poem, seafaring accounts would often celebrate the first sighting of an albatross, and nobody ever worried if they were killed – it signified a tasty dinner. One writer who tasted albatross after the publication of *The Rime of the Ancient Mariner* wrote, 'If Coleridge had ever made a meal of roast albatross, English literature would have been the poorer for the loss of a great poem.'

Samuel Taylor Coleridge was described as a 'very gentle bear'. He signed himself S. T. C. or Estese. Other pen names were Silas Tomkyn Comberbache, Nehemiah Higginbottom and Gnome. The famous story that he didn't finish 'Kubla Khan' because a 'person on business from Porlock' interrupted him is also doubtful. By his own admission, he'd just woken from an opium-induced sleep and two of the classic symptoms of opium addiction are memory loss and the inability to concentrate. And the 'person from Porlock' was probably Coleridge's physician, P. Aaron Potter, who regularly supplied him with laudanum – liquid opium distilled in alcohol.

STEPHEN *The young wandering albatross will set off and will be in the air for ten years before it lands again.*

JIMMY CARR *Why does it land after ten years? It must feel like a bit of a fool. It must go, 'I think I can go eleven!'*

The sirens were half-woman, half-what?

Not half-fish but half-bird.

According to Homer's *Odyssey*, the sirens lived on an island — in a flowery meadow strewn with the bones and rotting flesh of dead sailors. They had lured them there by singing excruciatingly beautiful songs in 'honey-sweet voices' and then 'warbled them to death'. Homer doesn't say what they looked like, but contemporary Greek vases from the late eighth century BC show them as women from the waist up and birds from the waist down.

Odysseus wanted to hear their song, so he blocked his men's ears with wax and had them lash him to the mast, with strict instructions not to free him, no matter how much he begged. His plan worked and that was the end of the sirens: they were condemned to die if a mortal heard their song and survived.

Perhaps because of the nautical setting, the sirens have often been confused with mermaids. The French, Italian and Spanish words for mermaid are all variants of the word 'siren'. But sirens were birdy rather than fishy. Scholars compare them to the human-headed *ba* birds of Egyptian mythology, which hovered over tombs, the embodiment of the human soul (*ba*) after death.

The first half-human half-fish creature was a merman, not a mermaid: Ea, Babylonian god of the sea, was adopted by Greeks as Poseidon and by Romans as Neptune. His association with water meant he doubled up as the god of cleaners.

More recently, in the 1840s, crowds flocked to see showman P. T. Barnum's 'Feejee Mermaid', a wizened creature that was actually the head and torso of a monkey stitched to the tail of a fish.

In 1493 Christopher Columbus claimed he saw mermaids from his ship. They were probably manatees, or 'sea-cows', aquatic relatives of the elephant but with pendulous breasts. ('Manatee' is from a Carib word meaning 'breast'). Columbus wrote that they were 'not as pretty as they are depicted'.

If he was wrong about mermaids, so is science. Manatees belong to the scientific order *Sirenia*.

STEPHEN *What did Odysseus do so that he could hear the siren song?*

ALAN *Downloaded it.*

JACK WHITEHALL *Along with the Harry Potter audiobooks.*

What did the Birdman keep in Alcatraz?

Not birds: it was against prison rules.

The 'Birdman of Alcatraz' was Robert Franklin Stroud (1890–1963). Our image of him is as a gentle eccentric, spending his years of incarceration befriending the birds that congregated at his cell window to be fed, like a latter-day St Francis of Assisi. In fact, Stroud was a murderer and a psychopath, whose record of violence was so extreme he spent 42 years in solitary confinement.

In 1909 working as a pimp in Juneau, Alaska, he shot and killed a barman who'd attacked one of his prostitutes. He was found guilty of manslaughter and sentenced to 12 years in the federal penitentiary on McNeil Island in Puget Sound. After stabbing two inmates there, he was transferred to Leavenworth Penitentiary in Kansas. Soon after he arrived, he murdered a prison guard with a screwdriver, and in 1920 he was sentenced to hang. His mother appealed to President Woodrow Wilson and the execution was stayed just a week before it was due – the gallows had already been built. Stroud's sentence was commuted to a lifetime in solitary confinement.

It was in Leavenworth that he began to keep birds, collecting injured sparrows and breeding pet canaries. From his cell he built a successful business and became a respected ornithologist, publishing two ground-breaking books on avian diseases, and inventing two bird medicines. 'Stroud's Avian Antiseptic' and 'Stroud's Effervescent Salts' were sold as cures for indigestion, pox and diarrhoea in poultry. However, when prison guards found he'd been using his lab equipment to make alcohol, he was transferred to the maximum security prison on Alcatraz Island, 1½ miles off San Francisco. He had less than ten minutes to say goodbye to the birds he had tended for more than 20 years.

His story was made famous by the 1962 movie starring Burt Lancaster, which ended with a statement that Stroud was still in prison and had always been denied parole. The film painted him in such a positive light that more than 100,000 movie-goers signed a petition for his release. Lancaster even offered to have Stroud stay with him if he was granted parole. The film was criticised for the mild-mannered characterisation of its hero, but for others it represented one of the best examples of self-improvement and rehabilitation ever seen in a US prison. Stroud never saw the movie and died the year after its release.

In Spanish *alcatraz* means 'gannet', but it once also meant 'pelican'. When the island was mapped by the Spaniards in 1775, a colony of pelicans lived there. The Spanish is from Arabic: either *al-qatras*, 'white-tailed sea eagle', or *al-qadus*, the leather bucket on a waterwheel that resembles a pelican's bill. From a combination of these we get the English word 'albatross'.

Prisoners at Alcatraz always had hot showers. The authorities feared that if they had cold ones, it might toughen them up and make them more likely to brave the 1½-mile swim to the mainland. In the 29 years of its operation no one successfully escaped from Alcatraz.

Where is most of America's gold kept?

Thirty feet below the New York subway.

Most people think Fort Knox, the Kentucky stronghold formally known as the US Bullion Depository, has more gold than anywhere else – and it does hold America's official gold reserves of 4,000 tons. But there's much more at the rather pedestrian-sounding Federal Reserve Bank of New York, which holds 7,000 tons.

No gold has been transferred to or from Fort Knox for many years, except in tiny quantities to test its purity. This has led conspiracy theorists to claim there's no gold in there at all. (They're wrong.) Other items kept in the vault at Fort Knox over the years include the Magna Carta (during the Second World War); several volumes of the Gutenberg Bible; the US Declaration of Independence; and the crown, sword and cape of St Stephen, king of Hungary in the eleventh century. There is also a huge cache of morphine and opium, originally stockpiled so the government could guarantee a supply of emergency painkillers in the event of a war.

Although it might seem unwise to put the Federal Reserve in the middle of New York (it was knocked off pretty thoroughly in the third *Die Hard* movie), it's completely secured. The only way in is through a 10-foot passageway made of a steel cylinder embedded in a huge steel and concrete frame. This rests on solid granite, which would be virtually impossible to tunnel through; one reason the Fed stores the immensely heavy piles of gold there is that the bedrock of Manhattan is so exceptionally solid. Whenever a compartment is opened, three members of the Federal Reserve staff must be present – even if it's just to change a light bulb. When moving gold bars, workers wear metal shoes in case they drop one on their feet.

The Bank of England has 400,000 bars of gold, worth £140,000,000,000. As with the Federal Reserve, most of it belongs to someone else – of the 4,500 tons, only 300 tons are owned by the UK, with the rest owned by central banks or international bodies. One of the most impressive things about these places is their scales – the Federal Reserve has a set that can accurately weigh anything from a single dollar bill up to 22 bars of gold. The Bank of England's scales can weigh items as small as half a postage stamp.

Gold bars are not 100 per cent gold; they always contain small amounts of other metals like copper or platinum. If they didn't, they'd be so malleable they wouldn't stay bar-shaped.

STEPHEN *What's the name of the highly fortified building where most of the gold in America is kept?*
SHAPPI KHORSANDI *The Beckhams' house?*

How did Roman soldiers receive their salary?

It wasn't in salt.

Pliny the Elder was the first to claim Roman soldiers were paid in salt. In his *Natural History* he writes that 'in Rome . . . the soldier's pay was originally salt and the word "salary" derives from it.'

As usual with Pliny, there's a grain of truth in his assertion. Of course, some of a soldier's salary went on food, and this would have included salt. But it's likely the word *salarius* was used metaphorically, as someone today might say they were paid 'peanuts'. Roman soldiers were definitely paid in money – the word 'soldier' is usually said to derive from *solidus*, a Roman coin that had once been gold but in medieval Latin came to mean a shilling. (It's interesting that the phrase 'to take the king's shilling' means 'to join the army'.) Rather than salt, Roman coins were valued by the amount of bread or wheat they could buy (a Roman soldier ate two pounds of bread a day). It is also possible that 'soldier' is from the Celtic *soldurii*, a word mentioned in Julius Caesar's *Gallic Wars*, meaning 'an elite corps of warriors attached to a chieftain'.

Whether or not Pliny was right, salt was very important to the Roman Empire. One of the first great Roman roads, the Via Salaria, leads from Rome to the Adriatic, where salt was gathered. It was an essential part of the Roman diet: 'salad' comes from the Latin *salata* – vegetables dressed with salt. And they called a person in love *salax*, literally 'salted', the origin of the word 'salacious'.

It had political significance too. The government often manipulated the price of salt, subsidising it to increase their popularity, and artificially inflating it to raise money for military campaigns. During the Punic Wars (264–146 BC), Rome's century-long struggle for control of the Mediterranean against the Carthaginian Empire of North Africa, Marcus Livius, the censor (part of whose job was to act as the Roman equivalent to the Chancellor of the Exchequer), introduced a new salt tax. This resulted in him acquiring the nickname *Salinator*, 'salt-dealer' – a title eventually given to any government minister in charge of salt prices.

In sub-Saharan Africa, salt has been used as currency for centuries. The Afar people of Sudan make their living by mining and trading it. They transport it in blocks by camel to Ethiopia, and use it as payment for goods and services.

The salt comes from a lake called Bahr al Assal, 'the Sea of Honey', an ironic name given that it's the planet's saltiest lake outside Antarctica. Salinity levels are ten times higher than normal seawater. Lake Assal is the lowest point of Africa. It's part of the Great Rift Valley that runs from Syria to Mozambique, a huge gash in the Earth's crust created by volcanic activity more than 8 million years ago. In 10 million more years, this will split Africa in two completely and a large chunk of land will become East Africa, the world's newest continent.

STEPHEN *Yes, it's true that the word derives from the Latin for salt, but Roman soldiers were never paid in salt.*
NOEL FIELDING *We're getting paid in salt, though, aren't we?*

What killed most of the population of Pompeii?

It wasn't the explosion; it was what came afterwards.

So far about 3,000 bodies have been found under the ash at Pompeii, but the town had a population of around 20,000, so almost everyone survived.

Before the catastrophic eruption of August AD 79, there had been several days of small earthquakes that were mostly ignored. Then, at lunchtime on the 24th, Vesuvius violently exploded, blasting a mushroom cloud 12 miles into the sky. That evening ash and pumice rained down: the townsfolk went about with pillows tied to their heads, but some were trapped in their homes or killed by collapsing ceilings.

Much more dangerous was the pyroclastic flow, an avalanche of intensely hot ash and rock accompanied by clouds of toxic gas travelling at up to 150 miles an hour. But this didn't arrive until between 6 o'clock and 8 o'clock the next morning, giving people 18 hours to escape. Most of them did, but anyone left behind was incinerated by the pyroclastic flow and would have died in a second.

Among the victims was Pliny the Elder. He was asphyxiated after bravely sailing to the town to offer help. He had a meal, a bath and a nap between arriving and succumbing to the volcanic gases.

In a lot of the houses there aren't many household objects left behind, partly because fleeing residents took them, and partly because, as soon as the ash had settled, people came back and started digging to loot whatever they could. At least some of the bodies found at Pompeii are those of looters whose tunnels collapsed onto them.

The famous preserved 'bodies' of Pompeians – which include children, pigs and a dog – are actually plaster casts. When people are buried in ash or lava, the soft tissue of their bodies decomposes, leaving a person-shaped hole in the rock. In the nineteenth century an Italian archaeologist called Giuseppe Fiorelli worked out that if you found a cavity and poured in plaster of Paris you could precisely reconstruct the shape of a living person. The technique is named after him.

Pompeii was completely obliterated and remained hidden for over 1,600 years. Since its rediscovery in 1748 it has revealed a brothel with erotic paintings, the earliest surviving Roman amphitheatre and a mosaic saying *cave canem*, 'Beware of the Dog'. Analysis of wheel ruts suggests the town had a one-way traffic system.

Vesuvius remains unstable. Millions of people live close enough to be at risk if it explodes again, as it will. It last erupted in 1944, when 88 Allied aircraft in a nearby airfield were wrecked by falling ash. The most serious injury on that occasion was a sprained wrist during the evacuation.

How many Spartans died at the Battle of Thermopylae?

299.

Sparta was one of the most powerful city states in ancient Greece, famed for its military prowess. Public and private life revolved around the army – Spartan boys went into training from the age of five. As a result, it became a dominant player in the defence of Greece from invaders, particularly the Persians under Darius the Great (550–486 BC) and then his son Xerxes (519–465 BC). For 50 years, between 499 and 449 BC, they made the conquest of Greece their priority. Having been defeated soundly in their first attempt (at the Battle of Marathon in 490 BC) the Persians waited a decade before trying again.

The second invasion force set off in 480 BC. It was much bigger than the first – as many as 300,000 troops. The Greeks decided their best strategy was to block the Persians at the narrow pass of Thermopylae on the eastern coast of mainland Greece, on the main route linking north to south.

The small army of Greeks, led by the Spartan king Leonidas, held off the vastly bigger Persian force for two days. But then a local Greek named Ephialtes betrayed the existence of a secret path behind the Greek lines. Realising that he now risked losing all his men, Leonidas elected to remain with his elite bodyguard of 300 Spartan foot soldiers to hold the pass long enough for the rest of the Greeks to retreat. This they did, until every last Spartan perished, taking 20,000 Persians down with them in the process. This gave such a boost to morale that, a year later, the Greeks comprehensively defeated the Persians at the Battle of Plataea, and 'Leonidas and the 300 Spartans' passed into legend as one of the greatest 'last stands' in history.

Except that only 299 Spartans fought to the death at Thermopylae.

For a start, the '300' doesn't include Leonidas himself, which bumps it up to 301. But two other Spartans missed the fight. One, Pantites, was sent off on a diplomatic mission to deliver a message: on his return home, he hanged himself out of shame. The other, Eurytus, went off with the other retreating Greeks because of an eye infection. He also committed suicide, throwing himself on the spears of the Persians at the Battle of Plataea.

The 299 Spartans weren't alone: 700 Thespians and 400 Thebans fought side by side with them – 1,499 men in all. Not that it matters how many there were: everyone agrees they did a great job. Through their self-sacrifice, 5,000 Greek soldiers lived to fight another day, more than two-thirds of the original army.

The Spartans were noted for their pithy manner of speech. Hence the English word 'laconic', after Laconia, the province of

Greece in which Sparta stood. In the fourth century BC, Alexander the Great's father, Philip II of Macedon, sent a blustering letter to the city saying, 'If I enter Laconia, I will level it to the ground.' The Spartans drily replied with the single word: 'If'.

Even on the morning of the Battle of Thermopylae the Spartans managed some crisp comebacks. When the Persians demanded the Spartans hand over their weapons, Leonidas replied, '*Molon labe*' ('Come and get it!'). This is now the motto of the Greek First Army Corps. Later in the day a Spartan called Dienekes heard reports that Persian arrows would be so dense they would blot out the sky. 'All the better', he said, 'to fight in the shade.'

STEPHEN ... *the Spartans sent back a one-word reply* ...
ALAN *'Bothered?'*

How many people were at the feeding of the 5,000?

Perhaps as many as 15,000.

The miracle of the five loaves and two fishes is the only one of Jesus' miracles that appears in all four gospels. Incredible though it would have been to eke out such meagre rations among 5,000 people, it was many more than that. According to Matthew (14: 21) 'the number of those who ate was about 5,000 men besides women and children.'

The Gospel of Matthew also records an entirely different miracle called 'The Feeding of the 4,000'. It gets less attention because there were 1,000 fewer followers (plus women and children) and Jesus had two extra loaves to feed them with.

Jesus' miraculous catering skills extended to drinks as well as food. One of his most famous feats took place at the wedding feast of Cana, where he turned water into wine to keep the party going. In the early twentieth century this troubled religiously minded temperance campaigners. One of them, Frederick Lees, found a way round it by announcing that the Hebrew word for wine was the same as the one for unfermented grape juice. He decided that whenever it appeared in the Bible in a negative light it was referring to the alcoholic drink, and whenever it was positive, it meant grape juice. He retranslated the entire Bible, amending it accordingly.

The drinking of wine during Holy Communion horrified Lees. His theory was that, as the Jews in Egypt were poor and Nile water was pure, it must originally have been water. His argument took hold and convinced several churches to swap their wine for water, but others found it ridiculous. Quite an achievement, they said: 1,800 years after Jesus turned water into wine, Frederick Lees had managed to change it back again.

In Mark (5: 1–20) Jesus performed an exorcism on a man inhabited by a large number of demons. He transferred these into a herd of nearby pigs, which ran into a lake and drowned. In Matthew (21: 18–20) a fig tree cursed by Jesus immediately withers and dies. In the Gospel of John, Jesus raises Lazarus from the dead four days after his burial. More playfully, in Matthew (17: 24–27), Jesus tells Peter to cast his line into a lake, correctly predicting that the first fish he catches will have a 4-drachma coin in its mouth.

The fourteenth-century Spanish mystic St John of the Cross coined the phrase 'the dark night of the soul'. After many years of struggle with himself, he decided there was an even greater miracle than the resurrection of the dead – and that was the achievement of patience.

What did Mary Magdalene do for a living?

She was a hairdresser. Or maybe a fishmonger. Or she dyed cloth.

There's no evidence that Mary Magdalene was a prostitute. She is mentioned in all four gospels, she was present at the crucifixion and the resurrection, but at no point does anyone cast aspersions on her virtue.

The myth of Mary-as-prostitute probably arose because she was confused with two other Marys. One was the sister of Lazarus, whom Jesus raised from the dead; the other was a sinner called Mary who washed Jesus' feet with her hair. In the sixth century Pope Gregory the Great declared all three Marys were the same woman. The Catholic Church didn't correct the mistake until 1969.

In the 1971 musical *Jesus Christ Superstar* it is implied that Mary is a prostitute when Judas sings, 'It's not that I object to her profession / But she doesn't fit in well with what you teach and say.' This has no basis in the gospels either.

She might, however, have been a fishmonger. Mary Magdalene is also known as 'Mary of Magdala'. *Magdala* means 'tower' or 'fortress' in Aramaic, and there are several places of that name in and around Galilee. One is Magdala Nûnîya, 'the tower of fish', which was famous for its salted fish. Another translates as the 'tower of dyers', so Mary (who is several times described as wealthy) might have made her money from dying cloth.

It's also possible that *magdala* was being used as an adjective, where it can mean 'hairdresser' (from the Aramaic *gadal*, 'to plait hair'). Or perhaps she wore a braid. Or maybe it was an affectionate nickname – Mary 'the tower' (like Peter 'the rock') because she was tall; or a prophetic one – 'Mary the watchtower', because she was the first disciple to see Jesus after he rose from the dead. There's more evidence for any of these options than there is for her being a prostitute.

There are plenty of genuine prostitutes in the Bible. There's Rahab, who helps Joshua by hiding his spies before the Battle of Jericho; the Moabite women who use sex to tempt the Israelites to worship Baal (Joshua 2: 1–21. Numbers 25: 1–3); and the Midianite harlot who gets speared with her lover in flagrante. Most memorable of all are the sisters Oholah and Oholibah, who lusted after Babylonians 'whose genitals were like those of donkeys and whose emission was like that of horses' (Ezekiel 23: 1–21).

Many books have claimed Jesus and Mary Magdalene were married. There's no hard evidence for this, although in the gospel of Philip, one of the many apocryphal gospels (i.e. those unapproved by the Church), Jesus kisses Mary on the '. . .'

Unfortunately at this point the papyrus has been eaten by ants, so we'll never know exactly where.

What did Lady Godiva do?

She certainly didn't ride naked through the marketplace in Coventry.

Lady Godiva was a real person: an Anglo-Saxon noblewoman who lived around the time of the Norman Conquest. She's in the Domesday Book as Godgifu ('God's Gift' in Anglo-Saxon), and listed as the only female Anglo-Saxon major landowner. She was married to Leofric, Earl of Mercia.

Together they were the power couple of late Anglo-Saxon England.

According to the legend, Lady Godiva begged Leofric to lift the heavy taxes he'd imposed on the people of Coventry. He said he'd do it if she rode through the city naked. So she stripped

and set off on her horse, her modesty covered by her floor-length hair. Leofric kept his word and removed the taxes.

There are no contemporary accounts of this story. It first appeared in 1237, almost 200 years later, recorded by Roger of Wendover, a gullible monk who collected anecdotes. The historical record shows that taxes in Coventry were no worse than anywhere else, and for peasants they would have been negligible, and the earl wasn't responsible for them anyway – Coventry belonged to Lady Godiva. It was barely more than a hamlet at the time, with only 69 families and too small to have a marketplace. The earl and his lady didn't live there: none of the houses were grand enough.

In fact, Lady Godiva and her husband were pious benefactors of the Church. A credible origin of the story is that she did once take a symbolic ride through the village as a penitent (wearing only a plain shift dress) to the Benedictine monastery she had founded and endowed there.

In one version of the legend Lady Godiva ordered the people of Coventry to stay indoors with their windows shuttered while she rode. But one person in the town, a tailor known ever since as Peeping Tom (from whom we get the expression) bored a hole in his shutters so he could have a look – and was struck blind (or blinded by the townsfolk). No written accounts of this story exist earlier than the eighteenth century. And Thomas isn't an Anglo-Saxon name.

Coventry has re-enacted the legend once a year on and off since 1678 with a 'Godiva Parade' or 'Procession'. It was a bit coy to start with: in the first one Lady Godiva was played by a boy, and on another occasion, in Puritan times, the horse wore trousers.

KATHY LETTE *Do you think that would work today, if we suggested to Boris Johnson that if we rode naked through the town we could stop paying our taxes?*
STEPHEN *Or maybe we could pay him not to ride naked through the streets of London.*
ALAN *I prefer that idea.*

When did the first woman vote in Britain?

It wasn't in 1918.

Some British women – those who owned property and were over 30 – won the right to vote in parliamentary elections in 1918. But they weren't the first. Lily Maxwell, a widow who ran a crockery shop, beat them to it in 1867 when she voted in a by-election in Manchester. An administrative error landed her name on the electoral register, so she turned up at the polling booth.

Maxwell's vote was later declared illegal, which it was – but it wouldn't have been if she'd voted before 1832. It was the 1832 Reform Act that legally limited parliamentary voting to 'male householders'; before then, if a woman was the householder then she could vote. Technically, votes for women were only illegal in Britain for 86 years, from 1832 to 1918.

There was more confusion in 1867 when the Reform Act was reworded, changing the words 'male person' to 'man'. Some women connected this to a law declaring that 'words importing the masculine gender shall be deemed to include females' – in other words, 'man' could technically mean either a man or a woman – and argued that women now had the franchise. Over 5,000 women in Manchester alone demanded the right to vote as a result. They were denied, and the loophole was swiftly closed.

Women gained the right to vote in local elections in 1869, and they have always been able to vote in certain parish elections. In 1843, in the parish of St Chad in Lichfield, Staffordshire, 25 out of 395 registered voters were women. One of them, Grace Brown, was so wealthy she was entitled to four votes. Almost 300 years earlier, in 1572, a landowning widow named Dorothy Pakington personally elected the two parliamentary representatives for Aylesbury (at a time when parliamentary 'elections' were won on the basis of whomever the local lord preferred).

When women were finally allowed to vote in national elections in 1918, many opposed the idea. The Women's National Anti-Suffrage League, established in 1908, had over 100 branches in Britain. Its members argued that women had no practical experience of important matters of state, and so couldn't be trusted to vote sensibly. They also claimed that if women gained the franchise, couples would start arguing about politics, and families would break down as a result. In 1910 they merged with the Men's League for Opposing Women's Suffrage.

Winston Churchill was firmly on the anti-suffrage side of the argument, saying at an election rally in 1905, 'Nothing would induce me to vote for giving women the franchise.' Fortunately, the decision was never his to make.

What's the most dangerous sport for girls in America?

Cheerleading.

Two-thirds of all serious sports injuries suffered by girls in the USA are caused by cheerleading. More than 20,000 cheerleaders are admitted to emergency rooms across the country every year, and that number is increasing because, despite the dangers, the sport is booming: in 1990 there were 600,000 cheerleaders in the USA. Today there are more than 3 million.

Most US cheerleaders – 96 per cent, to be precise – are female. One man who bucked the trend was George W. Bush, who was the head cheerleader for his high school in his senior year. This is often taken as evidence of Bush's lack of athletic ability, but in reality he was a decent sportsman, playing fullback for the Yale rugby union team that famously beat Harvard in 1968.

Before that, at the exclusive Andover Academy, a private all-male boarding school near Boston, Bush set up a stickball league. Stickball is a bit like baseball or rounders, played by American street kids with a broomstick handle and a tennis ball. Native Americans played a version of it, but it wasn't the kind of sport encouraged by an exclusive school like Andover. Bush appointed himself 'High Commissioner', wore a top hat and gave the teams risqué names like the Beavers and the Nads (he led the cheerleading for the latter with the refrain 'Go Nads!'). Biographers see this as an early indication of Bush's ability to combine being a charismatic leader and the class clown.

Bush wasn't that unusual as a male cheerleader. Cheerleading started in 1898 and was originally an all-male affair. There were no pom-poms or miniskirts – just a group of men leading a series of supporters' chants. In 1911 *Nation* wrote that 'The reputation of having been a valiant "cheer-leader" is one of the most valuable things a boy can take away from college.'

Women were actively banned from cheerleading until 1923 – there were concerns that females would develop 'loud, raucous voices' and learn how to swear. Even when they were allowed, their costumes consisted of ankle-length skirts and big sweaters. Other notable male cheerleaders include Dwight D. Eisenhower, Franklin D. Roosevelt and Jimmy Stewart.

The National Football League (NFL) is the most powerful sports league in the USA, if not the world. It generates $10 billion in revenue every year, and a 30-second commercial during the Super Bowl costs approximately $4 million. Cheerleaders for the NFL, however, struggle to earn the minimum wage of $8 per hour, and earn considerably less than the mascots in funny costumes who entertain the crowd.

In response to the number of injuries, some cheerleaders have taken to wearing helmets, especially during training. Helmets are controversial in American football. There is a growing opposition to their use on safety grounds: when wearing a helmet, the players tend to use the head as a weapon, barrelling themselves head-first into a tackle. The argument is that going bareheaded would make players much more careful when tackling, and less likely to suffer head injuries. But not everyone agrees and it remains a sport whose popularity rests on the 'big hits'.

How good was Kim Jong-il at golf?

Nowhere near as good as we've been led to believe.

The story goes that Kim Jong-il scored 11 holes-in-one the first time he played golf, and that 17 bodyguards witnessed him doing it.

Often cited as an example of absurd North Korean propaganda, in fact it was mainly spread by the Western press.

The claim originated when Australian undercover journalist Eric Ellis visited North Korea's only golf course, and asked the resident pro whether Kim Jong-il played. Under close scrutiny from security officials, he obviously said Kim was terribly good at golf and that he'd scored five holes-in-one.

Reports by Western news agencies soon inflated the story to 11 holes-in-one. Later additions included the 17 armed bodyguards, the fact it was Kim's first time, and his score of 38-under-par. (For non-golfers, this is twice as good as the best score ever achieved by anyone, anywhere, since records began.)

One North Korean propaganda expert said he'd never seen the claim made officially and that, because golf was perceived as an elitist capitalist sport, even if Kim had played, the regime were unlikely to want to broadcast the fact. Any story going around was being spread by tour guides and definitely not authorised. The North Korean government press office refuses to answer any questions on the subject of golf.

North Korea is not beyond making exaggerated propaganda claims: the state news channel once claimed sailors in a violent storm found the waters grew calm when they sang songs in praise of Kim Jong-il. But many of the reports can be explained by the problems of translation. When one described how the 'sky grieved' when Kim Jong-il died, many people in the West thought it was meant literally. This is a little unfair: if a Western newspaper wrote something similar, we'd naturally assume it was a metaphor.

North Korea has only one golf club, in the hills near Pyongyang (although there is rumoured to be a private course in Myohang, the mountain villa of Kim's father, Kim Il-sung).

Another country with only one golf club is Afghanistan. King Habibullah introduced the game there and founded Kabul Golf Club in 1919. He loved it so much he was buried on the course.

It's so rocky that players carry chunks of artificial turf with them for fairway shots. The 'greens' are smoother areas made from sand and engine oil and are referred to as 'browns'.

What is the brake man's job in a bobsled race?

To accelerate.

A bobsled's brakes should only be used once the race is over. Teams can be disqualified for using them during a race as it damages the track. The brake man is usually the fastest and strongest member of the team and sits at the back of the sled. He's the last person to jump in, and has the chance to give the sled a final take-off boost. So, despite their name, brake men make the sled go faster.

Once all four team members are in the sled, the driver is in control. The others don't have much to do at this stage – some teams used to bob back and forth to try and build speed, but this can interfere with the sled's streamlining. The best policy for the other three members of the team is to stay still and adopt an aero-dynamic shape.

Bobsledding got a boost from the 1993 Disney film *Cool Runnings*, loosely based on the true story of the first Jamaican bobsled team, who competed in the 1988 Winter

Olympics at Calgary. The film took some liberties. John Candy's character, Irving 'Irv' Blitzer, was based on the real coach Howard Siler. Although Siler had coached the US bobsled team, he hadn't won any gold medals, wasn't an alcoholic, and hadn't been shunned by the bobsled world for cheating. In the movie, the team is assembled from elite sprinters; in fact, none of the Jamaican sprint team wanted to do it, so the bobsled team was recruited from the Jamaican military.

Dudley Stokes, the Sandhurst-trained officer who was the driver of the real Jamaican bobsled team only heard about the sport in 1987, less than a year before the Calgary games. Just four months after his first time on the ice he was racing in the Olympics.

Jamaica still competes at bobsled. At Lillehammer in 1994 they came fourteenth, beating Russia and the USA, but didn't qualify in 2006 or 2010. A two-man bobsled team qualified for the Sochi Winter Olympics in 2014 but struggled to find the funds to get there. So they set up an online appeal hoping to raise $80,000 — and made over $184,000 in just four days. Sadly, they came last.

JOSH WIDDICOMBE *I haven't been recycling for the last month, because someone stole my recycling bin.*
ALAN *Are they good for sledding? I bet they're great for sledding.*
JOSH *Was it you?*
ALAN *I just got the lid.*
STEPHEN *Were you luging on Josh's lid? How wrong of you.*

What's the main rule of walking races?

You can have both feet off the ground at the same time – as long as no one sees you.

Rule 230 of the International Association of Athletics Federations (IAAF) says, 'Racewalking is a progression of steps so taken that the walker makes contact with the ground so that no visible (to the human eye) loss of contact occurs.'

If you freeze-frame a walking race you'll regularly see people with both feet off the ground. This results in lots of outraged emails but technically it's not against the rules. So long as the officials can't see the gap between the foot and the ground, there is no infringement.

At present there's no technology involved in monitoring walking races: judges just record any infractions they spot. If a walker racks up three of these the head judge holds up a red paddle to disqualify them. A high-tech shoe that detects when race walkers have both feet off the ground has so far failed to make an impact.

In the nineteenth century walking races were America's most popular spectator sport. Then known as 'pedestrianism', competitions lasted for up to six days (the longest time possible without competing on a Sunday). Competitors walked for 21 hours a day and for distances of up to 600 miles. To keep going they drank champagne, which was believed to be a stimulant. They were allowed short naps – the trackside was fitted with cots for them to sleep in. And they were even allowed to run if necessary, to relieve cramp. Two of the game's greatest rivals were Dan O'Leary, nicknamed 'The Plucky Pedestrian', and the sport's founder, Edward Payson Weston, a.k.a. 'The Wily Wobbler'.

In Britain the craze was given a boost by Captain Robert

Barclay Allardice, a Scottish laird, better known as 'the Celebrated Pedestrian'. He came from a family who wrestled bulls, carried flour sacks with their teeth, uprooted trees with their bare hands and founded Barclays Bank. In 1809 Captain Barclay walked 1,000 miles in 1,000 hours to win 1,000 guineas. Wearing a top hat, a thick woollen overcoat, flannel breeches, lambswool stockings and heavy leather shoes, he stopped once an hour for a brief sleep and a meal of roast fowl, mutton and beer. His 607th hour was the hardest: semi-comatose, his brother and a friend dragged him along and his groom whacked him with a stick to wake him up. By the middle of the nineteenth century, to walk in a 'Barclay fashion' meant to walk quickly.

Walking races began in London in 1897 and became part of the Olympics in 1906. Today the 20-kilometre and 50-kilometre walking races are Olympic events, although Britain hasn't had success for many years. In Tokyo, in 1964, Ken Matthews won gold for Britain in the 20-kilometre race. His winning time of 89 minutes was six minutes slower than the 83 minutes you now have to beat in order to qualify.

How long are Olympic swimming pools?

50 metres . . . and 2 centimetres.

An Olympic swimmer travels 50 metres for every length of a pool that they complete, but there's a 1-centimetre-thick touch pad at each end. This means the pools are built 2 centimetres longer, to make sure the swimmers travel exactly 50 metres. Touch pads were introduced at the Mexico games in 1968. Before then, competitors were scrutinised by poolside officials holding stopwatches.

According to an ongoing myth, some swimming pools contain a dye that changes colour if urine is present. Fortunately, this magic substance doesn't exist – which is good news for Olympic swimmers, who routinely pee in the pool. Multiple gold medal winner Michael Phelps has said, 'Everybody pees in the pool. It's kind of a normal thing to do for swimmers.'

People have been swimming for at least 10,000 years – as shown in the rock paintings in 'the cave of swimmers' at Wadi Sura in Egypt. Swimming is seen in early Minoan, Incan and Babylonian art, and the Egyptians, Persians and Greeks were all keen swimmers: Plato said anyone who couldn't swim lacked a proper education. The Japanese were holding competitive swimming galas as far back as 36 BC. To demonstrate one of the 'seven agilities', medieval English knights swam in armour.

The first book on swimming was more cautious. *Colymbetes*, written in 1539 by Nikolaus Wynmann, a German professor of languages, recommended three buoyancy aids: bundles of reeds, belts made of cork, and air-filled cows' bladders. In 1595 the scholar Everard Digby wrote *A Short Introduction for to Learne to Swimme*. He claimed men swam better than fish because they can also swim backwards, on their sides and upside down. He recorded various styles of 'exhibitionist swimming' – how to sit on the water, or swim while carrying things, or how to swim while cutting your toenails.

Doggy-paddle was the first stroke people learned: newborn babies perform it instinctively. Breaststroke was the first of the four main strokes to be swum competitively. Front crawl made its UK debut in 1844 in London at a race meeting that featured a number of Native American swimmers. The winner was Flying Gull, who covered 45 metres (150 feet) in 30 seconds, closely followed by his compatriot, Tobacco. The British thought the stroke and the splashing that accompanied it 'barbaric' and it wasn't adopted for another 30 years. Despite this, front crawl, or freestyle, remains the fastest way to get across a pool – the 50-metre record is currently 20.91 seconds and is held by César Cielo from Brazil.

The 1900 Olympics featured a 200-metre obstacle swimming course, where competitors had to climb over and swim under three poles and rows of boats.

Name *either* the starting point *or* the finishing point of the Paris–Dakar rally

Neither Paris nor Dakar is involved.

The Paris–Dakar rally is a famously tough motor race over near impossible terrain, but it has been held nowhere near Paris or Dakar (the capital of Senegal) for more than five years. The race was relocated to South America in 2009, after threats from al-Qaeda in 2007 and several murders in Mauritania in 2008. It is now officially known simply as 'The Dakar Rally', but in 2014 would have been more correctly called the Rosario–Valparaíso Rally, as it ran between the third-largest city in Argentina and the third-largest city in Chile.

The rally is so testing that fewer than half the teams ever finish. The most challenging year was 1986, when 79 per cent of the teams pulled out before the end. At over 9,300 miles, it was the longest course ever set and

seven competitors died – four of them in a helicopter crash, one of whom was the rally's founder Thierry Sabine. In 1982 Margaret Thatcher's son Mark took part and got lost for six days. He was eventually found 31 miles off-route.

It isn't the world's only extreme rally. India has the Blind Man's Car Rally, a 40-mile race in which blind navigators use a Braille map and give instructions to the (thankfully) sighted drivers. The drivers are obliged to follow their navigator's instructions, and aren't allowed to turn any corners on their own instinct.

The Mongol Rally is more than 10,000 miles long. It starts in England, crosses Mongolia and ends in Ulan-Ude in Russia. It doesn't even have a route – the organisers say it would cramp the style of the drivers.

The Baja 1000 Rally in Mexico has its own set of difficulties. Although the course length is a relatively modest 930 miles, it traverses very rough terrain, made even worse by locals who amuse themselves by placing booby traps like hidden holes and diverting rivers along the way. Competitors are warned that a likely sign of an impending trap is a large crowd along a particular part of the route, especially if many of them are holding video cameras.

The world's first long-distance car event was the 1894 Paris–Rouen Horseless Carriage Competition. It was more of a test of reliability than a race – prizes were allocated based on safety, handling, and low running costs, rather than speed. Only 21 out of 102 entrants survived the qualification trials. The car that crossed the line first wasn't declared the winner because it was so inconvenient to drive – it was a steam tractor towing a carriage, which needed someone to continually stoke the boiler. First prize went to a Frenchman, Albert Lemaître, driving a 3-horsepower Peugeot that covered the 78 miles in 6 hours 51 minutes, at an average speed of 12 miles an hour.

Which country is the world's largest producer of Brazil nuts?

It's not Brazil.

Half the world's Brazil nuts are now produced by Bolivia. Brazil produces 40 per cent and Peru the other 10 per cent.

Until recently Brazil did produce the most Brazil nuts. Bolivia has only been number one since the 1990s. Production grew rapidly when the government paid farmers to grow the nuts instead of coca leaves, which were being used for cocaine production.

Brazil nut trees are 150 feet tall and each one produces up to 450 kilograms (nearly 1,000 pounds) of nuts per season. They grow in so few countries because they are incredibly difficult to cultivate. They have to be pollinated by the Euglossine ('good-tongued') bee, which is found in pristine rainforest. Its long tongue means it's the only insect that can get to the nectar in the flowers. But the bees are in turn dependent on a particular rainforest orchid, whose nectar gives a special colour to the male bees' wings, making them more attractive to females and allowing them to reproduce. Brazil nut trees grown outside the rainforest lack the necessary orchids and bees and never bear fruit.

Brazil nuts are seeds, not nuts; the nut is the coconut-like casing around it. Inside this pod 20 to 30 seeds fit together like the sections of an orange. The pods fall off the trees when ripe and are easily heavy enough to kill a person. Fatal accidents are not uncommon and collectors stop work in strong winds.

The Portuguese name for Brazil nuts is *castanhas-do-Pará*, 'chestnuts from the vast ocean'; the pods they come in are called *ouriços*, or 'hedgehogs'.

Brazil nuts are one of the world's most radioactive foods, and the only one with an allergic reaction that is sexually transmissible. The semen of a man who has eaten them can trigger a response if his partner is allergic.

In a bag of muesli or mixed nuts, Brazil nuts always rise to the top. This is known as 'granular convection' or the 'Brazil Nut Effect'. It's an interesting phenomenon that helps us to understand why flints and stones rise to the surface of fields and why asteroids are covered in large, mysterious boulders.

What are the prickly bits of a rose called?

Prickles.

Thorns are the modified branches or stems of a plant, whereas prickles are part of its skin. Roses have prickles: the sickle-shaped hooks defend them against predators and help them grip when climbing. Holly and thistles have neither thorns nor prickles: their sharp bits are modified leaves.

There are about 200 species of wild rose, only a few of which have been used to breed the thousands of hybridised varieties known as 'cultivars'. The most important is *Rosa gallica officinalis*, from which most modern varieties of rose descend. It is native to central and southern Europe and comes in shades from pink to deep red. Its name means 'French medical rose' and from the thirteenth century it was grown in France to make rosewater and perfume, but it seems likely that it was the original red rose of antiquity. 'Rose' derives from the Latin *rosa*, from Greek *rhodon*, words the ancient Greeks and Romans used for both the flower and the colour red. According to mythology, roses sprang from the blood of the goddess Aphrodite's lover, Adonis, who was gored to death by a wild boar. Ancient roses were much prized and grown in great quantity. Their fragrant petals were spread across feasting tables, and roses were used to decorate graves or woven into celebratory wreaths.

They were also useful. Pliny the Elder recorded in his *Natural History* that they could cure 32 diseases, including the bites of rabid dogs. In the tenth century the Islamic physician Avicenna first distilled attar of roses – at 60,000 petals an ounce, the most expensive of all natural perfumes. In medieval Europe *Rosa gallica* was known as the 'apothecary rose': a floral first-aid kit. Its petals were made into oil to mask the taste of bitter medicines; its fruit (rosehips) were used to cure scurvy, colds and flu; and its leaves were a laxative. It was regarded as medicine for centuries. *Rosa gallica officinalis* appeared in the *British Pharmacopeia* (the annual list of approved drugs) up until the 1930s.

Rosa gallica was also the 'red rose' of Lancaster. Henry VII combined it with the white rose of York (probably the wild field rose, *Rosa arvensis*) to create the Tudor rose, the national flower of England. This became a symbol of unity after the 'Wars of the Roses' – although they weren't called that until Sir Walter Scott coined the name in the nineteenth century. From Roman times a rose suspended above a table bound anyone present to secrecy, which is why the ceilings of dining rooms or staterooms often sport plaster roses. This is the origin of the Latin tag *sub rosa* ('under the rose') which UK Special Forces still use to refer to covert operations.

New varieties of rose are bred for scent, colour, resistance to disease and cold, climbing ability and regularity of flowering. More than 30,000 have been created – though no one has yet managed to produce a blue one.

Finding names for so many varieties means that many of them don't sound much like flowers, from Absolutely, Bubble Bath and Chuckles to Wow!, X-Rated, Yorkshire Bank and Zebra. Many roses are named after celebrities and some even after

♪ *Every rose has its ... er ...* ♪

politicians, such as Ronald Reagan, Helmut Kohl and Arthur Scargill. But the English rose grower loves a home-grown actress best: you can order and plant a Felicity Kendal, a Jane Asher, a Susan Hampshire, a Hannah Gordon, a Charlotte Rampling, a Penelope Keith, a June Whitfield or a Thelma Barlow (Mavis Riley in *Coronation Street*).

STEPHEN *Rose bushes don't have thorns.*
ALAN *Thorn bushes have roses then? Is that it? Is it a trick?*

What was the main use for pepper in the Middle Ages?

a) To hide the flavour of rotten meat
b) As a nice seasoning
c) To appease warlords
d) To stuff up the nostrils of corpses

Full marks if you chose b), c) and d). Pepper was hugely popular in the Middle Ages but not because it helped disguise the taste of putrefaction.

In medieval times anyone who could afford pepper could probably also afford good meat. To this day the Dutch word *peperduur*, literally 'pepper expensive', means 'very expensive'. Pepper was so valuable people bequeathed it in their wills.

People also understood perfectly well about the dangers of eating spoiled meat. Medieval markets were subject to health and safety inspections; anyone caught selling rotten food risked being fined, put in the pillory and permanently losing their vendor's licence. Then, as now, rotten meat was thrown away, not seasoned and served up for dinner.

Pepper is the berry of a tropical vine, one of more than a thousand other members of the *Piperaceae* family, and native to Southeast Asia, although it has been traded for over 3,500 years. When Alaric the Goth besieged Rome in AD 408, he was persuaded not to sack the city by being paid a tribute in gold, silver, silk and more than a ton of peppercorns. In the nineteenth century pepper was so valuable fraudsters manufactured fake peppercorns out of clay and oil, mixed with the much cheaper powdered cayenne pepper.

Pepper's exotic reputation in the Middle Ages was enhanced by the claim that it was harvested from snake-infested bushes. Supposedly, venomous snakes had to be burned out of these bushes before the spice could be obtained, giving it its black colour. Cinnamon, often used as a pepper substitute, had a similarly far-fetched origin story: the historian Herodotus claimed the only source was the nests of huge 'cinnamon birds' that lived on inaccessible mountain precipices.

Black, white and green peppercorns are all the same berry. The black pepper is the unripe berry dried with the pulp left on. This gives it what food historian Harold McGee calls its 'fresh, citrusy, woody, warm and floral aroma'. White peppercorns are ripe berries soaked, de-pulped and dried. The soaking leads to fermentation which leads to a 'horsey or stable-like' note. Green peppercorns are harvested the week before the berry is fully ripe and then preserved in brine. Pink peppercorns are the berries of an unrelated evergreen shrub from Peru called *Schinus molle*.

Piperine – the compound in pepper that gives it its spice – has anti-inflammatory and anti-arthritic properties. It can help one to cool down because, like other spicy foods, eating enough of it causes 'gustatory facial sweating'. It also increases the flow of saliva and gastric juices – so the more pepper you put on your food, the more of it you'll want to eat. On contact with air or light, piperine degrades into isochavicine, which smells of nothing – that's why pepper is best kept in dark, airtight containers.

Pepper has had a variety of uses outside the kitchen. The Egyptians used it as part of mummification rituals, and it was stuffed up Ramesses II's nostrils when he was buried in 1213 BC. In the fifth century BC Hippocrates recommended it as a treatment for fever, and in eighteenth-century China it was mixed with vinegar and poured into the eyes of those suffering from lethargy. In traditional Indian medicine it was mixed with cow's urine and taken to treat flatulence. Black pepper (*Piper nigrum*) is now the world's most traded spice, accounting for 20 per cent of all exports. Today over a third of all the world's black pepper comes from Vietnam.

Under contract law, 'consideration' is a requirement in order for a contract to be valid. This can be a payment, or an exchange of promises – historically, the nominal consideration required to give a contract legal effect was something small but valuable: a peppercorn.

Would you rather drink pure water or treated sewage?

You'd be better off with sewage: really pure water is bad for you.

'Ultrapure' water has no impurities at all. It's just pure H_2O. That might sound like a good thing, but it can kill you if you drink too much of it.

Human blood contains electrolytes – chemicals which conduct electric currents that enable the body to function. Nerve impulses, muscle contractions, even our heartbeat all involve the use of electricity. If these electrolytes come into contact with ultrapure water, they leave the bloodstream by osmosis – and the loss of too many of them can be lethal.

Pure water is not only deadly dangerous, but extremely dull. All the (very subtle) flavours in water actually come from its impurities. 'Reclaimed' water, on the other hand – as treated sewage is known – is perfectly good for you. Its main problem is public perception, but after a major PR campaign in 2008, people in Orange County, California, have been drinking it with no complaints. In Namibia's capital, Windhoek, used water has been recycled directly into tap water since 1968. One Australian skiing resort reuses its toilet water by treating it and turning it into snow 'so clean you could eat it'. Thames Water says we may be drinking recycled water in Britain within 15 years.

The recycling process has three stages. The waste water is first passed through fine microfilters to remove solids and oils. It's then forced through a dense plastic film which admits water molecules but not others, such as tiny salt molecules – the film also blocks microbes like viruses and bacteria. Finally, the water is subjected to strong ultraviolet light to break down any remaining organic compounds. The result is clean, safe water.

Carried out on a major scale, this could save hundreds of millions of litres of water each year. We may soon have no choice: population increase, climate change and poor water management have created an acute global shortage. Only 3 per cent of the world's water is fresh, and half of it is locked in the ice caps. It's in even shorter supply in space – astronauts recycle 93 per cent of the water they take with them.

What's the quickest way to look healthy?

Eating carrots is better than sitting in the sun.

People who eat lots of fruit and vegetables each day have a pleasing, golden skin colour. This is thanks to carotenoids, organic pigments found in plants. When volunteers were asked to judge the health of faces either tanned by the sun or high in these pigments, they preferred the latter. This may be an evolutionary response; it benefits our offspring if we mate with healthy individuals.

This is something we share with other species. Male house finches have orange in their plumage, which is brighter if they consume higher-quality seeds, which also contain more carotenoids. When scientists artificially brightened these males' feathers, females were more attracted to them. For the same reason, birds with more vibrant orange beaks are more successful at attracting mates.

The highest concentration of carotene found in the natural world is in crude palm oil, which is bright red as a result. But eating too much can completely change your colour. The actress Marlene Dietrich once put her whole family on an all-carrot regime; after two weeks they had all turned yellow. In 1999 the hands and face of a four-year-old from Rhyl turned orange after it was revealed that she had been drinking 1.5 litres (3 pints) of Sunny Delight a day. The condition, whose medical name is carotenaemia, is harmless: sufferers return to normal colour within a few weeks.

The tiny village of Berlotte in Belgium has a Carrot Museum, which is so small it's impossible for visitors to enter. The entire museum can only be viewed through a window. By turning a wheel outside, you can rotate the display as you peer through the window. Exhibits include a carrot weather vane, carrot clock and carrot light.

The Spanish word for carrot, *zanahoria*, also means 'nerd'.

How many portions of fruit and vegetables should you eat a day?

Nobody really knows.

Although we're told to eat five a day in Britain, the number is entirely arbitrary. In Denmark it's six; Australia says seven; America suggests 'five to nine', and in Canada it's between seven and ten. Spain recommends five too, but a British 'portion' of

vegetables is about half the size of a Spanish one.

There is heated debate over whether five is enough: several studies have recommended seven for women and nine for men. So why is it 'five a day'? First, the recommendation is actually 'at least' five. Second, it was picked because it seems like an attainable target.

'Five a day' started in America in 1991 with a campaign by Californian nutritionist Susan Foerster to promote fruit and vegetable consumption. (California produces a lot of both of these.) This was adopted by the UK's Department of Health. The World Health Organization already recommended eating 400 grams (14 ounces) of fruit and vegetables a day to combat obesity and diabetes. Dividing this into five smaller portions seemed reassuringly manageable. 'Five a day' was as much a product of marketing as nutritional science.

Three recent surveys recommended three different figures – one for seven portions, one for ten and the third concluded that five was about right. (Extra health benefits, it argued, drop off after the fifth portion.) Every serving of fruit or vegetables (at least up to five) helps to lower the risk of heart disease, strokes and mortality generally, and there is broad agreement among scientists that we should all eat more than we currently do.

According to the latest data from the National Diet and Nutrition Survey, just 10 per cent of teenage boys and 7 per cent of teenage girls manage five a day. It rises to 30 per cent among adults aged 19 to 64, and people older than that do slightly better. Britons eat half as many fresh green vegetables today as they did during the Second World War.

Chips don't count as one of your five a day. In fact, no potatoes do, no matter how they're cooked. They are a starchy food – like rice or pasta. Baked beans do count, but no matter how many you eat, they only count as one portion.

What did the Famous Five have lashings of?

Enid Blyton never used the phrase 'lashings of ginger beer'.

The line is from the 1982 BBC television show *The Comic Strip Presents* . . . parody, 'Five Go Mad in Dorset', where it appears four times in 30 minutes.

The Famous Five did encounter 'lashings', but mostly of food. In *Five Go Down to the Sea* they enjoy a high tea of 'lettuce, tomatoes, onions . . . and lashings of hard-boiled eggs'. Later in the same book there are lashings of peas and new potatoes. In *Five Have a Mystery to Solve* pudding is served with 'lashings of treacle' and in *Five Have a Wonderful Time* they face the alarming prospect of 'lashings of poisonous snakes'.

Half a million copies of the Famous Five stories are sold every year, and Enid Blyton is still one of the top 25 most-borrowed authors in British libraries. She was phenomenally prolific: in a 46-year career she wrote over 4,000 short stories and 700 books – 37 of the books in 1951 alone.

The author was not as cosy as her work. She was cold to her own children and had a bitter divorce from her first husband – her daughter Imogen later wrote that she was 'arrogant, insecure, pretentious . . . and without a trace of maternal instinct'. She also liked to play tennis in the nude, and spent her twenties answering to the names Cabin Boy or Richard. George from the Famous Five – the strong-willed girl who wanted to be a boy – was based on herself.

In 2010 Blyton's publisher, Hodder, announced plans to issue revised editions of the Famous Five stories to make them more comprehensible to modern children. This meant removing out-of-date language. 'Mercy me' became 'oh no'; 'very peculiar' was changed to 'very strange'; 'school tunic' to 'uniform'; and 'awful swotter' became 'bookworm'. Fans concerned about political correctness gone mad can take comfort in the fact that there are still characters called Dick and Aunt Fanny.

Elsewhere, the censor has been less forgiving: in Enid Blyton's Faraway Tree series, Fanny and Dick have been rechristened Franny and Rick.

Where was Juliet standing when she was wooed by Romeo?

She wasn't on a balcony.

There is no 'balcony scene' in *Romeo and Juliet*. Shakespeare wrote that Juliet appeared at a window. He wouldn't have mentioned a balcony. There were no balconies in Elizabethan England.

In 1611, 14 years after *Romeo and Juliet* was written, the English traveller Thomas Coryat described a balcony in his book *Coryat's Crudities* – 'a very pleasant little tarrasse [terrace], that jutteth or butteth out from the maine building' – but he didn't know the name for it. The first recorded use of the word 'balcony' in English was in 1618, two years after Shakespeare died.

The 'balcony scene' was the brainchild of a playwright called Thomas Otway (1652–85), who rearranged *Romeo and Juliet* as his own *The History and Fall of Caius Marius*. It stole the characters, plot and much of the dialogue from Shakespeare and placed them in an ancient Roman setting. It became far, far more popular than *Romeo and Juliet*, which Samuel Pepys saw in 1662, noting in his diary, 'It is a play of itself the worst that I have ever heard in my life, and the worst acted that I ever saw these people do.' The play fell out of fashion, and by the time it was revived in the 1750s Otway's balcony scene was so ingrained in everyone's minds that it was added to Shakespeare's original.

The story wasn't Shakespeare's in any case – he'd got it from a version published in 1562 called *The Tragicall Historye of Romeus and Juliet*. This too was based on older stories, in the oldest of which the leading characters are called Mariotto and Giannozza.

Today's Verona has made a tourist attraction of the balcony. Casa di Giulietta (Juliet's House) has a real balcony for tourists to step on to, despite the fact Juliet never existed (nor Romeo, for that matter). Even so, people visit in their thousands and send sacks of lovelorn letters from around the world each year. A local society of volunteers called the 'Juliet Club' replies to them.

A 'Juliet balcony' is a modern architectural term, but it isn't actually a balcony – more a wooden gate in front of a window. Juliet's balcony at the Casa di Giulietta isn't a Juliet balcony.

What did Napoleon say to Josephine?

Not 'Not tonight, Josephine'. He never said that.

There are no contemporary historical sources for such an exchange. The phrase is first recorded in an 1898 play called *The*

Royal Divorce by the Irish dramatist W. G. 'Willie' Wills (1828–91). From the moment Wills coined it, the phrase took on a life of its own, becoming the punchline of satirical music hall sketches about Napoleon and Josephine, and inspiring at least two popular songs. From there it has settled down as a stock joke, in which a small, unattractive man spurns the advances of a sexually rapacious woman.

This is ironic, given the extraordinarily passionate marriage that Napoleon and Josephine shared. His letters to her after their wedding in 1796 are explicit: 'You know very well, the little black forest . . . I kiss you there a thousand times and wait with impatience for the time I can be there again.' As well as 'little black forest', his pet names for her pudendum include 'little Oscar', 'little Quiquette' and, most enigmatically, 'the Baron de Kepen', a private joke that no one has been able to shed light on.

This erotic obsession has fed another Napoleonic myth, that he wrote to her after the Battle of Marengo in 1800 with the blunt request, 'Home in three days – don't wash.' No one has been able to produce the letter and there are no references to it before the 1960s. That doesn't mean it didn't happen, but there is plenty of documented evidence that both Napoleon and Josephine

bathed every day and enjoyed keeping clean and fragrant. Josephine grew up on the Caribbean island of Martinique and loved exotic scents such as vanilla and cinnamon, and Napoleon himself had an official eau de cologne supplier, using 8 quarts (16 pints) of the perfume a month for his rubdown. He even went as far as to commission two scents from the perfumier Jean François Rancé – one for him called 'Le Vainqueur' (the Conqueror) and one for Josephine called 'L'Impératrice' (the Empress). The brief was that they should harmonise perfectly when the couple were together, and Rancé was forbidden from selling them to anyone else for 200 years (both have recently been brought back into production by Rancé's company, now based in Milan).

Josephine's real name was Marie Josèphe Rose. She usually went by the name Rose, but Napoleon made her change it: he couldn't bear to call her by the name her other lovers had used. 'Rose' also loved roses: she published the first written history of their cultivation and helped create the first artificially pollinated roses in her gardens at Malmaison.

Napoleon had a thing about Josephines. He had two other lovers similarly named: Josephina Grassini and Josephine Weimer. Grassini was an opera singer who was paid 70,000 francs by the French state every year from 1807 to 1814. Weimer was a beautiful and well-endowed actress (Napoleon once pushed 40,000 francs down her cleavage). Napoleon's arch-enemy, the Duke of Wellington, seems to have felt the same way – he seduced both Weimer and Grassini during his stay in Paris in 1814/15.

Wellington obsessively copied Napoleon's life. He made friends with the emperor's sister Pauline before buying her house and hanging a saucy picture of her on his bedroom wall. He tried to seduce Napoleon's brother's mistress and even hired Napoleon's cook – although it's said he cared so little for food he could scarcely tell rancid butter from fresh.

After the final defeat of Napoleon in 1815 Wellington was presented with his sword, three paintings of him and an 11-foot statue of the emperor as Mars, god of war, naked except for a fig

leaf and a cloak. Wellington installed the statue at the bottom of
the stairs at his house in London for visitors to hang their hats
and coats on. During the Blitz the fig leaf fell off.

Who coined the phrase 'Elementary, my dear Watson'?

Not Sir Arthur Conan Doyle, but P. G. Wodehouse.

In all the Sherlock Holmes stories, Holmes uses the word
'elementary' only once – in *The Crooked Man* (1894) – and he
doesn't address Watson after it:

> 'Elementary,' said he. 'It is one of those instances where the
> reasoner can produce an effect which seems remarkable to his
> neighbour, because the latter has missed the one little point
> which is the basis of the deduction.'

The words 'Elementary, my dear Watson' were first used 21
years later in *Psmith, Journalist* (1915) by P. G. Wodehouse, gently
mocking Holmes's slightly pompous manner. The phrase
appeared again at the very end of *The Return of Sherlock Holmes*
(1929), the first Holmes movie to be made with sound.

The Internet has made it easier than ever for mangled
quotations to spread around the world. The quotations expert
Nigel Rees dubbed the tendency to credit catchy lines to famous
speakers 'Churchillian drift'. Fred Shapiro, editor of *The Yale
Book of Quotations*, calls such people 'quote magnets'. Churchill is
Britain's greatest quote magnet; Mark Twain is America's. (The
line 'Golf is a good walk spoiled' has been misattributed to both
Churchill and Twain.)

Churchill never said, 'The only traditions of the Royal Navy
are rum, sodomy and the lash' (though he did say he wished he

had). The famous exchange where Lady Astor said, 'Winston, if you were my husband, I'd poison your coffee', and he replied, 'If you were my wife, I'd drink it' wasn't Churchill's either: it dates back to 1900, almost 40 years before he supposedly said it. Nor was the quip 'This is the kind of English up with which I will not put' a Churchill original – it had already appeared in *Strand* magazine.

Oscar Wilde never wrote, 'I am not young enough to know everything' – that was J. M. Barrie – and it's very unlikely he said, 'I have nothing to declare except my genius' when going through New York Customs. (We advise readers against trying the same thing.)

Einstein never said, 'Two things are infinite – the universe and human stupidity. And I'm not sure about the former.' In 1980 Andy Warhol admitted that he did'nt come up with his famous line about 15 minutes of fame. He did use it in a brochure he distributed in 1968, but was quoting someone else: a Swedish museum curator named Pontus Hultén, the painter Larry Rivers, or photographer Nat Finkelstein. Finkelstein claims it was him: Warhol said everyone wanted to be famous, and he replied, 'Yeah, for about 15 minutes, Andy.'

Churchill definitely met Bessie Braddock, a Labour MP, who told him, 'Winston, you are drunk'. And he did reply, 'Madam, you are ugly, and I will be sober in the morning.' But this, too, was adapted from an old gag – the earliest version dates to 1882, when Churchill was eight years old.

So rather than quote Churchill, remain silent. For as he said himself, 'Too often the strong, silent man is silent only because he does not know what to say, and is reputed strong only because he has remained silent.'

Who invented Pythagoras' theorem?

It wasn't Pythagoras.

Everyone is taught Pythagoras' theorem at school – that in a right-angled triangle, the square of the longest side (the hypotenuse) is the same as the sum of the squares of the other two sides. This can be expressed by the formula: $a^2 + b^2 = c^2$.

But this formula was known to the ancient Babylonians and Egyptians at least a thousand years before Pythagoras was born in 570 BC, and one Indian text from a century before Pythagoras contains the first mathematical proof. Also, even if he had come up with a new proof, it would be impossible to be sure that Pythagoras himself had made the breakthrough. For centuries after his death his followers attributed all their new mathematical theories to their erstwhile teacher.

Pythagoras was one of the most important and influential of the Greek philosophers known as the Presocratics, so called because they lived and taught in the century before Socrates. Like most of the others in the group, he didn't leave behind any written texts: our knowledge of his philosophy is entirely based on fragments of his teaching which appear in the work of his followers or other philosophers, in Pythagoras' case, most notably Plato.

At the core of his thinking is an almost mystical belief in mathematics. Pythagoras taught that physical reality could be expressed in numbers and that the proper study of mathematics

and geometry would reveal all the secrets of the universe. Music was an essential part of this. Inspired by the different sounds of a blacksmith's hammer, he developed a theory of harmonics. A keen player of the lyre, he observed that the pitch of a musical note was in proportion to the length of the string that produced it, and that intervals between harmonious sound frequencies formed simple numerical ratios. By applying this insight to everything from human emotions to the movement of the planets, he created a holistic vision of a musical universe where opposites were constantly striving towards harmony. The underlying order, the secret 'music of the spheres', was the mathematically determinable series of notes each planet made as they orbited the Earth.

Born on the island of Samos in the Dodecanese archipelago, he spent time in both Egypt and Persia studying with priests and philosophers before establishing his own school in the city of Croton on the south-eastern coast of what is now Italy. Perhaps because of this breadth of experience, the scientific and the mystical are indivisible in the Pythagorean world view. The school he founded became more of a cult, or at the very least a monastic community. As well as the dedication to mathematics and music (different songs, in different keys, would start and end each day), there was a very strict behavioural code. There were no personal possessions, the diet was strictly vegetarian, everyone worked on their theories communally, everyone did gymnastics, and all of it was underpinned by the belief that the soul was immortal and would be reincarnated in another form upon death. There are striking parallels in this philosophy with that of Pythagoras' exact contemporary, Gautama Buddha (about 563–about 480 BC), and some historians think Pythagoras might even have reached India.

But as with many cults, secrecy breeds suspicion. This wasn't helped by his followers claiming that Pythagoras had special powers: he had a thigh made of gold and could be in two places at once. They also said he could tell the future, bite snakes to death, and that a river once spoke to him. The movement's rules became more eccentric: never urinate towards the Sun, never marry a woman who wears gold, never pass an ass lying in the street, never eat beans. Eventually this esoteric aloofness brought the sect into conflict with the local people of Croton and the school was attacked and burned to the ground, killing many of Pythagoras' pupils. No one knows whether Pythagoras survived the attack, but one account has him escaping to the nearby town of Metapontum, where he starved himself to death.

Despite this, Pythagoras' influence is still felt today across many disciplines, including mathematics. And whether he actually produced his theorem or not, we now have 350 different ways of proving he was right.

Fill in the blank: 'The Man in the __ Mask'

The answer is 'velvet'.

The 'man in the iron mask' was a political prisoner in France under Louis XIV. No one is quite certain who he was, but his mask was made of velvet. Only after he died did people start the myth that he wore an iron one.

He was imprisoned in 1681 and died in the Bastille 22 years later. There are many theories as to who he was: an English nobleman, one of the king's sons, or – according to Voltaire and Alexandre Dumas – the king's elder brother. In the 1998 movie starring Leonardo DiCaprio, he is Louis XIV's identical twin. The most likely candidate is a valet called Eustache Dauger. It's not known what crime he committed (if any), but we do know that he was the servant of another prisoner, Nicolas Fouquet, once Louis XIV's superintendent of finances and court favourite. Fouquet was imprisoned for embezzling and it's possible that Dauger was imprisoned with him so he wouldn't reveal Fouquet's secrets and embarrass the king.

Many years after the mysterious prisoner is supposed to have died, Voltaire claimed to have met him while he too was imprisoned in the Bastille in 1717. He reported that the prisoner's mask was made of iron and was 'riveted on', and that it had a hinge so he could eat while wearing it. There's no evidence for this: the one genuine eyewitness account is the diary of Etienne de Junca, the deputy of the Bastille at the time, who stated the mask was made of black velvet.

Another story went that the prisoner had two soldiers constantly by his side, ready to shoot him if his mask ever came off. This wasn't true either. Nor was he kept in solitary confinement: he was allowed to go to Mass on Sundays, but only if he wore the mask. Unless new evidence is unearthed, the mystery of his identity is unlikely ever to be solved.

There was a 'man in the iron mask' who wore an actual iron mask and whose name we do know. He was an Edwardian called Harry Bensley, who in 1908 wagered £21,000 that he could circumnavigate the globe without showing his face. According to the terms of the bet, he had to wear an iron mask, take no luggage except a change of underwear, push a pram at all times and pay his way by selling postcards. Bensley claimed to have got through almost all the world's countries when the First World War broke out and he had to abandon the trip. Unfortunately, there's no evidence of him actually leaving Britain, so the odds are that this too is just a good story.

Which of the following is true of corrugated iron?

a) It's corrugated iron
b) It's not corrugated iron
c) It's corrugated but not iron
d) It's neither corrugated nor iron

It's c). Corrugated iron hasn't been made of iron since the 1890s. Since then it's been made of steel – 'galvanised mild steel', to be precise.

Steel is iron that has been purified and had carbon added to make it stronger: the less carbon, the 'milder' the steel. Iron ore, coke and limestone are heated to a very high temperature and blasted with hot air – hence the name 'blast furnace'. To make stainless steel, chrome is added. Chemical reactions cause the molten metal to trickle to the bottom and the impurities to float to the top as slag. Galvanised steel is finished steel that has been dipped in molten zinc to give it a scratch- and rust-resistant finish. So what we still call 'corrugated iron' is made of two metals, neither of which is actually iron.

Galvanisation originally used electricity and was named after the eighteenth-century Italian scientist Luigi Galvani, who used an electrical current to make dead frogs' legs twitch. Corrugated iron was invented in 1829 by Henry Robinson Palmer (1795–

1844), who also invented the monorail. Trained by Thomas Telford, he had worked with Brunel and was resident engineer at the rapidly expanding London Docks. Corrugated iron was his inspired solution to the need to erect large sheds and warehouses quickly. He named it 'corrugated' from the Latin *ruga*, a 'wrinkle', but soon sold the patent, unaware that his invention would revolutionise construction across the globe. By the end of the twentieth century more people lived under corrugated iron than any other building material.

Corrugated iron is cheap, strong, light, long-lasting, easy to transport and to recycle. You don't need much skill to use it and the corrugations make the sheets much stronger in one direction but easy to bend in the other. By the 1840s, not just roofs but whole buildings were being made of the stuff. Many were pre-fabricated and could be bought by mail order. You could have corrugated iron stables, gymnasia, hunting lodges, billiard rooms and laundries. In 1890 the catalogue of David Rowell & Co. was offering a cricket pavilion for £63.50 (£6,000 today), a two-storey cottage for £166 (£16,000 today) or a theatre for £695 (£67,000 today). Corrugated iron churches (or 'tin tabernacles') sprang up all over the British Empire: several are still in use as listed buildings today. The craze reached its height in 1851, when Prince Albert ordered a corrugated iron ballroom for Balmoral Castle. It's still there, now used as a carpenter's workshop.

It wasn't universally popular. William Morris, founder of the Arts and Crafts Movement, wrote that it was spreading 'like pestilence over the country', and some bishops were reluctant to consecrate iron churches. But the critics were in a minority. The Australian and Californian gold rushes were made possible by corrugated iron, and things really took off with its enthusiastic adoption by the military. The engineer and soldier Peter Nissen (1871–1930) invented his eponymous hut in 1916, and by the end of the First World War over 100,000 had been built. In the Second World War millions of British people sheltered in the 200,000 Anderson air-raid shelters assembled in back gardens.

Humble corrugated iron may not be iron any more, but it remains one of the cleverest, most practical inventions of this or any age.

STEPHEN *Why does your body need iron?*
ALAN *Because otherwise it'll go all floppy and wobbly.*

What happens if you hit a diamond with a hammer?

It will shatter.

Diamond is one of the hardest natural materials known to man. But to avoid shattering, a material needs to be tough rather than hard. 'Hardness' simply means something that can't be scratched; toughness is the ability to absorb shocks without breaking. A diamond's lack of toughness means it can easily break along one of its 'cleavage planes'. Cleavage is the splitting of a crystal in the direction of its faces where the atoms have weaker bonding. A diamond has four cleavage planes: if you hit it with a hammer, it will shatter into shards along those planes. A skilled cutter uses this same characteristic to create the beautiful facets of a cut and polished gemstone.

During diamond rushes, like the one at Kimberley in South Africa in 1871, unscrupulous traders exploited the confusion between 'hard' and 'tough'. They would 'test' diamonds that the miners had brought them with a hammer – when they smashed, they would say it couldn't have been a real diamond, but they'd offer to buy the splinters for a small price anyway.

Hardness is measured by the Mohs scale: if one mineral can scratch another then it has a higher Mohs rating. The scale is named after the nineteenth-century German mineralogist Friedrich Mohs, but the idea of scratching two minerals against each other to determine their hardness was first described by the ancient Greek philosopher Theophrastus (about 371–about 287 BC) in his work *On Stones*.

Diamond has always been the mineral against which all others are tested. Because of its structure, where each carbon atom shares four strong bonds with its neighbours, diamond is the best naturally occurring conductor of heat but the worst conductor of electricity. It's also the most transparent naturally occurring material and one of the least compressible.

For a long time diamond was the hardest known natural substance (it scores a perfect 10 on the Mohs scale). Then in 2009 researchers at Shanghai University found that a material called 'lonsdaleite' was even harder. Only tiny amounts have ever existed – it is created when the heat and pressure of entering Earth's atmosphere transforms the graphite in meteorites into a diamond-like crystal that still has graphite's hexagonal structure. This makes it denser and up to 58 per cent harder than diamond. It's named after Kathleen Lonsdale (1903–71), the pioneering Irish crystallographer and pacifist.

Despite all the superlatives, the one thing diamonds aren't is 'for ever'. They can burn up when torched by specially oxygenated flames, and ultraviolet light causes them to evaporate – but very, very slowly. It would take 10 billion years (almost the age of the universe) before you'd notice any difference.

What shape is a snowflake?

The average snowflake is not six-sided. It's not even symmetrical.

The next time it snows, go outside and try to find a six-sided flake. You'll be remarkably lucky if you do. The vast majority of snowflakes found on the ground are irregularly shaped crystals, which look nothing like the ones children make with white paper and scissors.

The first person to research the shape of snowflakes scientifically was the German astronomer Johannes Kepler (1571–1630). In 1611, two years after publishing the laws that govern the movement of the planets, he wrote *On the Six-cornered Snowflake*, which he hoped would provide him with funds to buy a Christmas present for a friend.

Kepler's essay, which also looked at the shapes of beehives and pomegranates, didn't quite manage to explain how snowflakes are made. But it did contain an important mathematical statement, the 'Kepler Conjecture', which states that the most efficient way of packing spheres is in a pyramid. Greengrocers have always stacked oranges this way, so it may seem obvious but four centuries later Kepler's conjecture has still not been proven.

The reason Kepler couldn't explain the shape of snowflakes was because he didn't know about the chemical structure of water, which wasn't discovered for another 70 years. The two hydrogen atoms and single oxygen atom of a water molecule always attach to each other at a very specific angle: when these molecules freeze together into a lattice, they form regular hexagons.

This makes it sound as if snowflakes should all be this shape. In fact, there are 35 basic shapes of snowflake including needles, hollow columns, dodecahedra and even triangles. Perfect hexagons form a small minority. This dazzling variety can be explained by two facts. First, each of a flake's arms grows independently, and second, single snowflakes can melt, freeze and clump together. It's a chaotic world up there in the clouds, and perfection is hard to come by.

STEPHEN *Describe a typical snowflake.*
ALAN *They're cold, and they're made of snow.*

What happens if you shout in the mountains?

You won't start an avalanche, but you might get rescued if you're caught in one.

Noises don't usually trigger avalanches, and certainly no noise the human voice can make. In theory a sonic boom or a low-flying helicopter could set one off – but only if it's already poised to happen. In almost all cases where people cause avalanches, it's because they've ventured on to an unstable layer of compacted snow, which detaches and starts a chain reaction.

Another key factor is wind. There's a limit to how much snow any snowstorm can deposit, but a strong wind can cause it to pile up extremely quickly. The resultant huge increase in weight over a short amount of time makes the snow very unstable. Most avalanches happen 24 hours after a heavy snowfall.

There are two main types of avalanche – 'sluffs' and 'slabs'. A sluff is loose snow that gathers pace and volume as it tumbles down a steep slope; a slab is a large block of snow or ice that splits and slides off the mountainside.

The Utah Avalanche Center compares the experience of a slab avalanche to standing on a magazine as it slides off a table, except the table is 10,000 feet high and the magazine can reach speeds of 300 kilometres (186 miles) per hour. The slab shatters as it falls and slams into anything in its path with the force of solid concrete. Slabs account for 90 per cent of avalanche fatalities.

A large avalanche can deliver 230,000 cubic metres of snow, enough to cover 20 football pitches 3 metres (10 feet) deep. If you find yourself covered in loose snow it will be 70 per cent air, so you should be able to shout for help. If you are dug out quickly, you have a good chance of survival: more than 90 per cent of avalanche victims are recovered alive if rescuers reach them in the first 15 minutes.

Though shouting doesn't cause avalanches, people do. A 1996 study by the Canadian Avalanche Association showed that 83 per cent of avalanches on ski slopes were the fault of someone involved in them.

The most extreme example of people causing avalanches took place on the Italian Front in the First World War. In the three-year campaign artillery exchanges between Italian and Austro-Hungarian troops regularly triggered lethal snowfalls, causing the deaths of over 40,000 soldiers. On 'White Friday', 13 December 1916, particularly heavy bombardments set off a huge series of avalanches in the Dolomites, killing 10,000 men in a single day.

When did the First World War get its name?

In 1918.

It might seem odd to refer to anything as the 'first' before there's been a second one, but in September 1918, British journalist and soldier Charles Repington wrote in his diary that he'd had a chat with a military historian from Harvard to discuss what the war should be called. They rejected 'the War', 'the German War', 'the Great War' (which then meant the Napoleonic Wars) and settled on the 'First World War', 'to prevent the millennium folk from forgetting that the history of the world was the history of war.' To call it the 'first' would also serve as a warning against future world wars. In 1920 Repington published a book called *The First World War 1914–18*.

There had been occasional earlier mentions of the war being a 'first'. In 1914 German philosopher Ernst Haeckel wrote in an American newspaper that 'There is no doubt that the course and character of the feared "European War". . . will become the first world war in the full sense of the word.' But that's not quite the same as actually naming it 'the First World War'.

Repington's full name was Lieutenant Colonel Charles Henry Wyndham à Court Repington. A brilliant soldier, he was kicked out of the army after a sex scandal, and then became a successful war correspondent. In 1915 his piece on the disastrous Battle of Aubers Ridge hastened the collapse of Britain's last Liberal government. Repington wrote in *The Times* that 'the want of an unlimited supply of high explosives was a fatal bar to our success.' The resulting furore – known as the 'Shell Crisis' – forced Asquith to form a coalition with the Conservatives, with David Lloyd George as minister for munitions.

Most people called the First World War the Great War until 1939. When the Second World War started, people were quick to assume the worst – *Time* magazine wrote, 'World War Two began last week,' even though at that stage neither Russia nor America was involved. Some called it 'the Second Great War'. President Roosevelt called it 'the War for Survival' but it didn't catch on. Other suggestions sent to the White House from across America included the 'Fatherland War', the 'Tyrant's War', the 'European War' and the 'War of Individual Liberty'.

The so-called 'Phoney War' of 1939 (when Britain and France had declared war on Germany, but didn't deploy troops) was also nicknamed 'the Little War that Wasn't There', 'the Word War' and 'the Nervy Nazi War'.

Other oddly named wars include the War of the Two Peters, the Flower War, the Cologne War, the Beaver Wars, the Peach Tree War, the Ragamuffin War and the Pastry War. Part of the Seven Years War between Britain and France (1754–63) was known as the Fantastic War.

STEPHEN *When was the First World War first named as such?*

BILL BAILEY *Before it started.*

STEPHEN *Before it started?!*

DAVID MITCHELL *It would be an act of a pessimist to call it the First World War that early, surely.*

What happened to crime during the Second World War?

It shot up.

Between 1939 and 1945 Britain's crime rate increased by 57 per cent. This would be remarkable at any time, but during the patriotic years of the 'Blitz Spirit' it seems unimaginable.

The vast majority of Britons did pull together, and proved astonishingly resilient throughout the Blitz. But the chaos caused by the war offered golden opportunities for the few bad apples. Gangster 'Mad' Frankie Fraser called it a 'criminal's paradise', not least because, when war broke out, all prisoners with fewer than three months of their sentence to serve were released.

Blackouts meant police couldn't chase criminals and the dark nights made pickpocketing easy. Looting was a regular occurrence – there were over 4,000 cases in London between September 1940 and May 1941 – and gangs of children would invade bombed-out houses after a raid, to filch the coins out of people's gas meters.

Some people regularly pretended they'd been bombed out of their homes to qualify for the £500 compensation. One man, Walter Handy, claimed the fee 19 times in five months. Some thieves disguised their getaway cars as ambulances. Others wore stolen Air Raid Precaution wardens' helmets and armbands to fool ordinary citizens into helping them with their robberies or roped innocent passers-by into helping load up cars with stolen goods.

Con men could easily exploit the rationing system. By 1945, a staggering 114,000 people had been prosecuted for black-market activities. Doctors took bribes to pass people as unfit to serve, and disabled people rented themselves out to attend the medicals of healthy friends and relatives so they could avoid conscription.

Prostitution rocketed: one popular innuendo-laden song was called 'I've got the Deepest Shelter in Town'.

Although everyone associates the Underground with the Second World War, nearly twice as many Londoners sheltered in it during the First World War. On a single night in 1918, more than 300,000 people sheltered in Tube stations. By the Second World War, a third of Londoners had built private shelters, and most of the rest simply stayed in their homes and hoped for the best.

What was the average age of US combat troops in Vietnam?

N-n-n-n-n-not 19.

In 1985 Paul Hardcastle released the anti-war song '19', which topped the UK charts for five weeks. The song, which included bugle calls and interviews with veterans, pushed the idea that the average age of an American combat soldier in the war was 19.

Hardcastle said he'd taken the claim from the 1984 ABC documentary *Vietnam Requiem*, but that statistic never appears in it. All the sampled interviews were taken from the same documentary.

Soldiers in the Vietnam War were undoubtedly young. The average soldier in the Second

World War was 26, which is at least three years older than the average American who served in Vietnam. Figures from the Southeast Asia Combat Area Casualties Current File suggest the average age at death was between 22 and 23, so we can assume the average age of all US combatants was about the same.

In Vietnam the war is known as the Resistance War Against America. In America it's not officially considered a war at all: for legal and political reasons, the government preferred to declare it a 'conflict'. It was a disaster for the USA – 58,000 American soldiers died and over 303,000 were injured. Three-quarters of Americans now believe it was a mistake for the USA to have been involved.

The war was tortuous, and so were the negotiations to end it. In 1968 all the parties got together in Paris. Eight months later all they had agreed on was the seating arrangement. The USA wanted people on two sides; the Communists wanted them on four. Then the North Vietnamese wanted a round table, to allow the Viet Cong (or National Front for the Liberation of South Vietnam) to be treated equally. The South Vietnamese demanded a square one so the two national governments could sit opposite each other. The eventual compromise was two rectangular tables, with a round table between them in the middle.

The Paris Peace Accords were finally signed in 1973, guaranteeing a swift withdrawal of US troops but ongoing aid and air support for the South. Henry Kissinger won the Nobel Peace Prize for his role, but his North Vietnamese counterpart Le Duc Tho, who was awarded the prize jointly, refused to accept it. In fact the award was premature: the war dragged on for two more years until the fall of Saigon on 30 April 1975, after the US Congress refused to sanction any more military assistance. Communist victories in Cambodia and Laos followed.

The song '19' reached number one in 13 countries, selling

4 million copies worldwide. Paul Hardcastle's collaborator Simon Fuller, creator of *Pop Idol* and manager of the Spice Girls and S Club 7, named his company 19 Entertainment after it. Hardcastle's next single, 'Just for Money', about the Great Train Robbery and the St Valentines Day Massacre did less well. Coincidentally, it peaked in the UK singles chart at number 19.

Which country's national anthem is 'The Land of the Free'?

Belize.

Belize is a tiny Central American nation – the smallest on the American mainland. It sits on the east coast, wedged between Mexico, Guatemala and the Caribbean. Its population is 330,000 – about the same as Leicester.

The national anthem of Belize is called 'The Land of the Free'. If it sounds familiar it's because it's the penultimate phrase of the American national anthem ('O'er the land of the free and the home of the brave'), whose official title is 'The Star-spangled Banner'.

The author of 'The Star-spangled Banner' was an American lawyer and poet called Francis Scott Key (1779–1843). He first jotted it down on the back of a letter during the War of 1812, inspired by an American flag still flying over Fort McHenry in Baltimore after a bombardment by the British. Originally called 'Defence of Fort M'Henry' and set to the tune of an English drinking song, it wasn't adopted as the national anthem for 117 years. By that time Key was already famous. His distant cousin F. Scott Fitzgerald was named in his honour: the novelist's full name was Francis Scott Key Fitzgerald. It's just as well Key's song was picked rather than other patriotic songs of the War of 1812, like 'Kidnapped Seamen', 'Huzza, for the American Tars' and 'Hull and Victory'.

The War of 1812 was the first time the USA had declared war on another nation. It was widely seen as a 'Second War of Independence'. It lasted 2½ years and at times was a close run thing – the British burned down the White House in 1814 – but the Americans eventually won and this initiated a period of intense nationalism known as 'the Era of Good Feelings'. It is now a largely forgotten conflict in Britain and America, but is still spoken of with pride in Canada, where the Canadian militia saw off several invasion attempts by the Americans.

Belize is the only country to have people on its national flag – it features two woodcutters, symbolising the national logging industry. Spanish is the most widely spoken language but not the official one, which is English. It was the last British colony on the American mainland, and known as British Honduras. It's still a member of the Commonwealth with the Queen as head of state.

Belize is a beautiful place, with a pristine rainforest, a huge barrier reef and the world's only jaguar reserve. It has several animals found nowhere else on the planet, including the Belize gemmed satyr (a butterfly), the mountain molly (a fish), the orangeflag blenny (a fish) and the Mayan knobtail (a dragonfly).

STEPHEN *'O say can you see by the dawn's early light, etc., etc.'*
Who wrote that?
ALAN *Jay-Z.*

What were the inhabitants of Mexico called before the Europeans arrived?

Not the Aztecs.

The people we call 'Aztecs' called themselves Mexica (pronounced 'Mé-shee-ka'). To the Mexica, 'Aztecs' were the inhabitants of their ancestral home of Aztlan in the north of the country, which they had left three centuries earlier. (Calling the Mexica 'Aztecs' is a bit like calling the Germans 'Prussians'). After years of wandering the Aztecs arrived at a great valley over 7,000 feet up, ringed by volcanoes and studded with lakes and marshes. They had been guided there by their great war god Huitzilopochtli, who revealed to them that they should build at a place marked by an eagle, holding a snake, perched on top of a cactus (this image still forms the centre of Mexico's coat of arms).

Unfortunately, the fulfilment of this rather precise prophecy led them to the middle of a marshy lake called Texcoco. Undeterred, the former nomads began to build one of the great cities of the world: Tenochtitlan, 'place of the fruit of the prickly pear cactus'. That was in 1325 and, within a century, its population had grown to more than 250,000, four times the size of London at the time. In 1521 it fell to the Spanish, and by 1585 was known as Ciudad de México (Mexico City), the name it still bears.

The Mexica took their name from the Mexihco valley, but the word's ultimate origin is uncertain. It may come from Mextli, a secret name for Huitzilopochtli; or from *metztli* ('moon') and *xictli* ('navel') because the city was at the centre of a set of connected lakes that formed the shape of a rabbit. Where we see a 'man' in the Moon, the Mexica saw a rabbit.

There are still Mexica in Mexico today. They are known as the Nahua and there are about 2.5 million of them: about a tenth of the population of Mexico at the time of the Spanish conquest. English words of Nahuatl origin include 'avocado', 'chili', 'chocolate', 'coyote', 'axolotl', 'tequila' and 'tomato'. In 2008 Nahuatl was made compulsory at schools in Mexico City, in an attempt to preserve the indigenous culture.

Until recently, historians assumed the majority of the Mexica were either killed by conquistadors or wiped out by newly introduced European diseases. But, while smallpox brought by the Spanish did kill around 5 million people three decades after they arrived, even worse epidemics of a mysterious disease took the lives of a further 17 million Mexica.

The disease was called *cocoliztli*, Nahuatl for 'pest', so it could be anything.

But the symptoms of raging fever, delirium and blood flowing from the ears don't sound like any European disease of the time. It is now thought to have been a haemorrhagic fever virus similar to Ebola but indigenous to Mexico. While contact with Europe undoubtedly destroyed their culture, it may be that the Mexica would have been decimated with or without the Spanish invasion.

Name the first great civilisation to mummify its dead

It wasn't the Egyptians.

The ancient Egyptians did mummify their dead, but they weren't the first to do so. A group of prehistoric coastal hunter-gatherers from Chile and Peru called the Chinchorro were making mummies in 5000 BC – over a thousand years before the earliest Egyptian attempts.

In Chinchorro society everyone was properly mummified;

in Egypt it was reserved for the wealthy and powerful. The Chinchorro removed the organs and replaced them with a paste made of ash, water and sea-lion blood. The same paste was used to make a mask (and a model of the sexual organs) before the whole corpse was painted black, polished until shiny, and adorned with a wig made from human hair.

Archaeologists have now recovered 149 Chinchorro mummies and studying them has revealed much about their lifestyle. Life expectancy was about 25 years – which is longer than that of most prehistoric peoples – perhaps because of their healthy diet of seafood and vegetables. This meant they had more time to spend on the elaborate ritual of honouring their dead by mummification. It's likely that the practice started because the surrounding landscape is so dry that almost anything that dies ends up in a semi-mummified state instead of decomposing. The Chinchorro mummies lasted for seven millennia but are now falling victim to climate change. As the region becomes more humid, bacteria are slowly turning them to black ooze – hence the word 'mummy', which comes from the Persian *mummiya*, meaning 'bitumen'.

Roman troops from North Africa brought the knowledge of mummification with them to Britain. The northernmost mummies, dating from about AD 300, were discovered in Barnsley. In the intervening centuries mummies haven't always been treated with proper respect. They've been recycled as fertiliser, rag fibre for newsprint, bruise powder and even a popular paint called 'Mummy Brown'.

But the Victorians were obsessed with them. Public unrollings were festive occasions with speeches by Egyptologists to set the scene and brass bands playing. They didn't always go smoothly: in Boston in 1850 Egyptologist George Glidden unwrapped a 'princess' who turned out to have a penis.

Where would you find the world's largest pyramid?

Mexico.

The great pyramid of Khufu at Giza in Egypt is the world's tallest pyramid but, by volume, the world's largest pyramid is in Mexico. The Cholula pyramid was built in AD 100 from sun-dried brick and earth. Although it's only 177 feet high – less than half the height of the tallest Egyptian pyramid – its volume is more than 141 million cubic feet, 25 per cent larger than any pyramid in Egypt.

According to legend, the Cholula pyramid was built by a giant named Xelhua, and used by Quetzalcoatl, the god of air, as a place to shelter from the wrath of the other gods (Cholula derives from a Nahuatl word meaning 'place of refuge'). Archaeologists have found that its size and shape evolved over centuries and that it performed many different roles: as a temple to a rain god, a shrine to the god of commerce, and finally a place to worship Quetzalcoatl in the years immediately preceding the arrival of the conquistadors.

When the Spanish arrived, they built a church on top of it, and made it a destination for Catholic pilgrims. The pyramid itself is now completely overgrown and looks like an unusually symmetrical hill. Latin-American pyramids are still being discovered – a new one was found near Mexico City in 2006. Unfortunately, they're still being destroyed too: in Belize in 2013, a road-building crew accidentally demolished one of the country's largest pyramids while looking for gravel to use as road filler.

The widely held belief that the Egyptian pyramids were built by slaves is not true – most were paid labourers, respected enough to be buried near the pyramids themselves. Pyramids are much more widespread than was once thought. As well as Egypt and Mexico, they can be found in Spain, China, Nigeria,

Peru, India, Indonesia and Sudan. There are nearly twice as many pyramids in Sudan as in Egypt, many of them built by the ancient Nubian Kingdom of Kush, which flourished for 1,200 years until conquered by the Ethiopians in AD 350. Kushite pyramids are much smaller than Egyptian ones – ranging from 20 to 100 feet in height.

In 2005 a new candidate for the world's largest pyramid emerged. Bosnian businessman Semir Osmanagic nominated the 650-foot Visocica Hill in the centre of Bosnia-Herzegovina, and he set up a charity to fund the research to prove it. In 2011 he mounted an international dig 'to break a cloud of negative energy, allowing the Earth to receive cosmic energy from the centre of the galaxy'. However, several archaeologists he claims worked on it said they never agreed to participate and never visited the site. A leading 'Oxford archaeologist' referred to by Osmanagic turned out to be an undergraduate.

Mark Rose, editor of the magazine *Archaeology*, dismissed Osmanagic's claims as nonsense. 'If it were true,' he wrote, 'it would be the equivalent of finding a 747 airliner in a Roman period site . . . It doesn't take a trip to Bosnia to know this is not going to happen.'

How did Vikings bury their dead?

There's no evidence that Vikings disposed of their dead by pushing them out to sea in blazing funeral ships.

The Up Helly Aa festival in Shetland stages Viking sea cremations each year. But, according to Gareth Williams, curator of the Viking collection at the British Museum, these date no further back than the late nineteenth century and make no claim to historical accuracy. The only known Norse reference to one concerns the god Baldur, but that was a mythical event not an actual funeral.

Prominent Vikings did have ship burials, but they happened on land and the vessel wasn't burned. The body was put aboard along with ritual offerings – sometimes including sacrificed slaves – and the whole ship was buried. Many of the Viking longships that survive today were preserved this way and were uncovered when the burial sites were excavated. The first complete boat burial site on British soil was found in the Scottish Highlands in 2011. In it was the thousand-year-old body of a chieftain with a shield on his chest and a sword and spear by his side.

In Old Norse a *víking* was a raiding expedition and a *víkingr* was someone who took part in one. But the word 'Viking' wasn't used in English until the early nineteenth century, following the translation of *Frithiof's Saga* from Swedish in 1825. Until then Vikings were 'Danes' or 'Norsemen'.

The Vikings came from Scandinavia, but they went everywhere. Between AD 800 and 1050 their territories stretched from the Middle East to Canada. The men were heavily tattooed, with piercings, patterns filed into their teeth, eye make-up and

flamboyant clothing. They took personal hygiene very seriously, bathing at least once a week – more often than their foreign contemporaries. Excavations of Viking sites have turned up tweezers, razors, combs and ear cleaners made from animal bones and antlers.

The first European to reach America was a Viking: Leif Eriksson landed there 500 years before Columbus. He and his crew named it Vinland – 'Wineland' – after the wild grapes they found, but left after ten years due to tension with Native American tribes.

The first European to see America was another Norseman, Bjarni Herjolfsson, but he didn't land there. His story is told in *Grænlendinga*, the oldest and most reliable of the Norse sagas. Attempting to sail from Iceland to Greenland, he was blown off course. He sighted land three times, but none of the shorelines matched what he'd been told to expect of Greenland, so he kept on sailing, reaching his destination on the fourth attempt. His descriptions of the land he saw on the first three occasions exactly match the North American coastline. It was his reports of this strange coast that inspired Leif Eriksson's expedition.

By the middle of the eleventh century the Viking age was over. As Scandinavia adopted Christianity and settled into the kingdoms of Denmark, Norway and Sweden, raiding tailed off. The lucrative trade with the Islamic world had fallen sharply as a result of the rise of the Khazar Empire, which occupied the land between the Black and Caspian seas, cutting off Viking trade routes to Byzantium and Baghdad. But Viking culture didn't disappear overnight. The Normans were a Viking colony in northern France (the Bayeux tapestry clearly shows they invaded Britain in 'Viking' ships). And the king of Norway colonised Scotland until the mid-thirteenth century – and the Western Isles until 1469.

The Vikings gave us the English words anger, birth, cake, dirt, freckles, hell, ugly, weak, husband, wife, skill, skull and slaughter. And the official English medical term for a hangover is 'veisalgia', which derives from *kveis*, the Old Norse word meaning 'uneasiness after debauchery'.

What can you legally do if you come across a Welshman in Chester after sunset?

Put away that bow and arrow . . .

The website of the Law Commission, the independent watchdog of UK law, clearly states, 'It is illegal to shoot a Welsh or Scottish (or any other) person regardless of the day, location or choice of weaponry.'

The Welshman in Chester myth is just one of hundreds of so-called 'dumb laws' that infest the Internet, most of which are nonsense. Another is that London black cabs have to carry a bale of hay for a no longer existent horse (they don't) or that it's illegal to die in Parliament (it isn't). However, it is still illegal, under the Statute Forbidding Bearing of Armour 1313, to enter the Houses of Parliament in a suit of armour, so don't risk it.

That's not to say that none of these laws were ever true; the 'shooting a Welshman' one was, at least partly. It dates back to 1403 when Henry, Prince of Wales (the future Henry V) was Earl of Chester and facing a rebellion from supporters of the Welsh hero Owen Glyndwr. After one uprising, he imposed a curfew on any Welshmen living in the city, stating that none should enter the walls of Chester before sunrise or stay after sunset, on pain of decapitation.

According to dumb law proponents, this law was never

repealed. But a law doesn't have to be specifically repealed to stop being the law. There's a legal maxim known as *lex posterior derogat priori* (literally, 'a later law repeals an earlier one') which ensures that when a new law is introduced, it is presumed to overrule any earlier legislation on the subject. Killing people (even Welshmen) is illegal under the Homicide Act 1957, as well as Article 2 of the European Convention on Human Rights on the right to life. These apply to Chester, just the same as everywhere else.

In 2013 the Law Commission shepherded the Statute Law (Repeals) Act through Parliament to purge the legal system of more than 800 antiquated laws. One such law allowed French refugees to own land worth no more than £500 in London, while another said forgers should be transported to Australia. But some ancient laws can create trouble if they aren't dealt with. In the 1970s an estimated 50,000 squatters occupied properties in London by exploiting the Forcible Entry Act of 1381, which prevented the legal owners from reclaiming their property by force. It was repealed by the Criminal Law Act of 1977, which made it a criminal offence for a squatter not to leave a property if asked to do so by the legal owner or resident.

What landmark formed the northern boundary of Roman Britain?

It's not Hadrian's Wall.

Nor (for the clever-clogs among you) is it the Antonine Wall, 100 miles north of Hadrian's Wall, and the answer to a popular trick question in pub quizzes. The actual answer is the Gask Ridge, a line of forts and watchtowers that lies even further

north, running between Perth and Dunblane.

Built between AD 70 and 80, 40 years before Hadrian's Wall and more than 50 years before work started on the Antonine, the Gask Ridge was Rome's first fortified land frontier. The two walls are much further south and much shorter than the ridge, to take advantage of Scotland's narrow 'neck'.

At 73 miles long Hadrian's Wall is the longest continuous wall the Romans ever built, but it took 15,000 men just six years. The most impressive parts of it were well defended, with a 15-foot wall and a deep ditch on the north side. But nobody knows what it was for. The only ancient source to mention it, the *Augustan History*, claims it was to separate northern barbarians from civilised southerners, but that theory doesn't fit the evidence.

First, a third of it was barely a wall – more of an earthen bank that wouldn't keep out the average ten-year-old. Second, there is very little evidence anyone ever tried to breach it. Third, important bits of Roman infrastructure like aqueducts were built north of it, implying that the Romans were confident they controlled the land beyond the Wall too. And it seems like the southern side wasn't particularly 'civilised' – there was another huge ditch there as well, suggesting there were security problems in both directions.

So what was it for? The practical answer is that it was probably a customs frontier, and anyone trying to pass it would have had to pay tax. With a cart full of goods, even the earthen bank would have been hard to cross.

Hadrian also built the wall as a symbol of Rome's power. He'd recently become emperor and one of his first acts was to pull his armies out of what is now Iraq. Some things never change. A large stone wall at least gave the impression that he was still in control of the empire's boundaries. Hadrian himself never saw the wall finished. He only visited Britain once, in AD 122, several years before it was completed.

At its peak Hadrian's Wall was patrolled by 9,000 men. They came from all over the Empire, including modern-day Belgium, Austria, Germany, Spain, Croatia and Algeria. At the mouth of the Tyne there was even a group of Iraqis – the last and only time Iraqi troops occupied Britain. After the Romans left, generations of locals and military road builders used the wall as a quarry, which explains why there's so little of it left today. The sections you can walk along were probably 'rebuilt', for romantic reasons, by Victorian antiquarians.

ROB BRYDON *You know, there is a map; there is a map which shows not just Hadrian's Wall, but you see Hadrian's conservatory, and Hadrian's water feature.*

STEPHEN *Yes. Carlisle is in a sense Hadrian's sliding patio door, isn't it?*

What's the nearest Third World country to the UK?

The Republic of Ireland.

French historian Alfred Sauvy coined the term the 'Third World' in 1952. But he didn't intend it to refer to what we would now call 'developing nations', only to those countries that were neutral in the Cold War. The 'First World' was the group of countries that sided with the capitalist USA; the 'Second World' was the satellites and allies of the communist Soviet Union. The 'Third World' was everyone else. It was an echo of the structure of Revolutionary France, where the First Estate was the nobility, the Second Estate the clergy and the Third Estate the people, the emergent power that had previously been overlooked.

Gradually, through the 1960s, the phrase 'Third World country' came to mean a poor one. But, according to its strict technical meaning of non-alignment, the nearest 'Third World' country to Britain is Ireland. By the same definition, other 'Third World' countries include Sweden, Finland and Switzerland.

Ireland's decision to stay neutral in the Cold War was partly due to the issue of Northern Ireland. Because of its differences with Britain, Ireland did not feel able to become a member of NATO. It did try to arrange a separate pact with the USA but this was never ratified, so it remained officially non-aligned.

Today there is also a 'Fourth World', comprising ethnic groups and indigenous peoples who are stateless, like the Kurds and Romanies. According to the Center for World Indigenous Studies, there are now more than 5,000 'Fourth World' nations, which together make up a third of the world's population.

STEPHEN *It's only more recently that it became a term meaning poverty. And nowadays, of course, it's not a politically correct word to use anyway. We don't say a Third World country, we say . . . ?*
ALAN *We say a vibrant tourist destination.*

What's the world's most overweight country?

Nauru.

Nauru is a tiny South Pacific island. The 10,000 people there have an average Body Mass Index of 34 to 35 (the healthy BMI range is 18 to 25). Almost 80 per cent of adults there are not just overweight but obese.

Pacific Island nations occupy most of the top spots in global obesity rankings; others often in the top ten include the Cook Islands, Tonga, Micronesia, Palau, Niue and Samoa. (Figures vary: another contender for the prize of 'most overweight' is American Samoa, where one airline has started charging passengers by weight.) All these islanders live mostly on imported foods, which have replaced the traditional, much healthier diet of fish, coconuts and root vegetables.

Nauruans are unhappy with the 'most overweight' label, saying they're genetically stocky and muscular (indeed, the island has produced lots of weightlifting champions). But although precise definitions of 'obesity' differ, the island definitely has a health problem, also topping the world list for diabetes. In the 55 to 64 age group diabetes rates are running at 45 per cent.

Nauru is tiny: you can drive around it in 20 minutes. Only the Vatican and Monaco are smaller. It doesn't even have a capital city.

In the 1970s and 1980s the country had the world's highest Gross National Product per head of population. Education, healthcare and housing were all free; the police chief bought himself a yellow Lamborghini and presidents had their suits flown almost 3,000 miles to Melbourne to be dry-cleaned.

The source of this amazing wealth was bird shit. Over millennia hundreds of thousands of migrating birds had visited the island to eat, and left their guano behind. Gradually it built up into a rocky landmass covered in tropical forest. When it was discovered that the guano-rock was full of phosphate – an incredibly powerful fertiliser – the Nauruans started mining.

Several decades of frantic excavation later, Nauru is a wasteland: the interior is largely uninhabitable and almost everyone lives on the edge. There is little phosphate left, and the island's wealth was poorly invested (including the disastrous bankrolling of a West End musical, *Leonardo: A Portrait of Love*).

Now climate change means the sea levels are rising and the future for Nauru looks very uncertain indeed.

Which country has the most time zones?

France.

You might expect it to be the USA, Russia or Canada, but it's France because its far-flung overseas territories are all legally part of the French mainland.

The world's clocks are set according to Coordinated Universal Time (UTC). The 12 French time zones stretch right around the world, from UTC minus 10 hours in French Polynesia to UTC plus 12 in the Wallis and Futura Islands.

The full list is as follows: French Polynesia (UTC –10 hours), the Marquesas Islands (UTC –9 ½ hours), the Gambier Islands (UTC –9 hours), Clipperton Island (UTC –8 hours), Guadeloupe, Martinique, St Barthelemy and St Martin (UTC –4 hours), French Guiana and Saint-Pierre and Miquelon (UTC –3 hours), French Metropolitan time (UTC +1 hour), Mayotte (UTC +3 hours), Reunion (UTC +4 hours), the Kerguelen Islands (UTC +5 hours), New Caledonia (UTC +11 hours) and finally the Wallis and Futuna Islands (UTC +12 hours).

The USA has nine time zones. As well as Pacific, Mountain, Central and Eastern times on the US mainland, it has Alaska time, Hawaii time and zones that cover its possessions in the Pacific: American Samoa, Guam and the US Virgin Islands. Canada stretches over six time zones and Russia 11, but it's on the French empire that the sun nowadays never sets.

It's still true that the sun never sets on the British Empire – but only just. The UK currently covers nine time zones. The most easterly is the British Indian Ocean Territory, a collection of atolls midway between Indonesia and Tanzania and home to the Diego Garcia military base. It is six hours ahead of the UK. The most westerly is the Pitcairn Islands, and it's thanks to these four tiny volcanic islands in the Pacific, inhabited by descendants of the mutineers from the *Bounty*, that the British can still make this claim. When the sun sets on the Cayman Islands in the western Caribbean, it's 13 hours before it rises on the British Indian Ocean Territory. But on Pitcairn it's still daylight.

The first person to use the phrase about the British Empire was the statesman and diplomat George Macartney (1737–1806). He wrote of a 'vast Empire, on which the sun never sets' after Britain had massively increased its overseas territories by defeating France and her allies in the Seven Years War (1754–63). Macartney made his remark in 1773, but variants of the phrase (about different empires) go back to Herodotus and the ancient Greeks.

Long before Britain took the title, the empire on which the sun never set was the Spanish Empire. During the time of Philip I and Philip II, Spain owned territories in South America, Africa, Asia and throughout the Pacific and Atlantic oceans. Over the years almost all of these were lost, or gained independence.

Today Spain covers only two time zones: mainland Spain and the Canary Islands. The Sun sets on today's Spanish Empire just one hour after it sets on Madrid.

When was 'time immemorial'?

6 July 1189.

Far from being a phrase referring to a vague period of history, 'time immemorial' is a specific legal term that originally referred to this date.

It was the first day of the reign of Richard I. The First Statute of Westminster in 1275 defined the beginning of his reign as 'the limit of legal memory'. In other words, if you had enjoyed a custom or practice (such as grazing your cattle on a piece of land) since before that date, it remained legal and you wouldn't have to go through re-establishing your right to it.

In 1832 the law was changed and time immemorial was redefined as 'time whereof the memory of man runneth not to the contrary'. These days, you don't have to prove that your rights date back to 1189 – only back 20 years (or 30 years if you're competing for them against the Crown).

Richard I, the Lionheart (1159–99), was one of Britain's most ferociously warlike kings. At the age of 16, he and his brothers led an army against their own father, Henry II, and they were at war (again) when Richard became king.

He spent only six months of his ten-year reign in England, and almost all the rest in France, with occasional jaunts to the Middle East. We don't even know whether he spoke English (neither of his parents did) though he certainly spoke French and Occitan. He raised the money for a crusade by selling official positions, and reportedly said, 'I would sell London if I could find a buyer.'

Since the 1950s it has been suggested that, because he ignored his wife and had no children, Richard was homosexual. He was very close to Philip II of France – they definitely spent one night in bed together, although historians claim this was nothing more than a PR stunt to display their friendship.

Shortly before Richard died of gangrene in 1199, he bequeathed his body to three different places – none of them in England – with the words, 'My corpse will be buried in Fontevrault, my heart in Rouen, and my bowels will stay in Chalus.' And that's what happened. His heart was rediscovered in 1838 during excavations in Rouen Cathedral. It was in a box with a Latin label that read, 'Here is the heart of Richard, King of England.' Recent analysis shows it had been embalmed with daisy, mint, frankincense, creosote and mercury.

How long is an epoch?

Anywhere from a fraction of a second to millions of years.

The word 'epoch' has two meanings. The original (and these days, rarer) one is 'a single point in time that begins a certain era'. For instance, the birth of Christ is the epoch that begins the Gregorian calendar.

Today most people use the word epoch to describe a period of time, although how long they last differs between disciplines. Geological epochs usually last for tens of millions of years. We are currently living close to the beginning of the Holocene epoch, which began around 11,000 years ago. Its name comes from the Greek *holos* ('whole') and *kainos* ('new'), meaning 'entirely recent'.

Even longer than an epoch is an 'era', which lasts several hundred million years. Longer still is an 'eon', of which there have been only four, each lasting half a billion years or more. On top of eons, we have supereons. There have been only two of those: the Precambrian, which encompasses the first 80 per cent of the time that Earth has existed, and the Phanerozoic, which is the last 20 per cent, and named for the abundance of life (it's from the Greek for 'visible animals').

Astronomers also organise their history into epochs, but an astronomical epoch can be much shorter. The first one, the Planck epoch, is the shortest: it lasted 0.000000000000000000 000000000000000000000001 seconds.

The Planck epoch wasn't just short: it lasted for the smallest amount of time possible. According to modern physics, no smaller division of time makes any sense. Nobody knows what happened in this first fraction of a fraction of a second after the Big Bang. The whole universe was unimaginably small, hot and dense. Time, space, gravity and matter didn't exist, yet everything and everywhere was contained in that tiny point.

We have to wait around drumming our fingers for three or four minutes before atoms begin to form. By then, six or seven other epochs have already passed.

How fast was the Earth's fastest mass extinction?

It took an absolute minimum of 12,000 years.

The Earth has had five 'mass extinctions' in its history. The worst and fastest – the 'Great Dying' – came at the end of the Permian period, 252 million years ago when 95 per cent of all species died out. But it was a slow process, taking between 12,000 and 108,000 years to complete.

The Great Dying probably started with a volcano – an eruption that went on for a million years, vomiting up 1.4 million cubic miles of molten magma, and creating a plain of volcanic rock the size of western Europe. This pumped carbon dioxide into the atmosphere, overheating the planet and thawing huge frozen deposits of methane, which cranked up the temperature even further. The seas turned to acid and the world became the domain of micro-organisms that didn't need oxygen to live. Almost all other living things were wiped out – including trees, trilobites and the eurypterids, sea scorpions over 8-feet-long. It took life on Earth 10 million years to recover.

Mass extinctions take many thousands of years. They're catastrophic, but they don't wipe everything out overnight, like the climax of a disaster movie. The extinction that killed the dinosaurs, for example, took 33,000 years. The 6-mile-wide asteroid that slammed into Mexico's Yucatan peninsula wasn't the only cause: the dinosaurs were on their way out anyway. In the million years before the impact, the temperature had rapidly shifted several times. Huge volcanoes in India had been pumping up toxic fumes and warming the planet. Had the asteroid arrived a few million years later, the dinosaurs might have survived – but if they had, humans probably wouldn't have evolved.

Before scientists knew about the asteroid, some believed that small mammals had eaten all the dinosaur eggs, devastating their numbers. Other theories for their disappearance included 'wars' between the dinosaurs, or the idea of *Paläoweltschmerz* (ancient world-weariness) – that they simply got tired of life.

Today we are already in the middle of the sixth great extinction, and many scientists believe it's a man-made one. Species are dying out 1,000 times faster than they did before humans arrived. Until recently, like all the other extinctions, it's been a slow burn – 12,000 years so far. But it's speeding up: 322 species of mammal have gone extinct since 1500 and, if current rates continue, 75 per cent of mammal species may be gone in the next 300 years.

A NOTE ON SOURCES

*Nothing is more important than to see the sources of invention which
are, in my opinion, more interesting than the inventions themselves.*

This book conceals more than 2,000 discrete pieces of
information and we take great care to make sure all our facts
and observations come from reliable and accurate sources.

To verify anything in the book, go to qi.com/genig3. The
online sources also provide a wealth of additional background
detail. Please do let us know if you have a quibble or a
correction, or add your own discoveries via our Twitter account
@qikipedia.

Over the past ten years, QI has recruited a happy platoon of
fact-wranglers. Working behind the lines is the crack unit of
Anne Miller, Anna Ptaszynski and Alex Bell. They are backed
by the Great Elven supply train: Rob Blake, Will Bowen, Stevyn
Colgan, Mat Coward, Ben Dupre, Jenny Doughty, Mandy
Fenton, Piers Fletcher, Chris Gray, Molly Oldfield, Justin
Pollard, Dan Schreiber, Freddy Soames, Liz Townsend and
Richard Turner.

Each of them has contributed to the QI arsenal of research,
ideas, jokes and insights, and behind them all, acting as the
editorial exosphere, screening out the harmful rays of waffle and
repetition, stands the unflappable Sarah Lloyd.

Grateful thanks are also due to Faber & Faber, our publishers since the beginning. Stephen Page, Julian Loose, Charlotte Robertson, John Grindrod, Anne Owen, illustrator Dave Anderson, proofreader Anna Swan, indexer Jill Burrows and especially Paula Turner of Palindrome, have once again collectively redefined the meaning of 'grace under pressure'.

INDEX

Abbotsbury Swannery 185
abductive reasoning 98, 100
Abyss of Ophir 124
acacia trees 196
Accession Council 107
Adams, John 85
Addis, William 43
Addis Brush Company 43
Addison, Joseph 149
Adonis 234
Advent 52, 87, 90
Africa 7–8, 81, 137–8, 162, 170, 172, 179–80, 189, 212, 282
African Queen, The (film) 16
Afrikaans language 30
Agnes of Assisi, St 96
Aitken, John 54–5
Alaric the Goth 237
albatrosses 204–5, 208
Albert, Prince 42, 60, 107, 255
Alcatraz 207–9
alcohol 34, 77, 131, 201–2, 205, 208, 217
Aldrin, Buzz 49, 50
Alexander, Jason Allen 32
Alexander the Great 216
Alexandra, Princess 107
algae 166, 173, 193

Allahakbarries 97–8
allergies 233–4
al-Qaeda 231
Altamura 72
aluminium 49
Amazon, River 3, 7
Amazon rainforest 5–7, 175
America 3, 84, 141, 163, 173, 266–7
American Civil War 34, 89
American Declaration of Independence 85, 209
American War of Independence 47
amoebas 141
Anaya, Ignacio 18
ANCONA, RONNI 11
ANDERSON, CLIVE 79, 176
Anderson shelters 256
Andes 4, 177
Andrew, St 47
Angel, Jimmie 2
Angel Falls 1–2
Angel of the North 125
Anglo-Saxon period 109, 129
Antarctica 4, 23, 163, 166–7, 173, 212
Antonine Wall 276–7
ants 183–4, 196, 219
Aphrodite 71, 234

Apollo 11 49
Apollo 17 50
apples 25, 58
apriums 25
aquifers 3
Arabic language 97–8, 208
Aramaic language 218
Arctic 1, 4, 163, 165
Argentina 231
Arles 128
arm wrestling 131
arms 131, 185–6
Armstrong, Neil 49, 50
Asher, Jane 236
Asia 36, 74, 81–2, 95, 237, 282
Asquith, Herbert 261
Assal, Bahr al, Lake 212
Assissi 95–6
asteroids 154, 234, 286–7
Astor, Nancy 249
astronauts 179–80, 200, 240
Athena 147
Atlantic Ocean 1, 4, 174, 201, 282
atmospheric rivers 2–3
Aubers Ridge, Battle of 261
Augustus, Emperor 58
Australia 25, 68–9, 125, 137, 141, 164, 171, 192, 225, 239, 241, 255, 276

avalanches 259–60
Avicenna 235
Aztecs 74, 268
B & Bs 84
ba birds 206
Baal 219
Babylon 58, 250
backbones 190
Bacon, Francis 95
bacteria 119–20, 172–3,
    183–4, 188–9, 240
Badger Day 87
bagpipes 103
bags for life 22
baguettes 72–3
BAILEY, BILL 5, 67, 161,
    182, 262
Baja 1000 Rally 232
Bak 147
Baldur 273
baleen 158–9
Balmoral 255
Bamiyam 125
bananas 25, 54
Barbados 24–5
Barber, David 186
Barclay Allardice, Capt.
    Robert 228–9
Barlow, Thelma 236
Barnes, Marx Panama 36
Barnum, P. T. 206
barratry 202
Barrie, J. M. 96–8, 249
Bartneck, Christoph 20
Bastille 253
Bayeux tapestry 274
Beagle 202–3
bears 87
Beatrice, Princess 107
beavers 28–30
Beckham, David and
    Victoria 210

Bedford, James 200
Beene, Mr 64
Beerbohm, Max 112
bees 138–9, 195, 233
behaviourism 116
Beijing 27, 175
Belgium 241, 278
Belize 266–7, 271
Bellamy, Francis 45–6
Benedict, St 76–7
Benedict XIV, Pope
    105–6
Benedict XVI, Pope
    92–3
Benedictines 76, 220
Bensley, Harry 253–4
Berlin, Irving 90
BFF 149–50
Bible 58, 93, 95, 216–17,
    218–19
bichirs 162
Big Bang 285
Big Ben 126
biological warfare 12–14
Birdman of Alcatraz
    207–8
birth certificates 35–6
birth rates 51–2
bites 132
black market 263
Black Sea 172–3
blennies 162
Blind Man's Car Rally
    232
Blitz 248, 263
blood 13, 32, 54, 106, 142,
    143, 189, 193, 197, 200,
    203, 234, 239, 269–70
Blyton, Enid 243–4
boa constrictors 188
bobsledding 226–7
BMI 280

Boleyn, Anne 106
Bolivia 125, 233
Bollywood 11
Bonaparte, Pauline 247
Bondeson, Jan 114
Borneo 95
Bosnia-Herzegovina 272
Boswell, James 23
Bouthillier de Rancé,
    Armand Jean le 76–7
Bowler, Thomas and
    William 155
bowler hats 155
Boxing Day 87–8
Boyd, Samuel 18
brachiation 9
Braddock, Bessie 249
Braille 232
brain 40, 99, 135, 136,
    140, 199
BRAND, JO 31, 54
Brazil 1, 7, 124, 233
bread 56–7, 72–3
breakfast 22–3
breastfeeding 54
breathing 31, 55, 162–3, 191
BRIGSTOCKE, MARCUS
    3, 33
British Antarctic Survey
    167
British Empire 185, 255,
    282
British Indian Ocean
    Territory 282
British Isles 1, 157
Brooke, Frances 152
Brown, Grace 222
Brown, James 114
Brunel, Isambard
    Kingdom 255
Brunner, John 170
BRYDON, ROB 155, 278

Buckingham Palace
106–8
Buddhas 125
bulletproof custard 65
bullet-resistant glass
64–5
bullets 64–7
Burdett-Coutts, Baroness
113
Burnside, Ambrose 18
Burroughs, Edgar Rice
9–10
Bush, George W. 223
butterflies 122, 267
Byron, George Gordon,
Lord 40, 171

Caan, James 32
Cahn, Sammy 90
Caine, Michael and
Shakira 33
California 3, 89, 123, 126,
239, 242, 255
cambium 28
Cambodia 265
camels 29, 165–6
Canada 60–61, 127–8,
193, 241, 267, 273,
281–2
cancer 141, 144, 190–91
Candlemas 86–7
Candy, John 227
canyons 123–4
Captain Pugwash 100–101
capuchin monkeys 70
carbon 21, 254, 257
carbon dioxide 21, 73,
120, 286
Caribbean 24, 266
Carlisle 278
carotenoids 240–41
CARR, JIMMY 19, 27, 39,

66, 77, 144, 205
carrier pigeons 118–19
carrots 240–41
Carter, Steve 36
Carthaginian Empire 212
cartilage 190
Cassell, John 17–18
castoreum 30
Catherine of Siena, St 96
cats 117, 161, 197
cattle-branding 19
Cavallari, Arnaldo 72
Cawdrey, Richard 150
Central America 21, 127,
266
Cernan, Eugene 49
chainsaws 54–6
champagne 23
Chance, Edgar 138
Chang'e 48
Chang'e 3 48
Charles, Prince 110
Charles I, King 110
Charles II, King 71, 106
Charlotte, Queen 42
cheerleading 223–4
cheese 18, 53, 59, 146
chemical weapons 14–16
Chester 275–6
Chesterton, G. K. 97
chickens 118, 132
childbirth 54–5
Chile 231, 269
chimpanzees 139
China, 14, 26–7, 28, 33,
74, 82, 95, 97, 125,
168–9, 170, 175, 238,
271
Chinchorro 269–70
chlorine 15
chlorofluorocarbons 177
chocolate 146

Cholula pyramid 271
Chopin, Frédéric 37–8
chopines 71
chromosomes 140
Christianity 81–2, 86–7,
95–6, 105–6
Christmas 42–3, 52,
86–90, 93, 94, 131
Churchill, Winston S.
5, 15–16, 23, 148, 222,
248–9
ciabatta 72–3
Cielo, César 231
cinnamon 238, 246
Cistercians 76–7
citrus fruit 13, 24–5
clams 5
Clare of Assisi, St 96
Clarke, Jeremiah 38
CLARKSON, JEREMY 19,
64, 141
claws 134–5
Clement X, Pope 105
Cleopatra 120
Clinton, Bill 174
cloacal kiss 132
cloning 126
Club 18–30 34
coal-fired power stations
16
cobras 189
coca leaves 233
cocaine 233
Cochabamba 125
Cochran, Josephine
Garis 146
Cockerell, Christopher
144–5
cockroaches 49
coffee, 59
cognitive dissonance 40
Cold War 279

Coleridge, Samuel Taylor 204–5
COLES, RICHARD 8
Colosseum 105–6
colour 48–9, 50, 129–30
Columbus, Christopher 206–7, 274
comb jellies 173
Commonwealth 267
compost 7
Conan Doyle, Arthur 97–100, 202, 248
conception 51–2
conditioned response 115
conscription 263
conservation 130
Conservatives 261
contract law 239
Cook, Thomas 34
Cool Running (film) 226–7
COREN-MITCHELL, VICTORIA 8
Cornelius, Robert 147
Cornwall 16, 62, 79
corrugated iron 254–6
corsets 158–60
Corvan, Ned 79
Coryat, Thomas 244
Coutts, Thomas 113
Coventry 219–21
cowbirds 138
cowboys 71, 154–5
cows 26, 238
crabs 5, 135, 140, 194
Creighton, James George Aylwin 60
Crick, Francis 143–4
cricket 97, 100
crickets 136–7
crime rates 263–4
Croatia 278
crocodiles 133

Croton 251–2
Crown Court 67–8
crows 138, 139–40
crude oil 17
Cruikshank, John 204–5
Cruise, Tom 72
crusades 284
crushing 188
cryogenics 199
cryonics 199–200
Cuba 10, 12–13
cuckoos 137–8
Cup-a-Soup 121
Currey, Donald 126–7
Cyprus 130

Dakar Rally 232
damnatio ad bestias 105–6
dams 29–30
dangerous sports 223–4
Darius the Great 214
Darwin, Charles 60, 69, 116, 202–4
Darwin, Emma 203
Darwin, George 203
Darwin, William Erasmus 60
dating 72
dating systems 92–3
Dauger, Eustache 253
David, Jacques-Louis 45
DAVIES, ALAN 27, 57, 65, 70, 79, 95, 122, 133, 141, 152, 157, 160, 161, 182, 194, 197, 201, 207, 216, 221, 227, 236, 256, 259, 267, 279
Dead Sea 172–3
deductive reasoning 98
DEE, JACK 144
Denmark 1, 41, 241, 274
Dennis the Small 93

deserts 175–6
diabetes 242, 280
diamonds 256–7
diarrhoea 185, 208
DiCaprio, Leonardo 253
dictionaries 150–52
Dienekes 216
Dietrich, Marlene 241
Digby, Everard 230
dinosaurs 123, 131–3, 286–7
Dionysus Exiguus 93
dishwashers 146–7
Disney, Walt 199–200
DNA 36, 132, 140–41, 142–5, 184, 186
Doctor Who 101
Dodge City 156
dogs 31, 113–16, 117, 197, 213–14, 235
Dolbear, Amos 13–7
dolphins 139–40, 164
Don, Monty 23
Don Juan Pond 173
doves 118
dragonflies 267
Drake, Sir Francis 95, 177
drawings 147–8
driving tests 64
drowning 30, 38, 119, 163, 175, 217
drunkenness 32
dugongs 31
Dumas, Alexandre 253
dumb laws 275–6
Duncan, King of Scotland 112
dunce 18–19
Dunlop, John Boyd 20–21
Duns Scotus 18–19

Dürer, Albrecht 113
Dutch language 237
dyeing 26, 120, 157, 218,
    230

E. coli 22
Ea 206
Earth 4–7, 121–2, 132,
    169, 179–81, 182–3,
    285, 286–7
    atmosphere 17, 89,
        176, 178–9, 257
    magnetic field 17, 122,
        169
    orbit 50, 169, 179–80
    population 13, 170
    earthquakes 4–5
    earthshine 50
    earthworms 133, 193,
        203–4
Easter 90, 93
eating for two 53–4
Eaton, Cyrus 101
Ebola 269
echolocation 140
Edinburgh 113–14
Edward VII, King 60
Edward VIII, King 110
Edward the Confessor
    107
eggs 137–8, 166
Egypt 147, 154, 198, 206,
    217, 230, 238, 250–51,
    269–70, 271–2
Einstein, Albert 101, 249
Eisenhower, Dwight D.
    224
elasticity 168
Eleanor of Aquitaine 108
elections 221–2
electricity 16, 51–2, 239,
    254, 257

electrolytes 239
elephants 30–31, 132,
    195–6, 197, 207
Elizabeth I, Queen 102,
    111
Elizabeth II, Queen
    106–8, 109, 186, 267
Ellis, Eric 225
emissions standards 26
Empire State Building
    167, 172
energy 65, 67, 120, 166,
    168, 177, 181, 272
energy drinks 40
England 1, 15, 28, 30, 34,
    38, 42, 44, 47, 60, 62,
    68, 73, 83, 96, 102, 104,
    108–10, 113, 118, 149,
    150, 164, 182, 187, 203,
    205, 219, 232, 235–6,
    244, 266, 283–4
England, Bank of 210
English Civil War 46
English language 15, 17,
    36, 94, 95, 129, 150–53,
    215, 249, 267, 269, 273,
    275, 284
eons 285
Ephialtes 215
epigenetics 141
epochs 285–6
eras 285
ergs 175
Eriksson, Leif 274
Escoffier, Auguste 74
Ethiopia 7, 13
ethylene 21
EU 170
eucalyptus trees 125–6
Eugenie, Princess 107
euphemisms 30
Europe 7, 14, 28, 33, 52,

61, 71, 81, 87–8, 104,
    120, 127, 129–30, 134,
    137, 141, 172, 186, 189,
    234–5, 261–2, 268–9,
    274, 286
European Convention on
    Human Rights 276
Eurytus 215
Evening Birds 7
Everest (Churchill's
    nanny) 5
Everest (mountain) 23
Eves, Stuart 179
exosphere 179
extracellular matrix 198
eyelids 197

Fair Isle 158
Famous Five 243–4
Farrow, Mia 32
fascism 45–6
fashion 70–71
Faunce, Thomas 82
feathers 130
Federal Reserve 209–10
feeding of the 5,000
    216–17
female franchise 221–2
Ferrero Rocher 86
Ferris, George
    Washington Gale 19
ferris wheels 19, 146
FIELDING, NOEL 212
Fiennes, Sir Ranulph
    199
film-making 11–12
finches 138, 240
fingers 198–9
Finkelstein, Nat 249
Finland 279
Fiorelli, Giuseppe 214
fire extinguishers 75

First World War 14–15,
    149, 254, 256, 260,
    261–2, 264
Fisher, John Arbuthnot
    148–9
Fitzgerald, F. Scott 266
Fitzroy, Robert 203
flags 46–50, 63–4, 108
flash floods 175
flatworms 188
fleas 167–8
flint-knapping 69–70
floods 3
floppy trunk syndrome 31
fly ash 16
Flying Gull 230
Foerster, Susan 242
foetuses 54
fog pills 15
fog weapons 15
football 100, 103, 104
forceps 55
Forestry Commission 6
formaldehyde 27
Forrest, Edwin 113
Fort Knox 209
Fouquet, Nicolas 253
Fourth World 279
France 7, 13, 18, 41, 45,
    72–4, 78–9, 87, 95,
    104, 109, 119, 128, 148,
    232, 234, 247, 252, 262,
    276, 278, 279, 281, 284
Francis, Pope 65
Francis of Assissi, St
    95–6, 207
Franklin, Rosalind 143–4
Fraser, 'Mad' Frankie 263
French language 28, 94,
    103–4, 129, 151, 202,
    206, 284
French Revolution 45, 71

Friends (TV) 32
froghoppers 168
frogs 31, 54
frogs' legs 73, 254
frostbite 199
fruit salad tree 25
Fry, Bryan 188
Fuller, Simon 266
Fuller, Thomas 149
fungi 6, 193

Gagarin, Yuri 179
Gallipoli 149
Galton, Francis 116
Galvani, Luigi 254
galvanisation 254
gambling 33
Garland, Judy 32
gars 163
gas, 14–16, 21
Gask Ridge 276–7
Gaugin, Paul 128
Gauls 120
Gautama Buddha 252
gavel 67–8
Gellar, Sarah Michelle 32
George, St 47
gasoline 17–18
Gelasius I, Pope 93
Gemini VI 89
genes 140–41
genetic engineering 27
Genoa 201–2
genomes 141, 142
geometry 251
George III, King 42, 47
Georgia 89
Germany 14–16, 42–3,
    61–2, 120, 149, 262,
    278
gibbons 9
Ginsberg, Allen 139

Gir Forest National
    Park 7
Giza 126, 271
glass 64–5
Glidden, George 270
glycyrrhizin 75
Glyndwr, Owen 275
gobbledygook 19
Gobi desert 175
Godey's Lady's Book 53
Godiva, Lady 219–21
Goethe, Johann
    Wolfgang von 134
goethite 134
gold 126, 209–10, 252
Golden Rule 58
goldfish 140
golf 49, 80, 224–6, 248
gonorrhoea 183–5
Gordon, Hannah 236
goulash 155
Grace, W. G. 100
Grand Canyon 123–4
granite 16
granular convection 234
grapefruit 24–5
graphite 257
Grassini, Josephine 247
gravity 121–2, 169, 179,
    285
Gray, John 114
Great Britain 3, 5–6, 7,
    14–15, 17, 19–20, 42–3,
    47, 64, 67–8, 72, 74,
    79–80, 85, 88, 91, 100,
    107–8, 115, 120, 121,
    130, 137, 144, 145, 148,
    164, 186, 200, 204,
    221, 230, 240, 241–3,
    248, 254, 256, 261–2,
    263, 266–7, 270, 273,
    276, 278

Great Dying 286–7
Great Exhibition 43, 108
Great Green Wall 175
Great Lakes 174
Great Male
    Renunciation 71
Great Rift Valley 212
Greece 34, 71,77, 97, 99,
    120, 147, 206, 214–15,
    230, 250, 257, 282
Greek language 54, 75,
    94, 105, 133, 158, 187,
    191, 192, 199, 234, 285
Greenland 1, 124, 274
'Greensleeves' 102–3
Gregg, Justin 139–40
Gregorian calendar 93,
    285
Gregory the Great, Pope
    218
Grey, Lady Jane 110
Greyfriars Bobby 113–14
grissini 72
Groot, Jan de 80
Groundhog Day 86–7
Guaira Fall 1
guano 280–81
Guarneri (violin makers)
    39
Guatemala 266
guessing 116–17
Guns N' Roses 32
Gutenberg Bible 209
Gwennap Head 79

Habibullah of
    Afghanistan, King 225
Hadrian, Emperor 277–8
Hadrian's Wall 276–8
Haeckel, Ernst 261
haemorrhoids 54
haircuts 7

Haiti 202
HALL, RICH 185
hammerstones 70
Hampshire, Susan 236
hamsters 200, 283
Hamza, River 3
Hancock, John 85
hand-axes 69–70
Handy, Walter 263
Hangover, The (film) 32
H'angus the Monkey 78
Hardcastle, Paul 264, 266
HARDY, JEREMY 166
hare lip 53
hares 53
Harley Davidson 26
harmonics 251
Harris, Isle of 157
Harris tweed 157–8
Harry Potter 207
Hartlepool 78–9
Hatra 13
hats 155–7
Hawaii 3, 47, 50
Hawkins, Peter 101
Hawthorne, Nathaniel
    137
headaches 88
healthiness 240–41, 280
health hazards 16, 118
heartbeat 130
Hebrew language 94, 217
hedgehogs 87
Helms, Ed 32
Hendrickson, Sue 132
Hendrix, Jimi 164
Henley, Margaret 97
Henley, William Ernest
    97
Henry II, King 104,
    108–9, 284
Henry V, King 110, 275

Henry VII, King 103,
    110, 235
Henry VIII, King 102–3,
    106–8, 110
Henry the Young King
    104, 108–9
heredity 141, 143
Herjolfsson, Bjarni 274
Herod, King 58, 93
Herodotus 238, 282
Hesse, Herman 85
Heylyn, John 149
hibernation 200
Hideyoshi, Toyotomi 125
high heels 70–72
Hillary, Edmund 23
Hillel the Elder 58
HILLS, ADAM 160
Hinckley, John 66
Hinduism 26
Hines, Margie 28
Hippocrates 238
Hiroshima 169
Hitler, Adolf 15, 43, 62
holidays 34–5
holly 88, 234
Hollywood 11
Holocene epoch 285
Holy Communion 217
Homer 114, 206
Hoover Dam 29
Hoppe-Seyler, Felix 143
Horatii 45
horses 88, 220–21
hovercraft 144–5
Hughes, Reverend
    Griffith 24
Huitzilopochtli 268
Hultén, Pontus 249
Hume, David 111
hurricanes 52
Huxley, Aldous 115

Hyde Park 108
hydrogen 21
hydrothermal vents 5
hypersleep 200
hypothermia 200

ice 51, 60, 166, 178, 199
Ice Age 165
ice hockey 60–61
Iceland 1, 4, 36, 274
ICI 21
India 7, 11, 26, 95, 232,
    238, 250, 252, 272, 287
Indian Ocean 4
indigobirds 138
Indonesia 74, 95, 272,
    282
Industrial Revolution 6
inner tube 20–21
insects 12–13, 192
intelligence 139–40
IAAF 228
International Criminal
    Court 68
International Space
    Station 179
IOU 149
Iraq 278
Ireland, Republic of 17,
    22, 87–8, 157, 278–9
iron 27, 134, 254, 256
Irving, Washington 154
Islam 81–2
isochavicine 238
Israel 69
Italian language 72, 94,
    127, 129, 206
Italy 22, 45, 61, 72–3, 96,
    102, 197, 214, 251, 254,
    260

J (letter) 94–5

jalapeño peppers 18
Jamaica 226–7
James I, King 47, 107, 111
James II, King 106
James Bond 23
Jarvis, Anna 91–2
Japan 14, 27, 95, 230
Java 171
Javitt, Joan 90
Jay-Z 267
Jefferson, Thomas 111
Jelly Babies 75
jellyfish 173, 191
Jericho, Battle of 219
Jerome, Jerome K. 97
Jerusalem 58
Jerusalem artichokes 127
Jesus 41, 58, 86, 89, 92–6,
    124–5, 216–17, 218–19,
    285
jetlag 283
'Jingle Bells' 89–90
John the Baptist 95
John of the Cross, St 217
John o'Groats 79–80
John Paul II, Pope 65
Johnson, Boris 182, 221
Johnson, Gregory Lee 46
Johnson, Dr Samuel 23,
    150–52
Jones, Richard 102
Josephine, Empress
    245–7
Joshua 219
jousting 103–4
judges 67–9
juggling 56
jugular veins 197
Julian calendar 41
Julius Caesar 41–2, 94,
    211
jumping 167–9

Junca, Etienne da 253
jungles 7, 9
JUPITUS, PHILL 72, 86
juries 67–9

Kaario, Toivo 145
Kabul Golf Club 225–6
Kaffa 13
kangaroo court 79
kangaroos 193–4
Keiller's marmalade 23
Keith, Penelope 236
Kendal, Felicity 236
Kepler, Johannes 258
    and his conjecture 258
keratin 158
Kettilby, Mary 22
Key, Francis Scott 266–7
Khazar Empire 274
KHORSANDI, SHAPPI
    157, 210
Kim Il-sung 225
Kim Jong-il 224–5
Kipling, Rudyard 69, 97
Kissinger, Henry 265
kites (birds) 6, 130
Kleen Maid 56
knees 195
knights 103, 109, 230
knitting 158
Kohl, Helmut 236
Kowalski, Bernard L. 171
Kropotkin, Peter 146
'Kubla Khan' 205
Kush 272

Labyrinth of the Night
    124
Lacarrubba, Dennis 49
Laconia 215–16
Lake, Ricki 32
lakes 127, 174, 212, 268

Lancaster, Burt 208
'Land of the Free, The'
    266
Land's End 79–80
Laos 265
Las Vegas 31–3
lashings of 243
lassos 154
Latin America 81, 271
Latin 9, 19, 76, 94, 120,
    133, 158, 197, 211–12,
    234, 255, 284
LaTourette, Steven C. 174
lava 4, 213
Lazarus 217, 218
Le Duc Tho 265
leap years 41–2
Leary, Timothy 139
Lebedev, Pyotr 182
Lees, Frederick 217
LEGO 19–20
legs 136–7, 192–4
Lemaître, Albert 232
lemon juice 22
lemons 25
Lent 52, 90, 127
Lenz, Johann Georg 134
Leofric, Earl of Mercia
    219–20
Leonida, Gheorghe
    124–5
Leonidas 215–16
leprosy 13
'Let It Snow' 90
LETTE, KATHY 221
Levick, George Murray
    187
Levkov, Vladimir 144–5
Lewis, Isle of 157–8
Lewis Chessmen 158
lex posterior derogat priori
    276

Liberace 38
Liberals 261
Liberty, Statue of 126
lichens 166
light 180–81, 182–3
lightning 16, 118, 177
Lilly, John C. 139
limes 25
limpets 134
Lincoln, Abraham 250
Lincoln, Battle of 104
Linda, Solomon 7–8
lions 160
literally 152–3
lizards 132, 188
'Lion Sleeps Tonight,
    The', 7
lions 7–8, 30
Liquorice Allsorts 74–5
Little Ice Age 40
Lloyd George, David 261
lobsters 134–5
LOCK, SEAN 119
Locke, James 158
locks 44
Lohan, Lindsay 85
LOL 149
Lombardo, Guy 90
London 1, 22, 62, 100,
    102, 107, 124, 125, 155,
    158, 164, 167, 171, 182,
    221, 229–30, 248, 255,
    263–4, 268, 275–6,
    284
London to Brighton
    Rally 63
London Underground
    264
Long Island Motor
    Parkway 61
Lonsdale, Kathleen 257
lonsdaleite 257

Lope de Vega 177
loudness 160–61
Louis XIV, King 71,
    252–3
Lovelock, James 200
LSD 139
luging 227
Lulach the Idiot 111–12
lumberjacks 56
Luna 24 48
Luther, Martin 42–3

Macartney, George 282
Macau 33
Macbeth 111–13
McCarthy, Tim 66
McCormick, Robert
    202–3
Macdonald viola 40
McGee, Harold 238
Macready, William
    Charles 113
magma 4, 124, 286
Magna Carta 209
magpies 140
make-up 71, 273
Malcolm III of Scotland
    111–12
Malmaison 247
mambas 189
manatees 31, 206–7
Mandela, Nelson 97
MANFORD, JASON 64
mangoes 25–7
Mao Zedong 27
Maracaibo, Lake 177
Marathon, Battle of 214
Marble Arch 108
Marconi, Guglielmo 125
Marcos, Imelda 85
Marcus Livius 212
Marengo, Battle of 246

Marks, Johnny 90
marmalade 22–3
marriage 32–3, 41
Mars 4, 124, 178, 183
Marshal, William 104
Martin, St 87
martyrs 88, 105–6
Mary Celeste 201–2
Mary Magdalene 218–19
Mary, Queen of Scots 111
Mary Tudor 106
mass extinctions 286–7
mathematics 250–52
Matthews, Ken 229
Matthias, St 41
Mauna Loa Observatory 50
Maverick, Maury 19
Maverick, Samuel 19
maverick 19
Maxwell, Lily 221
May, Robert 74
May, Ronald 90
May Day 52
Mayans 21
Mayflower 82–4
mealworms 139
Mecchi, Irene 8
medals 119
medicine 235, 238
mêlées 103–4
Mercer, Jack 28
mermaids 206–7
mesosphere 178
meteorites 257
methane 286
Mexica 268–9
Mexico 18, 232, 266, 268–9, 271, 286
mice 54, 195–6
Middle Ages 13, 105, 237
Middle East 70, 273, 284

midges 166
mid-ocean ridge 4
midwifery 54–5
Miescher, Johannes Friedrich 143
Milan 61, 247
milk 54, 57
Milne, A. A. 97
mind palace memory technique 99
mine detection 140
minstrel songs 89
misery whip 56
missing persons 35–6
missionaries 81–2
MITCHELL, DAVID 11, 24, 57, 70, 94, 262
mites 166, 184
Mohs, Friedrich 257
his scale 257
molluscs 133–4
Molloy, Doug 44
Monaco 280
monasteries 82, 109, 111
Mongol Rally 232
monks 105, 107
monkeys 78–9, 160
monogamy 186–8
Moon 48–9, 50–51, 96, 122, 179, 180, 201
Moon, Lottie 82
Moore, Demi 32
Moore, Patrick 201
Morgan, J. P. 89
morphine 209
Morris, William 255
mosses 6, 166
Mothering Sunday 90–92
moths 122, 155, 161
motoring 63–4
motorways 61–2

mourning 44
Mozart 37, 39
Mulcaster, Richard 150
Müller von Thomamuehl, Dagobert 145
mummification 238, 269–70
Murray, George 167
music, misattribution of 38, 102
music of the spheres 251
musical instruments 103
Mussolini, Benito 61, 150
mustard gas 15–16

nachos 18
Nahuatl language 269, 271
names 51, 94–5, 97, 109–10, 261–2
Namibia 176, 239
Nance, Nejdra 35
Napoleon Bonaparte 245–8
Napoleonic Wars 78, 261
NASA 50, 149, 154, 158, 177, 181, 200, 201
Nash, John 107
National Climatic Data Center (US) 87
National Football League (US) 224
National Rifle Association 18
Native Americans 127, 223, 230, 274
NATO 279
Nauru 280–81
Nazis 45–6, 61–2
Naylor, Robert and John 80

Neanderthals 144
necks 184
necrophilia 187
Nelson, Horatio 149
nematodes 192–3
nephrostome 31
Neptune 142, 206
Nero, Emperor 105
nests 137–8, 185
neuroscience 116, 139
New York 35, 51–2, 61,
    112–13, 209–10, 249
Newton, Battle of 47
Niagara Falls 1
NICE 53
Nicholson, William 98
Niépce, Joseph
    Nicéphore 148
Nigeria 11–12, 82, 271
Nile, River 3
Nissen, Peter 255–6
Nnebue, Kenneth 11–12
Nobel Prizes 101, 115,
    143–4, 265
NOBLE, ROSS 52, 157, 173,
    283
Nollywood 11–12
non-alignment 279
Norman Conquest 107,
    109, 219
North Africa 212, 270
North America 83, 86,
    127–8, 163, 165, 175,
    274
North Korea 224–5
Northern Ireland 279
Norway 100, 274
nose bleeds 54
nuclear disarmament 101
nuclear fusion 180
nuclear power stations 16
nuclear waste 16

oak 6
obesity 242, 280
O'BRIAIN, DARA 27
Observatoire du Pain 72
Occitan language 284
O'Connor, Sinead 32
octopuses 192
Oddi, Ruggero 197
Odon, Jorge 55
Odysseus 207
Odyssey 114, 206
oenology 40
Ohno, Susumu 142
Oholah 219
Oholibah 219
oil 21, 120, 154, 226, 227,
    240
Old Norse language 273,
    275
O'Leary, Dan 228
Olive Oyl 28
Olympic Games 10,
    226–7, 228–31
OMG 148–9
onions 141
opium 205, 209
orange (colour) 24,
    129–30, 240–41
oranges (fruit) 22–5,
    129, 258
orchids 233
organ, pipe 38
OSMAN, RICHARD 121
Osmanagic, Semir 272
osmosis 239
osteotome 54
Otway, Thomas 245
Oxford English Dictionary
    72, 149–50, 152–3
oxygen 21, 163, 166, 172–3,
    177, 178, 257, 258, 286
ozone 176–7, 178

Pacific Ocean 4, 282
package holidays 34–5
Paddington Bear 23
paedophilia 187
Page, Hilary Fisher 20
pain 199
Pakington, Dorothy 222
Pakistan 27, 95
Paläoweltschmerz 287
Palmer, Henry Robinson
    254–5
Pan 97
pandas 167
Pantites 215
paper bags 22
papples 25
parakeets 164
parasites 136, 137, 193
Paré, Ambroise 54
Paris 18, 72, 128, 214, 247
Paris Peace Accords 265
Paris–Rouen Horseless
    Carriage Competition
    232
Parker, Gilman C. 202
parrot fish 176
parrots 139
Parthenon 147
Partridge, Eric 149
PASCOE, SARA 24, 92
Passover 58
Pavlov, Ivan 115–16
Pechmann, Hans von 21
Peeping Tom, 220
pelicans 208
penguins 163–4, 166, 167,
    186–7
pepper 237–9
Pepys, Samuel 245
perfume 30, 234–5, 247
perihelion 179
PERKINS, SUE 36, 113

Permian period 286
Persia 28, 70, 214–15, 230, 251
Peru 233, 238, 269, 272
Peter the Great 127
Peter Pan 96–8
petrels 205
petrol 17–19
Pettway, Ann 35
Phelps, Michael 230
pheromones 155
Phidias 147
Philip I of Spain 282
Philip II of France 284
Philip II of Macedon 216
Philip II of Spain 282
Phoney War 262
phosphate 281
photographs 147–8
photons 180–81
physiognomy 203
piadina 72
pickling 26
piercings 43–4, 273
Pierpont, James Lord 89–90
pigeons 117–19
pigs 27, 116, 143–4, 198, 213, 217
Pike, Oliver 138
Pilgrim Fathers 83
pili 184
Pineapple Express 3
piperine 238
Planck epoch 285
plaster of Paris 214
plastic bags 21–2, 56
Plataea, battle of 215
platform shoes 71
Plato 230, 250
Pliny the Elder 136, 195, 211, 213, 235

plumcots 25
pluots 25
Plutarch 147
Pluto 51, 181
Plymouth, Massachusetts 82–4
Plymouth Rock 82–4
poisons 26, 133, 188–9
Poland 13, 124
polar bears 163–4
police 35–6
political correctness 244, 279
pollination 127
polyethylene 21
polyps 191–2
polythene 21
pomelo 24
Pompeii 213–14
Pontefract cakes 75
Popemobile 65
Popeye 27–8
Popeye (film) 28
pornography 148
Portuguese language 22, 233
Portuguese men-o'-war 191–2
Poseidon 206
postage stamps 123
potatoes 13, 243
Potter, P. Aaron 205
poultry 208
powder monkeys 78
Powell, John Wesley 123
pregnancy 52, 53–4
Presocratics 250
pressure 5, 132
prickles 234
primates 9
primogeniture 109
Prince Albert (genital

piercing) 43–4
Princess Royal 107
pronunciation 129
propaganda 225
prostitution 69–70, 105, 207, 218–19, 264
protein 73, 127, 142, 143, 168
pseudogenes 142
puffins 187
Pugwash Conferences 101
Punic Wars 211–12
Purcell, Henry 38
Puritans 83–4
pus 143–4
pyramids 126, 271–2
pyroclastic flow 213
Pythagoras 250–52
pythons 188

Quetzalcoatl 271
quinces 22–3

rabies 13
radiation 16–17, 49, 180
radon 16–17
radula 133–4
Rahab 219
rain 2, 6, 120, 126, 175
rainforests 5–7, 175, 233, 267
Ramesses II 238
Rampling, Charlotte 236
Rancé, Jean François 247
ransoms 103–4
raspberries 23, 141
Reagan, Ronald 66–7, 236
recycling 227, 240, 255
Red Bull 40
Rees, Nigel 248
Reform Act (1832) 221–2

Remington, Frederic 156
Repington, Charles 261
resilin 168
rhinoceroses 113, 158
Richard I, King 109,
    283–4
*Rime of the Ancient Mariner,
    The* 204–5
Rio de Janeiro 124–5
Rivers, Larry 249
robins (birds) 129–31
'Rockin' Around the
    Christmas Tree' 90
Rodger, N. A. M. 58
Roger of Wendover 220
Rohwedder, Otto 56–7
Rome 13, 22, 41–2, 45,
    105–6, 112, 120, 125,
    150, 206, 211–12, 235,
    237, 270, 276–7
Romeo and Juliet 244–5
Ronkonkoma, Lake 61
Roosevelt, Franklin D.
    46, 224, 262
Rose, Mark 272
roses 234–6, 247
Rouen Cathedral 284
Royal College of Music
    38
Royal Standard 48, 108
'Rudolph the Red-nosed
    Reindeer' 90
Rufus of Assisi, St 96
Russell Bertrand 101, 115
Russia 33, 115, 127–8, 145,
    232, 262, 281–2
Russian Orthodox
    Church 127
Ryan, John 100–101
RYAN, KATHERINE 72
Ryan, Mary 185

S Club 7 266
Sabine, Thierry 232
Sahara 175
Saigon 265
St James's Palace 106–7
St Paul's Cathedral 38
St Petersburg 33
St Sixtus Abbey 77
Salomons, Sir David
    Lionel 63
salt 53, 211–12
salt water 173
salutes 45–6
sand 175–6
Sandwich, Earls of 58–9
sandwiches 58–9
'Santa Baby' 90
satnavs 183
Saudi Arabia 82, 175
Sauvy, Alfred 278
Scandinavia 273–4
Scargill, Arthur 236
Schirra, Wally 89–90
scorpions 13
Scotland 6, 47, 79, 88,
    111–12, 274, 277
Scott, Captain Robert
    Falcon 23, 167
Scott, Walter 235
sculptures 147–8
sea cremations 272–3
sea level 4–5, 176, 178, 281
sea lions 139
sea mounts 4
seagulls 17
seals 31
seaweed 158
Second World War 10,
    14–16, 21, 46, 57, 91,
    101, 118, 209, 243, 256,
    261–2, 263–5
sedia gestatoria 65

Seeger, Pete 7
selfies 147–8
Sellafield nuclear plant 17
semen 234
SERGEANT, JOHN 168
servants 88, 91
SESSIONS, JOHN 43
Seven Years War 282
Seville oranges 23
sewage 239–40
sex 8, 34, 51, 70, 131–2,
    135, 151, 155
Shaddock, Captain 24
shadows 182–3
Shakespeare, William 8,
    94, 112–13, 244–5
shale 16
Shapiro, Fred 248
Shard 1, 167
sharks 133, 190–91, 197
Shearer, Douglas 10
Sheffield, John 107
Shelley, Mary 171
shells 135
Shelvocke, George 204–5
Sherlock 99
Sherlock Holmes 98–100
Shetland 272
ship burials 273
Shrapnel, Henry 19
shoe polish 75
shouting 259–60
shrapnel 19
shrimps 187
sideburns 18
Siegel, Jerry 9
Siemenowics, Kazimierz
    13
sign language 76
silence 76, 77
Siler, Howard 227
silkworms 107

Simonides of Ceos 99
Sinatra, Frank 32
Sioux 132
siphonophores 191
sirens 206
Sixtus V, Pope 105
skiing 260
Skye, Isle of 170
Slash 32
sliced bread 56–7
slugs 133, 194
Smallwood, Imogen 243
Smith, Dick 90
SMITH, LINDA 14, 134
smoking 71
snails 133–4, 194
snakes 132, 188–9, 197,
    252, 268
snow 258–60
Snowdon, 34
snowflakes 258–9
soap 75, 119–20
Socrates 250
soil 6, 16–17, 126
solar system 51, 154, 179,
    181
Sotheby's 40
Sotomayor, Javier 167
South Africa 7, 118, 256
South America 6, 127,
    154, 163, 175, 231, 282
Soviet Union 279
space 89–90, 121, 179,
    182–3
Spain 13, 28, 34, 241–2,
    268–9, 271, 278, 282–3
Spanish language 94, 154,
    156, 206, 208, 241, 267
Sparta 214–16
Spears, Britney 32
speed limits 63–4
sphincters 196–7

Spice Girls 266
spiders 155, 184
spies 78–9
spinach 27–8
SPQR 150
squatting 276
Stafford, Tom 89
stalker (motoring) 63
'Star-spangled Banner,
    The' 266
Starbucks 59
starfish 194
statistics 116–17
statues 124–5, 126
steel 254
Stephen, SS 88, 209
Stetson, John B. 156
Stetsons 156
Stevenson, Robert Louis
    97
Stewart, Ian 56
Stewart, Jimmy 224
Stiffkey, Vicar of 8
stigmata 96
Stokes, Dudley 227
Stone Age 73
Stonehenge 73, 126
Stradivarius 39–40
stratosphere 177, 178
strength 183–4
stridulation 136–7
strigils 120
Stroud, Robert Franklin
    207–8
Stuarts 111
sub rosa 235
Sudan 272
sugar 22, 28, 75, 77
Sullivan, David 80
sulphur dioxide 4
Sumatra 171
Sun 34, 41, 50, 96, 122,

    127, 176–7, 178, 179–81,
    182, 183, 252
sunflowers 127–8
sunlight 48, 51
Sunny Delight 241
sunscreen 182
suntan 240
supereons 285
Superman 9
SVBEEV 150
swans 185–6
Sweden 126, 152, 274, 279
Sweetie Scone Day 88
sweets 74–5
Swiebodzin 124
Swift, Jonathan 149
swimming 10, 29, 208–9,
    229–31
swimming pools 229–31
Swiss army 118
Switzerland 100, 279
symphysiotomy 55

table hockey 61
tails 29, 162, 193–4, 206,
    208
Taklamakan desert 175
Taliban 125
Tambora, Lake 171
Tarzan 9–11
Tatars 13
tattoos 273
taxes 212, 219–21, 277
tear gas 15
tectonic plates 4
teeth 28–9, 133–4, 135,
    189, 190, 273
Telford, Thomas 255
temperance campaigning
    17, 34–5, 217
Tenochtitlan 268
terra preta 6

testicles 31
testosterone 75
Texcoco 268
text-speak 149
Thames, River 60, 186
Thames Water 239
Thanksgiving 89
Thatcher, Margaret 232
Thatcher, Mark 232
Theophrastus 257
Thermopylae, Battle of
    214–16
thermosphere 178–9
Third World 278–9
thistles 234
Thomas Cook 34–5
Thomson, Charles 85
Thomson, Robert
    William 20
thorium 16
thorns 234, 236
Thrips palmi 13
thumbs 198–9
time 285–6
time zones 281–3
Titanic (liner) 5
Toba, Lake 171–2
tobacco 74
Tobacco 230
toes 198
toilet training 119
TOKSVIG, SANDI 25,
    164, 167
tool-making 69–70
tortilla chips 18
tournaments 103–4, 109
toys 20–21
traction engines 63
Trappist monks 76–7
tree canopy 6, 126
trees 56, 125–7
tricycles 63

troposphere 178
tubeworms 5
Tudor, Owen 110
Tudor rose 235
Tudors 110–11
Twain, Mark 248
Twelfth Night 86
Tyrannosaurus rex 131–3
tyre manufacture 19–21

Udry, Richard 51–2
Ueno, Hidesaburo 114
UFOs 89
ultimogeniture 109
ultrasound 161
ultraviolet light 176–7,
    178, 240, 257
UNESCO 11
unicorns 64
Union, Act of 47
Union Flag/Union Jack
    46–7, 108
United Kingdom (UK)
    1, 62, 67–8, 170, 278
United Nations (UN)
    12–13, 107
United States 2, 3, 10,
    11, 12, 17, 18, 26, 35–6,
    45–6, 47, 48, 56–7,
    61, 68–9, 81–2, 85, 86,
    89, 91, 95, 113, 123, 142,
    146–7, 154, 156, 174,
    202, 209–10, 223–4,
    228, 241–2, 248,
    261–2, 264–5, 266–7,
    280, 282
uranium 16
urine 15, 26, 151, 230, 238

vagina masculina 197
Van Gogh, Theo 128
Van Gogh, Vincent 128

Vanderbilt, Cornelius 61
Vanderbilt, William
    Kissam, II 61
vanilla 30, 246
varicose veins 54
Vatican City 65–6, 280
veganism 28
VEGAS, JOHNNY 133, 167
vegetable oil 127, 241
vegetables 27–8, 211,
    240–43, 270, 280
velvet 252
Venezuela 1–2
Venice 71
Venus 4
Verona 245
Vesuvius 213–14
Via Salaria 211
vicars 90
Victoria, Queen 42–4,
    106–8, 109–10, 113
Viet Cong 265
Vietnam 125, 239, 264–5
Vietnam War 264–5
Vikings 272–5
Vilhonneur 148
Vine, Allyn 5
VINE, TIM 59
vines 9
violins 39–40
viruses 240
vitamin A 27
Vitalis of Assisi, St 96
vitrification 199
volcanoes 4, 171–2, 268,
    286–7
Voltaire 253
voting 221–2
vultures 187

Wales 6, 88, 133, 176
walking races 228–9

walnuts 26
Warhol, Andy 159, 249
Warren, W. L. 109
washing 119–21
Washington, George
    47, 134
water 18, 29, 119–20, 126,
    162, 166–7, 172–3, 217,
    239–40, 258
water boatmen 136, 160
water flea 140–41
waterfalls 1–2
Watson, James 143–4
weather 86–7, 178
Weavers 8
WEBB, ROBERT 199
weddings 32–3
weight 53, 116–17, 135, 166,
    167–8, 169, 173, 182–4,
    190, 259, 280
weight-lifting 184, 280
Weimar, Josephine 247
Weiss, George 8
Weissmuller, Johnny 10
Wellington, Duke of
    247–8
Wells, H. G. 97
wells, poisoning of 13
Welsh language 133
Wendi, Emperor 97
Wendy 96–7

Westminster Abbey 107
Weston, Edward Payson
    228
Westvleteren XII 77
whalebone 158–60
whales 31, 133–4, 140,
    158–61, 197
'What a Wonderful
    World' 8
WEHN, HENNING 84
whisky 157
White, Carlina 35
'White Christmas' 90
White Friday 260
WHITEHALL, JACK 100,
    131, 207
Whitfield, June 236
Wills, W. G. 246
WHO 55, 242
whydahs 138
WIDDICOMBE, JOSH 227
Wight, Isle of 145, 170
Wild West 154–7
Wilde, Oscar 249
Wilkins, Maurice 144
William IV, King 107
William the Conqueror
    107, 109
Williams, Gareth 272
Williams, Robin 28
Willis, Bruce 32

WILSON, CAL 80
Wilson, Woodrow 91,
    207
wind 49, 259
Windermere, Lake 1
wine 40, 55, 217
wings 136–7, 166, 186, 233
'Winter Wonderland' 90
wisdom of crowds 116–17
witches' knickers 22
WMD 14
Wodehouse, P. G. 97,
    248
Wolsey, Cardinal 103
woodpeckers 6
words, misused 153
World's Fairs 146
worms 155, 192–3
Wren Day 88
Wynmann, Nikolaus 230

Xelhua 271
Xerxes 214

yeast 73, 77
yeti crab 5
yodelling 10
Yutu 48

Zanzibar 170
Zhaocun 125